# The Licensing Racket

# The Licensing Racket

## HOW WE DECIDE
## WHO IS ALLOWED TO WORK,
## AND WHY IT GOES WRONG

Rebecca Haw Allensworth

Harvard University Press

Cambridge, Massachusetts & London, England   2025

First printing

*Library of Congress Cataloging-in-Publication Data*

Names: Allensworth, Rebecca Haw, author.
Title: The licensing racket : how we decide who is allowed to work,
and why it goes wrong / Rebecca Haw Allensworth.
Description: Cambridge : Harvard University Press, 2025. |
Includes bibliographical references and index.
Identifiers: LCCN 2024014006 (print) | LCCN 2024014007 (ebook) |
ISBN 9780674295421 (cloth) | ISBN 9780674298699 (pdf) |
ISBN 9780674298729 (epub)
Subjects: LCSH: Occupations—Licenses—United States. |
Professions—Licenses—United States.
Classification: LCC HD3630.U7 A55 2025 (print) | LCC HD3630.U7 (ebook) |
DDC 331.7020973—dc23/eng/20240626
LC record available at https://lccn.loc.gov/2024014006
LC ebook record available at https://lccn.loc.gov/2024014007

*For my mother*

# Contents

# The Licensing Racket

# Introduction

## The Bargain

*Professional licensing is the most important labor regulatory institution in America, and it's broken in ways even its toughest critics don't recognize.*

On April 9, 2018, the Tennessee Board of Cosmetology and Barber Examiners met in downtown Nashville for their monthly meeting. I was there in the rows of chairs set up for observers, all of whom, other than me, were beauty-school instructors and students observing the board at work.

After approving the floor plans for two new proposed cosmetology schools, the board considered the licensure application of Omar Mahmoud. Mr. Mahmoud, a fifty-two-year-old Arabic-speaking immigrant, was a US Army veteran who served for seven years during the wars in Iraq and Afghanistan. Mr. Mahmoud was licensed as a cosmetologist in Michigan and had completed all the education required to be a barber in Tennessee. He explained to the board, in broken English, "I have been long, long time in this field." He had been cutting hair for more than thirty years. "This is my job . . . this is my business."

But if Mr. Mahmoud wanted to cut hair legally in Tennessee, he would need one more thing that, for him, was out of reach. He would need to pass an English-only written test on the theory of barbering. He had failed the exam twice. "I tried hard," he said. "I tried a lot." His cosmetology license in Michigan could not be transferred to Tennessee (through a process called reciprocity) because Tennessee had a policy of not recognizing licenses from states that allowed test-takers to use interpreters.

I watched as Mr. Mahmoud pled his case. "I want to work," he said. But the board would not budge. One board member suggested Mr. Mahmoud keep trying, noting she knew someone who had passed on the sixth try. As things stood, she said he had not tried and failed enough for the board to do something out of the ordinary to help him. "Unless you want to test, like, eight more times and then come back," she said, "we can talk then." I saw Mr. Mahmoud shaking with anger and frustration.

The chairman of the board offered these words to Mr. Mahmoud shortly before formally calling the vote: "I know sometimes people on your side of the fence feel like maybe we are trying to hold you back. We certainly aren't. We have a job that we have to do." The board voted unanimously to deny his application.[1]

## Bigger Than Unions, More Expensive Than the Sales Tax

The "job" to which the board member was alluding was administering a professional license, or deciding who gets to work in a given profession, defining appropriate practice, and identifying bad providers for professional discipline. The job is performed by some two thousand state licensing boards scattered across the country, each dominated by busy part-time volunteers from the very profession they are tasked with regulating. They interpret laws that have been passed, after heavy professional lobbying, by state legislatures unaware of, or indifferent to, the ways that their regulation affects workers, consumers, and the public at large. This is the system by which we regulate one-fifth of American workers, making it the most important labor regulatory institution in the country. This book is my attempt to explain the function—and dysfunction—of the professional licensing system, its effects on equality, public health, and the economy, and its role in the American Dream.

As I use the term, a professional license is a government-granted right to perform a service that can be obtained only through a significant investment in human capital, usually in the form of education and examination. I consider a profession to be licensed if you cannot practice at all without the government's permission—so a car mechanic certification is not a license because you can work on cars without one. And a professional license requires more than a brief online course or passing a CPR test; its educational requirements are considerable, measured at least in months and more often in years. Finally, a professional license is something held by an individual, not a company or a facility, and it's transferable when you change employers. Thus, a restaurant permit issued by a local health department is not a professional license as I use that term.

Professional licensing began with the so-called learned professions, or occupations "based on advanced, or complex, or esoteric, or arcane knowledge."[2] But it has expanded dramatically in the last fifty years to cover work that doesn't require knowledge we typically think of as advanced or arcane, including pest control application, court reporting, auctioneering, and alarm system installation.[3] According to my research, there are as many as *three hundred* professions licensed in at least one state.

The capaciousness of licensing extends not only to the number of professions covered, but also to the number of Americans whose working life is governed by the licensing system. My best guess is that almost 20 percent of American workers, or nearly thirty million, must hold a professional license to do their job.[4] That's more than ten times as many workers as are subject to the federal minimum wage.[5] And it's a larger share of the American workforce than public and private unions combined can claim.[6]

Professional licensing, so defined, is unique not only because of its reach, but because it is an especially onerous form of regulation, erecting high (and for many people, insurmountable) financial and educational barriers. Economists who have tried to measure the effect of this regulation often find that it raises prices to consumers by more than the highest state sales tax.[7] Its effect on wages is within the range estimated for union affiliation, yet it affects more workers.[8] Professional licensing cuts through every social class of American worker and touches all of us as consumers—not only when we buy a house or have surgery, but when we go to the salon or get a massage.

## Red Tape

Yet despite its place of prominence in the working lives of tens of millions of Americans, and in all our lives as patients or clients of professionals, professional licensing is poorly understood. It has avoided the kind of academic scrutiny focused on other labor regulatory institutions such as unions and the minimum wage. Media attention has been spotty; while a few outlets have done in-depth investigations into systemic failures of the system, most reporting on the subject focuses on one-off scandals.

To the extent professional licensing receives attention in policy circles, the lines of the debate are, by now, familiarly drawn. On the one side is what I will call the libertarian position—that professional licensing keeps out too many workers, innovators, and new forms of competition. Licensing is a web of "red tape," raising impenetrable entry barriers and reducing economic freedom and entrepreneurship. Libertarians argue that it excludes safe, competent providers and keeps licensees from fully competing with one another. The losers are the consumers who pay too much for professional services—if they can get them at all—and the millions of workers who can't practice their trade without fear of governmental sanction. The winners are the professions themselves. On this side of the debate can be found prominent conservative think tanks, like the Institute for Justice and the Mercatus Center, and funders, such as the Koch Brothers. But the red-tape thesis cuts across the aisle; for example, Obama's economic advisors and "liberaltarian" scholars like Brink Lindsey and Steven Teles have made similar arguments.[9]

The libertarians have on their side what little academic attention has been paid to the issue. The biggest contribution here is from the field of economics, and in particular the work of Professor Morris Kleiner, whose numerous economic studies of licensing show its tendency to increase prices with little in the way of a measurable effect on quality. His work, and that of a generation of economists it has inspired, also shows that it restricts the labor market for professional services by reducing participation and mobility.[10] Economists have also found that licensing reduces innovation and welfare, broadly construed. Legal academics, by contrast, have essentially ignored the issue, meaning very little was known before I began my research about the legal and administrative processes that gave rise to the tangle of red tape in the first place.

On the other side of the debate from the libertarians are those who defend licensing as essential to service quality and safety, as a traditional form of regulation designed to preserve the independence of the professions and to protect individuals from charlatans and incompetents. On this side can be found the professions themselves, and, above all, the state licensing boards they control. Although this side lacks the empirical academic support championed by the libertarians, it has largely succeeded in resisting widespread reform of the professional licensing system.

When I began my book research in 2018, I was an active participant in this policy debate. Like most other academics, my research supported the libertarian perspective that licensing goes too far. I dedicated the early years of my career as an antitrust law professor to studying the self-regulatory structure of professional licensing, incorporating empirical economic findings into my critiques of the laws and regulators we use to implement the licensing system. I learned that almost every licensing board is dominated by professional members, so I argued that the state licensing board is like a cartel—a group of competitors who conspire to insulate themselves from competition. My scholarship was cited by the Supreme Court and earned me invitations to testify before Congress and to speak at the White House.[11]

As research often does, my work led to more questions, particularly about what was lost in the "red tape" framing of which I was a part. First, the "red tape" idea, particularly as studied by economists, focused primarily on licensing laws and not on the larger system of regulation that implements them. To a legal academic, this was like studying law without studying the courts. From what I had learned in my previous research, the legal system that decides whether and how American professionals work was almost entirely self-regulated. To what extent did the structure of professional regulation explain the endurance of the more egregious examples of licensing-gone-too-far trotted out by the critics of licensing? In other words, how much did talking about professional red tape ignore the reasons *why* there is so much of it?

Second, the framing tended to focus attention on a subset of professions that were most susceptible to the regulation-run-amok argument, or what licensing reformers call the "low-hanging fruit" of professional licensing. Of all the low-hanging fruit (and to be fair, there is a lot), the examples that seemed most to capture the imagination of the libertarians came from the business of hair. It seemed that every policy-minded media outlet had a story about a barber, hair braider, or shampooer who had been unfairly treated by the licensing system. Catch phrases like "permission-slip culture" appeared in headlines and white papers, usually illustrated with examples from the beauty industry. But to me, licensing in the beauty industry was a small piece of a bigger picture. Given that the structure of *all* professional licensing is uniquely self-regulatory among American agencies, both state and federal, how confident could we be that the problem of too much red tape is limited to low-income professions like cosmetology and barbering?

## An Inverted Agency

Before I explain how I set about to answer these questions, I should elaborate on what I mean by the "uniquely self-regulatory" structure of professional licensing, a subject that has been largely absent from either the public or scholarly debate on the issue.

For the most part, states—not the federal government—license professionals. That's a product of history more than law. Until the 1940s, courts interpreted the Constitution as keeping the federal government out of our everyday lives. Regulating how and whether people could work was considered to be beyond Congress's powers. By the time the Supreme Court opened up its interpretation to allow for federal regulation of the workplace, like the minimum wage and antidiscrimination statutes, the states had already formed the regulatory infrastructure to govern the professions.[12] For reasons that will become clear in a moment, the professions were happy with that state of affairs. Congress has not rocked the boat in the last eighty years, although legally it could probably pass federal licensing statutes that would preempt state professional regulation.

State legislatures regulate the professions—with the notable exception of law—through "practice acts" that define the scope of a profession, outline basic entry requirements like testing and education, and establish ethics rules to define good practice.[13] Perhaps the most important thing that a state licensing law does is establish a board to oversee the nitty-gritty of professional regulation. State laws give these boards the power to interpret licensing statutes, create ethics rules and other regulations that have the power of law, and decide individual cases for application or discipline.[14] Crucially, these statutes typically mandate that most board seats go to currently licensed practitioners in the profession.[15] The regulation of lawyers is even more intensely self-regulatory in that legislatures are largely not involved. States regulate legal practice through their Supreme Courts, which are, of course, made up of lawyers. Supreme Courts delegate day-to-day licensing decisions to boards that are made up entirely or almost entirely of lawyers, whose decisions are ratified, usually with a rubber stamp, by judges—in other words, by yet more lawyers.[16]

Boards are incredibly powerful. Technically, boards are subordinate to state legislatures; they cannot directly alter the legislative compromises enshrined in state practice acts. But the idea that a state board's hands are tied, and its work is merely ministerial, does not reflect reality. It is the nature of laws that they cannot be fully determinate; they cannot capture every eventuality, every specific case, every set of facts that might occur. Like judges, boards have immense interpretive power—especially when resolving individual cases.[17] And actually, the analogy to judges *understates* the regulatory power of a board because legislatures tend to be especially generous in delegating regulatory authority to boards by writing particularly vague practice acts for boards to interpret.[18]

Boards are hopelessly under-resourced. State legislatures like delegating authority to licensing boards, in part, because it's cheap. The typical state agency—which a licensing board is not—requires state funds to operate. Most licensing boards are funded by application and renewal fees paid by licensees. Boards like to keep fees low for their licensees, so this exerts downward pressure on their own operating budgets. Board members themselves work for little or no pay at all, other than reimbursed travel and meal expenses.[19] Investigations, as we will see in the second half of the book, are slow and inadequate; underfunding is part of the problem. Ideally, boards should have systematic data on how their rules might affect prices, wages, employment, and safety, but there's almost nothing in the budget for data collection. With a different board for every profession in every state, there are no economies of scale to gather or interpret this information.

Boards are invisible. Another corollary of having a separate board for every profession is that they operate under the radar. With nearly two thousand boards in the United States, it's virtually impossible to study them in any systematic way or to generalize about their successes or failures. Though powerful in the aggregate, each board oversees an average of a few thousand licensees, and it's easy to dismiss observations about one board as idiosyncratic. It took me three years of attending meetings and interviewing board members before I felt like I had a handle on just one state.

Again, comparing boards to courts is useful. Judges may be seen as less accountable than elected politicians, but even judges operate under more scrutiny than licensing boards. Judges and their opinions are regularly studied by professors like me and observed by the general public. Go downtown to the courthouse on any weekday and you'll see all kinds of people observing courts: law students, reporters, community organizers, and court watchers. Contrast that with the typical state licensing board meeting—which is sleepy and sparsely attended. In my years of watching board meetings, I almost never saw someone in the audience who did not have business with the board. In fact, I was often the *only* person in the audience.

Most importantly, boards are dominated by members of the very profession they are tasked with regulating. I undertook a systematic study of the composition of all American licensing boards in 2017, which revealed that almost all of them had a majority of professionals as members. Of the 1,740 state boards that I identified, 85 percent were required by statute to be mostly comprised of members of the profession. Vacancies and quorum rules meant that the 85 percent number probably understated the degree of control that the professions had on boards.[20] Not only were most board members currently practicing in the profession, but they typically came from the ranks of their state or national professional association, organizations dedicated to the betterment of their profession and its members.[21] Many were past presidents.

The coziness between associations and licensing boards concerned me because of all the ways in which professional and public protection could conflict. The details of how these interests collide will be explored throughout this book. For the moment, it's enough to see that what's good for the profession isn't always good for the public—for example, higher wages mean higher prices; more professional prestige can mean fewer providers. Whatever bias may be created by using professionals as regulators, it's made all the more intense by stacking boards with people who have spent their careers advocating for their profession and its members. By the time a professional gets on a licensing board, the impulse to circle the professional wagons is somewhat ingrained.

Licensing boards, of course, are unlike associations in that they are not purely private entities; they are held to state law, their decisions are usually reviewable in state court, and board members serve at the pleasure of their governor and swear an oath to the state they serve. But in exchange for these nominal checks on their power, licensing boards receive immense power not held by an association. Their decisions have the force of law and can be enforced using the power of the state. The imprimatur of government also confers legitimacy on their decisions. A board tasked with protecting the "health, safety and welfare of the citizens of Tennessee" is presumed to do so, especially when its members frequently incant that mantra at meetings. Thus, licensing boards are public-private partnerships that in some ways combine the most dangerous features of a professional association and a governmental agency. Boards have all the interests and incentives of a private club, and the police power of the state to back them up.

There is another consequence, often overlooked, that flows from packing boards with currently licensed practitioners. This effect has less to do with what those board members *are* and more to with what they *are not*. Active professionals are not government bureaucrats. That may sound like a good thing, but consider what a bureaucrat is: a professional regulator, trained in how to balance the costs and benefits of policy choices. To be sure, bureaucratic regulation doesn't always rise to its full potential. But at least in theory, full-time state employees have what virtually no board member has: regulatory expertise, the ability to collect and analyze relevant data, and, perhaps most importantly, time to dedicate to the project.

In this way, the American licensing board is an inversion of the typical governmental agency, where bureaucrats take counsel from industry experts but make the final decision for themselves. At a licensing board, those with the most information about the regulatory consequences of a decision—its staff and lawyers—can only advise. In the end, the decision is made by the men and women who take a few days off every quarter from their busy professional lives to moonlight as their own regulators.

It may seem bizarre to give this much power to what amounts to a private association dressed up in governmental clothing. In any other area of government, we would not tolerate such a conflict of interest. We would look with suspicion at a judge deciding a case where the reasonableness of her salary was at issue, or a politician introducing legislation that would benefit his business. But for the professions, self-regulation is viewed as part of the deal. Sociologists tell us that one of the defining characteristics of a profession is its autonomy—the ability for the profession itself to decide what are its boundaries, what is appropriate practice, and who can join its ranks.[22] The American professional licensing system—self-regulated through and through—is a natural extension of this principle. And boards, like the professions they regulate, pursue the prototypical image of a profession: closed from the outside and autonomous within.

## No Free Passes

The risk of over-regulation that comes with this regulatory structure was obvious to me, and not only for lower-income professions like cutting hair. As an antitrust professor, I knew that competition was essential to keeping quality and innovation high and prices low. I also knew that when left to their own devices, industry members regulating themselves would find ways to avoid competing with one another. In the professions, this might mean heavy-handed regulation that protected professional income, suppressed the number of providers, or precluded new ways of delivering service. In trading off the things that consumers cared about—safety and quality on the one hand, availability and affordability on the other—professionals regulating themselves could be expected to discount arguments about access in favor of even very hypothetical claims about safety. That was true whether you were a doctor or a barber, an architect or an auctioneer.

Yet it seemed that in the debates over licensing, high-prestige professions got a bit of a free pass. For years I had heard a standard argument from people who believed in our licensing system. We needed licensing, and specifically professionally dominated boards, to protect us from harm. Only professionals could judge good or safe practice, so only professionals could truly protect the public. Since incompetent or predatory doctors and lawyers could inflict real harm, it was hard to argue that regulation of these professions ever went too far. Doing so would require putting a dollar value on life and liberty, which was as methodologically difficult as it was politically unpopular. Further, these professions were complex and difficult to understand from the outside, so it would seem that only self-regulation made sense.

The red-tape thesis was not well-positioned to challenge this narrative. By framing the problem as an economic cost / benefit analysis, where benefit was defined essentially as safety, the libertarian critique was most convincing when professions like medicine and law were left out of it. But I wondered: were rules that made legal and medical help more expensive and harder to find worth it just to keep out a few bad apples? (I did, at that time, take for granted the idea that these boards *were* keeping out the bad apples.) I wanted my book to interrogate the most prestigious professions along with the cosmetologists and auctioneers. So, for that reason, I started at the top.

The cosmetology board meeting where Omar Mahmoud was denied his license because he used an Arabic-language interpreter in the exam was therefore not the first licensing board meeting I attended in

Tennessee, but the second. My first meeting had been three weeks earlier, across town at the Tennessee Board of Medical Examiners, where I saw the board consider the application of Dr. Edward Owens.

Dr. Owens, an OBGYN from Memphis, had lost his license the previous year because he admitted to having had sex with eleven patients and prescribing some of them large quantities of drugs without documentation. He had told the board he knew the patients were likely reselling the prescription drugs for cash (the most reasonable inference, and one shared by several board members, was that he was compensating them for sex). He had admitted to the board that he had had sex with a patient in his office after performing a pelvic exam on her, and that he had invited another patient to have sex with him in the physician sleeping quarters of the maternity ward while he was on call. Dr. Owens had testified that he had come to work intoxicated and had taken drugs while on the job. He had twice lost hospital privileges after settling malpractice suits and accumulating ten hospital "peer-review" cases over bad outcomes, including one that involved a stillborn child.[23]

But at that hearing in March 2018, a few months after his temporary revocation, I saw him ask the board to put all that in the past. He appeared before the board as a changed man, he said, asking for a new license to practice medicine. He wore a pressed suit and brought his lawyer and the two psychiatrists that had shepherded him through an intense recovery process to address his addictions: drugs, sex, and gambling. (His recovery began in 2013—the year the medical board learned about his misdeeds, but four years before it took any action against his license.) As I watched from the back of the room, he approached the microphone to address the twelve-member board with his head bowed. "I'm deeply humbled," he said. "I'm truly sorry and I'd like to show I can be a better physician than I was the last time I practiced here in the state of Tennessee."

A physician board member said that what impressed her in the case was "a meticulous attention to recovery." Most board members agreed that Dr. Owens should be given a fresh start to symbolize his having shed what he described as the "narcissistic character traits" he used to have. Shortly before the board voted to give Dr. Owens a new license to practice medicine in Tennessee, one board member said, "I'm all about second chances."[24]

The Owens case turned out not to be an aberration, as I hoped it would be, but rather a mere example from a professional disciplinary system too forgiving to be safe. In the course of my research, I saw boards keep in practice lawyers who extorted sex from their indigent clients in exchange for their services, medical professionals who took guilty pleas in federal court for dealing opioids, and doctors who prescribed such dangerous quantities and combinations of drugs that patients died. I saw these decisions alongside ones that vindicated the libertarian hypothesis, that boards go too far in keeping providers out and competition down. An apparent contradiction emerged. When it came to barriers to entry and restrictions on practice, boards went too far; when it came to disciplining dangerous providers, they didn't go nearly far enough.

It may be hard to get into the club of the professionally licensed, but once you're in, you're in.

## Showing Up

This book is the product of the four years I spent embedded in my state's professional licensing system. I attended board meetings, transcribed meetings from videos pulled from the web, and gathered data on how boards make rules and disciplinary decisions. I tried to overcome my awkwardness as a nosey outsider at these meetings by actually getting to know licensing board members. In many cases I succeeded; board members were happy to chat with me during breaks, or over coffee or dinner. When COVID hit, my methodology went virtual and I interviewed board members on Zoom and on the phone.

I interviewed other players in the licensing game: board staff and administrators, board attorneys and administrative law judges, professionals seeking licensure and license holders facing board discipline, professional students and educators, advocates for licensure reform, state lawmakers, and federal law enforcement officers. My research took me from hair salons in Nashville to pill mills in East Tennessee. I got to know recovering addicts, doctors under federal indictment, and conscientious objectors to my state's hair-cutting laws. In all, I interviewed more than 180 people involved in the regulation of twenty-eight professions.

Some of the names of people I interviewed and whose cases I observed before licensing boards have been omitted or changed for this book. My goal here is to explain a system, not expose the misconduct of individuals who comprise it. In fact, one of my primary claims is that the failures of our professional licensing system are utterly banal, and even the most shocking stories of regulatory dysfunction found in this book are depressingly typical. Affording some anonymity to my subjects allows me to paint a picture for the reader without unfairly making examples out of the people who helped me learn the truth about licensing.

The state I got to know best was Tennessee, but my observations apply broadly across America. Publicly available information shows that Tennessee's professional regulatory system is unexceptional in almost every way. The regulatory process that Tennessee uses is typical—most professions in my state are governed by boards dominated by the very professionals the board is supposed to oversee, and Tennessee is not an outlier in terms of how stringent its licensing rules are or how well the medical board protects patients.[25]

To test whether these structural similarities between states created the same regulatory results I observed in Tennessee, I expanded my primary-source research and interviewed people involved in licensing in twenty-six other states. I attended multiday meetings of the Federation of Associations of Regulatory Boards—an umbrella organization that counts hundreds of professional licensing boards from all fifty states among its members. I went to conferences put on by national organizations like the National Conference of State Legislatures about professional licensing and the politics of reforming the system.

I also dove deep into the secondary literature on licensing. To the many economics papers I had read for previous work I added studies from sociology, medicine, and even a few from law. I also read countless news articles and investigative reports on licensing and its problems. In the end, I amassed more than eight hundred academic and media articles on professional licensing from around the country. This national literature on licensing, referenced throughout this book, confirms that Tennessee represents the norm.

There are some differences between states, such as how they use independent judges in disciplinary cases or how much oversight state government has over board decisions. I note these differences where they are relevant, but from my observations, no state is doing it right. There is, however, one important way in which Tennessee is an outlier. My state has liberal sunshine laws that mandate public access to meetings and, for all professions except my own (law), prohibit secret board deliberations. Even better, Tennessee livestreams its licensing board meetings and makes audio and video recordings available online. If my state is more transparent than most, and if sunshine is the best disinfectant, then my criticisms based on Tennessee's boards should be even stronger when applied to the rest of the country.

## What I Saw Where No One Was Looking

In my years with the licensing boards of Tennessee, I saw a lot of very boring things happen in meetings that probably should be a part of any well-functioning regulatory system. For example, I sat through an eight-hour disciplinary trial of an accountant accused of conducting a subpar audit (although the experience was worthwhile because it inspired the working title for this book—*Board to Death*). I also learned that the typical board member is well-meaning and of high integrity; I did not meet a single board member who did not take seriously his or her obligation to the people of the state of Tennessee. But I also found that when professional interests and public protection don't align, which is often, board members struggle to set aside their professional biases in the name of the public. The result is a regulatory system that is by and for professionals, and neither reasonable nor safe from a public protection point of view.

Part I, "Locked Out," tells the story of a regulatory system that goes too far in the name of public safety, and thus largely supports most of the libertarian hypothesis. Professional licensing boards, influenced by the professional associations from which they come, operate a one-way ratchet, increasing entry barriers to their profession over time and resisting competitive incursions on professional turf. As barriers grow and competition suffers, patients and clients pay more for less. What the libertarian focus misses here, and what was painfully obvious as I watched America try to cope with COVID with far too few healthcare providers, is that the pathologies of professional self-regulation go well beyond shampooers and hair braiders. And while we all pay for the overregulation of the hair professions with our money, the rural poor and otherwise underserved pay for overregulation in healthcare with their lives.

I also learned that the story about too much red tape for the low-income professions has a side not presented by the conventional accounts. Licensing does leave too many marginalized workers like immigrants, ex-offenders, and racial minorities out of the American Dream. But for members of those same marginalized groups who *do* make it into a profession, the fact that the profession is licensed—that the government has said that "not just anybody" can do it—is a big part of what makes it part of their American Dream in the first place.

I saw Black hair professionals from West Tennessee fight hard, and successfully, to defend their license against legislative threats, arguing that it served as a pathway to the middle class and to a dignified and respectable career. Several generations ago, sociologists claimed that licensure was the ultimate symbol of status for doctors and lawyers.[26] So it is for the lower-income licensed professionals of today. The fact that licensing benefits some workers like the hair professionals from West Tennessee does not by itself justify the ways in which it harms others, like Omar Mahmoud and Fatou Diouf, a hair braider from Senegal who appears in several chapters of this book. But seeing both sides of the story helped me see why reforming the lower-income professions, especially barbering and cosmetology, has been so fraught.

The chapters in Part II ("Locked In") reveal that the unexamined claim at the heart of licensing—that its high prices and scarcity are worth it for its benefits to public safety—are hard to square with boards' behavior as disciplinarians. Boards make little effort to discover misconduct and even when they do, they tend to protect the careers of manifestly dangerous and incompetent providers. These disciplinary decisions, so inexplicable from the outside, conform to an internal logic of board decision-making that is a product of poor system design and lack of resources. The professional disciplinary system uses board members primed to see the humanity in their fallen colleagues, gives them too little information, and asks them to go with their gut.

Moreover, I learned that the problem of inadequate discipline has a perverse twist. Bad doctors and lawyers who are allowed to stay in their professions after disciplinary proceedings tend to lose their ability to work for high-end firms or hospitals, or to take private insurance. They have few professional opportunities other than as doctors and lawyers to the uninsured, addicted and poor, the incarcerated or accused. The licensing system keeps the worst of the worst in practice, and then shunts them toward the most desperate members of the public. The criminal system has tried to compensate for an inadequate discipline by putting bad professionals behind bars, but it is a poor substitute for a functional system of professional licensure.

What we need is a coherent, defensible theory for when licensing is required; its absence is a troubling omission in the literature, and a product of too little legal academic attention to the topic. I fill that gap in the Conclusion with a novel theory of when to use professional licensing and how to do it correctly. The significant downsides of professional licensing can be justified only for work that implicates public safety *and* that requires individualized, case-specific application of complex knowledge that cannot be broken down into a set of bright-line rules of practice. In other words, licensing makes sense when a job is dangerous and requires professional judgment to be done right.

For the professions requiring this kind of governmental intervention (fewer than are licensed now), regulation should be more *governmental*— bureaucratic, accountable, and disinterested—than the unfettered self-regulation of the present-day state professional licensing board. Getting professional licensing right requires, at the very least, changes to board resources, personnel, and procedures. Boards should be given the funds and expertise they need to do their jobs, they should include more voices from outside the professions, and they should be held accountable through stricter decision-making procedures. But this may not be enough. State governments should also consider eliminating the board system altogether and claim for themselves the decision-making authority they enjoy over in almost every other area of regulation.

The arrangement between society and the professions is often described as the "grand bargain."[27] For its part, society agreed to leave the professions alone from governmental interference and to confer a high degree of trust and esteem on their members. In exchange, the professions agreed to regulate themselves in the public's interest, to police their own, and keep us safe. We were promised that the professions would "set and enforce standards for the quality of their work, and that they will only admit appropriately qualified individuals into their ranks."[28] Nowhere is this arrangement more apparent than in the design and structure of the American system of professional licensing. Every day, we hold up our end of the bargain by giving state licensing boards nearly unfettered autonomy over their profession.

Have the professions held up their end of the bargain? The board members I met would say yes. Every professional board member I met understood his or her obligation to protect the public; each held himself or herself to a high ethical standard. And yet I saw them do things that anyone from the outside could see put the public directly and unacceptably at risk.

Over the next two sections of this book, I will explain the failure of this bargain and its consequences for society. I will unpack the biases of licensing board members and explain how even the best professionals can remain blind to them. And I will show that although the spirit of altruism is alive and well within the professions, it is folly to believe goodwill alone leads to reasonable and safe professional regulation. By putting self-regulation at the heart of the most important labor regulatory institution in America, the professional licensing system is letting all of us down.

# Part I

---

# Locked Out

# 1

## The Ratchet

*Professional regulation creeps upward over time. The professions and the boards they control have a lot to do with that.*

On an unusually warm Saturday in November 2020, I drove to the south-east corner of Nashville to visit the African-style hair braiding salon of Fatou Diouf. It was a small storefront in a strip mall in an area of town dense with immigrant-run restaurants and businesses. As I walked through the door all eyes were on me. The white lady with smooth hair did not belong. When it became clear that I was there at the invitation of the boss, the braiders turned back to their work, fingers moving in a fast, intricate rhythm, sometimes two braiders to a client. Ms. Diouf was busy, too—she was braiding a client's hair, taking calls nonstop on the Bluetooth in her ear, and, ostensibly, giving me an interview.[1]

Ms. Diouf arrived from Senegal at age twenty-three to study business administration. Twenty-two years later, she still remembered the exact date she landed: October 18th, 1998. It was not only the day of her arrival, but it was the first day she braided hair in America. She went straight from the airport to a braiding shop to do what she had been doing since she was a girl: braid hair.

African-style hair braiding, as most commonly practiced in the United States, involves braiding synthetic hair—sold in long, unbraided form—into someone's natural hair, and then braiding the synthetic hair to the end. It requires no chemicals, sharp tools, or heat. "We do this with our bare hands," Ms. Diouf told me, holding up ten fingers to illustrate.

She started the business administration program, but quickly realized she could make a good living from doing her passion and so she quit school. She started braiding in a salon where the stylists—as was, and still is, common—were unlicensed. She had heard all about the state board inspector before she actually saw him. "You were hearing Nick, Nick, Nick, all the time," she recalled. "And then one day, it was 'Nick's here! Run! Run!'"

The scene was one repeated all over Tennessee—and the country— on a daily basis: stylists running out the back door as a hair board inspector stepped in the front. Diouf had heard that if they caught you, you could never get a license. "[We'd] give fake names," she recalled, "whatever sounded African. Fruits, vegetables." Later in our interview, when Ms. Diouf, who is Muslim, took a break to pray, her client leaned in, as if confiding, to tell me she was there all those years ago for one of the Nick raids. "I had to go home with my hair half-done," she remembered. "It was scary."

The raids kept coming, and Diouf kept braiding and running. To her and her colleagues, braiding was their heritage and culture. "Braiding started in Africa. . . . We didn't see ourselves going to school, it didn't make sense," she told me. The idea of needing hundreds of hours of instruction in an American beauty school and permission from state government to braid hair seemed, to Ms. Diouf, absurd. She thought maybe the state licensing board, comprised of fellow hair professionals, might be persuaded to see it that way, too.

Ms. Diouf learned that the board met on the first Monday of every month in Nashville. She and her colleagues (other unlicensed braiders also tired of running from Nick) drove downtown to make their case to the board that braiding was harmless and the constant raids were unnecessary to protect the public. They explained that braiding was a part of their African heritage, not a college major. It was a craft taught by mothers and grandmothers in living rooms, not by instructors in classrooms. A good braiding job—the product of practice and talent—meant your client came back. A bad braiding job meant she didn't. Neither scenario, they pointed out, implicated the health, safety, or welfare of the citizens of Tennessee.

The board held firm. "They kept repeating the same thing: 'You have to go to school,'" Ms. Diouf recalled. "They had no argument," she said, "they knew what we were saying was true." The experience left her without hope. "It's going to keep going," she remembered thinking about the raids and fines.

What Ms. Diouf didn't fully understand at that moment was that she was trying to relitigate a dispute that had been settled a decade before with the creation of the Tennessee "natural hair" license. The only way to stop the raids was for Ms. Diouf to navigate the obstacles put in place by the board for hair braiders in Tennessee: three hundred hours of classroom education, an application fee, and a two-part examination.[2] And far from the empathy she expected from colleagues in the beauty industry, it seemed the hair professionals on the board actually *wanted* to make it hard for her to become licensed.

The braiding license was the product of a fierce battle that raged in many states around the country, a battle that came down to simple economics.[3] In the 1980s, braiding became popular among African Americans looking for a natural hair style. For some, it was the ideological inheritor of the Afro—the next generation's offering in a movement that rejected the idea that Black hair needed to be smoothed and chemically damaged to appear more white. For others, it was simply a lower-maintenance look that offered variety and versatility.[4]

The rise of the Afro in the 1960s and 1970s created its own economic crisis in the Black hair industry, as cosmetologists saw their clients opting for a style that could be maintained at home with fewer trips to the beauty salon. But the crisis posed by braiding was different, because for most people it was not an at-home style. It required the services of a braider, and often this happened in shops, and often for quite a bit of money. Debra Nutall, who got her start braiding in Memphis in the 1980s, told the Associated Press, "I never imagined it would take me as far as it did. I was able to buy my first home, my first car, and my children did not have to grow up in public housing."[5]

The fact that braiding happened in shops for money gave the cosmetology profession its opportunity to neutralize the competitive threat. Boards around the country started raiding braiding shops, claiming that braiding was a form of cosmetology. Braiders like Nutall were fined and bullied into closing their shops. Some boards went further, using cops posing as clients to arrest unlicensed braiders.[6]

In their campaign against unlicensed braiding, cosmetology boards had one problem: their statutes did not obviously give them authority over the practice. "Cosmetology" included cutting, dying, and relaxing hair, but not braiding.[7] If braiding were to come under the ambit of these boards, a legislative change would be necessary, and a legislative change meant a public battle between cosmetologists and braiders. In Tennessee, that battle resulted in a compromise: a three-hundred-hour natural hair license—the license Ms. Diouf didn't have on the day she appealed to the board.[8]

When Ms. Diouf asked the cosmetology board to relax its licensing requirement for braiders, she was essentially asking a profession to lower its entry barriers in the name of entrepreneurship and opportunity. But once the license for braiding had been established, the board dominated by hair professionals wasn't about to give ground. As Ms. Diouf learned that day, the ratchet of professional licensing only went one way.

## The Proliferation of Licensing and Its Barriers

For many professions licensed today, elaborate educational and testing requirements and constant government surveillance is more than what's necessary to protect the public. It was not always this way. Sixty years ago, we licensed only a handful of occupations, mostly what we considered the "learned professions"—medicine, law, nursing, architecture, and engineering—where public safety was at stake and good practice was too complicated to be reduced to simple do's and don'ts that didn't require years of training. But over the last half a century, professional licensing has exploded as a regulatory intervention, now covering about three hundred professions, many of which do not obviously pose significant public risk or seem to require complicated knowledge.

When we drill down into the actual requirements for these licenses, the picture gets even worse, as the height of entry barriers over time has grown along with licensing's proliferation. Tennessee's hair braiding license is a good example—although three hundred hours of instruction was a fraction of the hours required at the time to become licensed to *cut* hair (1,800 hours), it was still more class time than a semester of college, and almost twice as many educational hours as it took to become an emergency medical technician.[9]

How do professions end up licensed in ways that defy common sense? Licensing starts out small, with a legislative proposal brought by the profession itself and often without any pushback from the consumers and the workers the license will exclude, who will ultimately experience its downsides. Busy legislators vote for it because it's presented as a win-win, and the lack of pushback contributes to the sense that it's an issue less deserving of their attention than more salient topics like education, abortion, or criminal law.

Once a profession secures for itself a licensing law—and control over the regulatory board that oversees it—it uses that influence to work the ratchet of professional regulation upward. Initial licensure works as a kind of "foot in the door," as one advocate for his profession told me; from there, professionally dominated boards drive an iterative process of increasing regulation through their own power, then push the legislature to enshrine their changes in statute.[10] For example, when they were initially licensed in the 1990s, alcohol and drug abuse counselors needed fifteen hundred hours of supervised practice to be licensed to provide counseling on their own. As the professionally dominated licensing board worked the ratchet over the years, that number doubled to three thousand; then again to six thousand. Thus, by the time I started watching the board as it considered relenting on another recent hike they had made in their entry requirements, the supervised practice requirement for addiction counselors was as long as a medical residency.

The notion that licensure works as a one-way ratchet is borne out by empirical data. A national study of licensing for electricians, dental hygienists, respiratory therapists, and real estate agents revealed that on average, over time, states tend to increase licensing requirements along three dimensions: experience required for licensure, the cost of licensure, and continuing education requirements. For example, it found that states had increased the experiential requirements for electricians by 4 percent year-over-year since 1980. The study also found that boards dominated by professionals increased requirements more steeply.[11] Understanding how this ratchet works requires knowing what professionals want out of government regulation and how they exercise control over it.

## Licensure Is Good; More Is Better

Professions want licensure, and more of it. In some ways it's surprising that professions want the government to limit their ability to practice, as it might have been to Ms. Diouf when she received no mercy from her professional board. But in fact, a governmental license provides professionals with three categories of rewards: reduced competition, increased professional prestige, and control and autonomy over their work.

First, licensure protects professionals from competition. Imposing the kinds of educational and testing barriers that go along with professional licensure reduces the number of people who can practice and compete with each other. Occasionally, professionals invoke financial protectionism explicitly, as when I heard a board member advocate for stronger certification and testing in his profession because he was "concerned about pay for our counselors in the trenches . . . if you flood the market, you will lower the pay."[12] Often, it's more oblique. At a legislative hearing about the Alarm System Contractors Board, a board member testified that high fees were set for applications in an effort to "clean up the industry."[13]

A more subtle way that licensure can reduce competition is through the promulgation of ethics and other practice rules. For example, the ethical rules in law against advertising or communicating with someone who already has a lawyer reduce competition among lawyers.[14] So, too, do rules that limit where and when providers can work. If cosmetologists were permitted to make house calls, then the whole profession would be under competitive pressure to offer them, disrupting the comfort and convenience of those who want to work in a salon. A similar phenomenon can be found in debates about telemedicine. Telemedicine is cheaper to provide than in-person medicine (and therefore a potentially competitive offering) but is less professionally satisfying for physicians. Until COVID forced their hands, professional groups had resisted it, citing quality-of-care concerns.[15] Unwanted competition was another explanation for its unpopularity.

Second, licensure confers prestige on a profession. Licensure gives a profession the imprimatur of the state, an air of exclusivity, and an association with the "learned professions" like medicine and law. Sociologists say state licensure is the ultimate step in professionalization, a sign that a line of work is more than a mere "occupation."[16] A barber may never achieve the social status of a lawyer, but requiring the same number of classroom hours for both licenses, as Tennessee does, puts them in the same ballpark. A licensing restriction also contributes to a profession's identity, setting it apart from related areas of practice. An art therapist is not just another therapist if you need a separate license for it. Even high-prestige professions fight to maintain high barriers to licensure, for example, by promulgating ethics rules that preclude low-cost alternatives (such as online automated legal help) in order to shore up a profession's status as elite or learned.[17]

I saw evidence that status and esteem were primary motivators for seeking licensure. The National Association of Alcohol and Drug Abuse Counselors provides a template statement for its members seeking licensure to use when lobbying state legislatures. "Adopting a licensing law for counselors will move this profession ahead. . . . Licensing will provide increased credibility and professionalism for this field," it says.[18] Similarly, interior designers identified "legitimacy," "affirmation," and "identity" as reasons to seek licensure.[19] Meanwhile, hair professionals especially chafe at the idea of deprofessionalization. When I asked a beauty school student at a cosmetology meeting about the recent push to delicense aspects of her profession, she said "something has to set us apart from the general public. In a world where everyone has a degree, [a license] gives you an edge."[20]

Finally, licensing is attractive to a profession because it's the best of both worlds: it confers the benefits of legal restraints (less competition and more esteem), while giving the profession itself autonomy over how those restraints will be used.[21] Licensing, because it usually goes hand-in-hand with a self-regulatory board, gives the profession the horsepower of the state and the reins to control it. Control is especially important for professions that feel they can end up playing second fiddle. The interior design profession believes it won't get out from under architecture's thumb until it has its own license. And a dental hygienist I interviewed explained the problem with using a board comprised of dentists to regulate hygienists: "Until we govern our own profession, we will always be looked at as someone's auxiliary."[22]

Professional interests like those in play in licensing are the focus of professional associations, or voluntary, private advocacy organizations comprised of professional members. There are national and state versions of these associations, and they all seek the betterment of the profession and its members. Sometimes these interests align with public safety, and indeed many professional associations take policy positions that do benefit patients, clients, and the public welfare in general. But at their core, they are an organized voice for the profession and its members, seeking to vindicate the things professionals care most about: working conditions, public esteem, financial security, and professional autonomy. There is nothing inherently wrong with groups like professions organizing to advocate for themselves; it is an important part of our democracy. But it is important to recognize that associations, by definition, approach regulatory and policy questions from the perspective of their professional members.

## Odysseus and His Lobbyists

Usually, behind any act of regulation is something that most people can agree is a problem. Mandatory seatbelts came out of car crash deaths; Congress created federal deposit insurance following waves of banking panics in the early 1930s.[23] Victims and advocates for change raise awareness and call for action, while regulatory targets (car manufacturers, banks) resist change. Since industry tends to have deep pockets and loud lobbyists, the pressure against regulation from its targets can be intense. Politicians, of course, have their own ideals and incentives. All of these interests and pressures get fed into the gears of our legislative system, along with a significant amount of sand. What comes out isn't perfect, but it can be close enough to do some good.

Since licensing works out well for those subject to it, the process of enacting a professional licensing law looks very different. It's not resisted by the target of regulation—it's usually their idea.[24] Economies of scale for a state-by-state push for licensure are provided by a national association, which designs the campaign and its arguments. Local professionals bring this template to their state legislatures and ask them to essentially bind their profession with a practice act setting entry barriers and restrictions on practice.

On the one hand, this can look like an act of self-control or self-sacrifice, as when Odysseus asked his shipmates to tie him to the mast so that he would not steer the ship toward the Sirens' enchanting song. But in the case of licensing, the incumbents don't usually feel the full restraints of the law for which they advocate. Either they already possess the requirements they seek to impose, or the proposed practice act "grandfathers" in existing providers by exempting them from the license requirement.[25] One researcher I talked to described this as the professions "rais[ing] a drawbridge."[26]

To the extent anyone identifies a problem that must be addressed through licensure, it doesn't come from consumer or patient groups. It's identified by the profession itself, often in the form of a hypothetical. I attended an interior design conference where a speaker on the "advocacy tools" panel suggested that designers meet one-on-one in legislators' offices to push for licensure. She said the "lightbulb moment" happened when you pointed out that "if someone were to come in here with a gun," the legislator's ability to exit safely was down to good interior design.[27]

These meetings can make all the difference. As organized groups, professionals and their lobbyists are able to make their opinions heard more loudly and forcefully on the proverbial "hill" (it happens that my state's capitol, like the United States Capitol, rests on a hill) than those of other groups who might also care, like consumers or marginalized workers.[28] These lobbyists can answer a legislator's questions about public protection truthfully if they answer them narrowly: licensure will probably keep at least some bad providers out and, theoretically, can lead to higher-quality practice. The legislator should ask questions about whether that quality improvement is worth it in terms of scarcity, higher prices, and fewer opportunities for workers. But more likely she will shrug and vote for it, figuring the professionals get what they want and consumers might be better off, too. To a state legislator, debates about licensing issues can seem one-sided, which helps the misperception that licensing is not an important issue.

State legislators don't care enough about licensing to do the kind of work it takes to hash out specifically worded statutes. They are busier than members of the federal Congress because they are responsible for a wider swath of regulation and are given an average of half the time to do it (in all but a few states, legislators are part-time).[29] They draw a modest salary and therefore maintain day jobs for when the legislature isn't in session. Busy state legislators welcome the opportunity to unload regulatory authority and interpretive leeway to licensing boards. And the professions and their lobbyists like it this way, too.

The story behind a 2018 bill to license art therapists illustrates the point. I interviewed the state representative sponsoring the legislation, and he said he first became interested in the issue when a friend of his told him his nephew was an art therapist and wanted licensure for his profession. "They came to me and made a compelling case," he said of the art therapists' lobby. They told him art therapy was especially effective for treating veterans with PTSD, and that licensure would "distinguish" them and allow for third-party reimbursement.[30] He explained that consumer protection was a secondary goal, "but there was some interest in providing patients with a sense of what they were getting."[31]

In the end, that bill failed, but not because art therapy was unlikely to implicate public health or because it would possibly increase costs for people who benefitted from it. It failed because art therapists insisted on regulatory control over the license, but the legislature balked at the cost of having a stand-alone board. The next time the bill came through, it presented a compromise that evidently the art therapists could live with: a three-member art therapy board made up entirely of professionals that would be "advisory" to the psychology board. It passed, and art therapists are now their own licensed profession in Tennessee.[32]

## Licensing Board as Professional Association

Once a profession has secured licensure—and the majority of seats on the board that will oversee it—the work on the ratchet continues at the board level. Association influence of board decision-making is profound, starting with the fact that associations pick who will be on the board. Associations often float slates of candidates for the governor's consideration; some states formalize this process into law.[33]

The reasons why most board members come from leadership in a state professional association are both practical and political. Most board members are appointed by their state's governor, and although a lot of board appointments are acts of political patronage, there are only so many midwives, accountants, and funeral directors who are owed a favor from the governor.[34] Professional association leadership is the perfect place to turn to find board members who are respected in their fields. It never hurts for a governor to curry favor with professional associations; they can have significant political clout in state government. Leadership in a professional association also signals some of the rarest qualities one can find in competent professionals: time and a willingness to serve one's profession without much in the way of compensation or recognition. "You have to find people who are service-oriented and altruistic," a former member of the chiropractic board told me. "And usually those are involved with associations."[35]

Once selected, board members are not prohibited from retaining their membership in their professional association while serving on the regulatory board. In fact, I heard board attorneys encourage sitting members to lobby the legislature on professional licensing issues, as long as they did so under the aegis of a professional association, not in their capacity as board members.[36] For example, at a meeting of the Board of Cosmetology and Barber Examiners, a board member asked about whether she should speak out against a pending bill that would roll back the high-school requirements for barbers. "I just want to know if I need to be the squeaky wheel on this," she said.[37] In another meeting, the chair of the physical therapy board told his fellow board members to work with the state's professional association to "get on the same page to decide what to bring to the legislature."[38] Board members cling tight to their influence over the legislature; a bill that would have prohibited licensing boards from using licensing fees to hire lobbyists failed during the time that I was watching them.[39]

When I asked professional board members about whether they saw their roles as association advocate and public regulator as conflicting, I got two answers. The first was that much of what the profession wanted for itself—strict entry requirements, strong ethics rules, and relaxed competition—was good for the public, too. This seemed to be the perspective of a former member of the chiropractic board whose brother was, at the time, the president of the state professional association of chiropractors. He told me they would get together to hash out the board's agenda, saying "we gotta get this stuff fixed."[40] Some board members told me they were on the board to protect the public and, in nearly the same breath, to "elevate" or "advocate for" the profession or simply to "keep us regulated."[41]

A full accounting of the claim that what's good for the profession is good for the public will have to wait for Chapter 3, but suffice it to say it's only sometimes true. High standards can theoretically lead to better service, although the empirical evidence of licensing's effect on quality is weak. Prestige and esteem prevent professional burnout, theoretically leading to more and better providers and greater public trust and confidence in what they are getting. In other ways, however, public and professional interests collide. The higher professional pay sought by associations generally must come out of the pockets of consumers and patients. The prestige and exclusivity of professional licensing also leads to provider scarcity, reducing access to services. Practice and ethics rules can ossify a profession and prevent innovation that would otherwise benefit the public. I heard a nice formulation of how the interests of a profession and of the public can conflict as I listened to a panel about nursing licensure at a national conference on licensing. The nursing advocate said he'd had to ask his constituent nurses, in culling down their desired licensing restrictions, "How many of these are about public protection, and how many are just nice to have?"[42]

The other answer I got when I asked professionals about the potential for conflicting interests was that when they stepped down from their association to assume a seat on their state's board, they changed hats. A few modified the sartorial metaphor and told me they removed their civilian clothes or doffed their proverbial white lab coat. But mostly I heard about hats.

Changing hats, board members told me, required constant reminders. A past president of the Tennessee Medical Association (TMA) and current member of the medical board said, "Your first instinct is to protect your colleagues—I was very involved in advocating for the profession. You have to change hats."[43] A few hours later I heard her slip up and call to order a meeting of the TMA, not the medical licensing board she was sitting on.[44]

If board members are constantly reminding themselves to protect the public, so too are their staff. At most discussions about rule or policy changes, I heard the state-employed lawyers and administrators who support the board try to draw the board back from professional protectionism by cautioning them to consider the public.[45] These admonishments often resulted in board members tacking on "the health, safety, and welfare of the people of Tennessee" as a reason for their decision, but it rarely changed the substance. Despite these admonishments, board members still felt comfortable prefacing comments during a meeting with a phrase like "coming from the Tennessee Dental Association . . ."[46]

As much as I respected the integrity of the board members I got to know, and as seriously as they seemed to take the need to change hats, I had my doubts that a professional—after years of association work and ingrained habits of professional advocacy—could by sheer force of will shed her hard-won professional identity and see things as a client or a patient would. And the frequency with which I saw boards let professional interests influence their decisions made me pessimistic about whether it *was* possible to change that particular hat.

For example, when boards spoke of their "constituency" or "stakeholders," or even "the public," they weren't talking about patients or consumers, they were talking about licensees and their advocacy groups. I asked a chiropractic board member what the most important thing was in making a regulatory decision and he said, "how it is going to affect individual doctors." (Chiropractors refer to one another as "doctors," to the chagrin of the medical profession.)[47] I asked a nursing board member about this conflation of the public and the profession, and he said that his board's mission was to protect the health, safety, and welfare of the citizens of the state of Tennessee. "Nurses are citizens of the state of Tennessee," he explained.[48]

Sometimes special treatment for this "constituency" is quite direct. Boards don't always operate on a completely balanced budget, and they can accumulate funds when their licensing fee revenue exceeds their operating costs. When this happens, a board generates a surplus. For example, in 2018, the Tennessee Real Estate Commission had a $4 million surplus *and* another $4 million in a consumer recovery fund (a fund ostensibly to compensate harmed consumers; in fact, compensation through recovery funds is notoriously rare).[49] In states like Tennessee, these surpluses can be "swept" by the governor into the general state fund. Boards in these states would rather spend down their surplus before the governor comes for it, and they sometimes find creative ways to do so. The Tennessee contractors board paid $1.7 million of its surplus to an industry organization called "Go Build Tennessee."[50] I learned at a conference that the Nevada State Contractors Board cut out the middleman and wrote checks out of its surplus to the state's licensees for a total of $3 million.[51]

## Working the Ratchet

Handouts aside, the most common way that boards pursue the interests of their association is by working the ratchet of professional licensing on their behalf. State law uses vague language to describe professional entry standards (another product of the political economy of licensing), giving boards "quite a bit of leeway" over licensing policy, as one sitting board member told me.[52] So long as the board follows the right processes for making the interpretive rule, it has the same force of law as the statute it interprets. The result is ever-increasing barriers to entry and a moving target for people trying to obtain a license.

It's not just entry rules that boards change on a dime. Boards use practice and ethics rules, too, to work the ratchet upward. Rules demanding higher degrees of supervision, ethical rules against advertising, and rules limiting the what, where, and when of professional service all potentially reduce consumer and patient satisfaction while increasing practitioner convenience or pay. Although this serves the profession as a whole, not all providers like it. I met a professional at a board meeting who was so stressed out by the prospect of losing his livelihood to board regulation that he said I couldn't use his quote if I revealed even so much as his profession. He motioned for me to follow him out into the hallway, away from the microphones recording the meeting. He whispered to me, "These guys can change one rule, and the whole way I practice is toast."

Licensing boards also use their interpretive authority to increase the costs of staying licensed. Most professions require their members to keep up their training with continuing education (often referred to as "continuing education units" or CEUs) as a condition of licensure renewal. Whether continuing education is a good way to keep up professional quality is an open question; a study looking at an increase in CEUs for real estate agents was unable to find a measurable effect on quality. But higher CEU requirements do measurably benefit professionals by reducing the number of competing professionals and increasing their wages.[53] Many boards reserve for themselves the right to approve CEU providers, sometimes down to the course and instructor. This allows boards to deal out market power over continuing education to professional groups they favor such as associations, schools, and even private businesses. And CEUs can be big money; the medical continuing education industry alone is a multi-billion-dollar industry.[54]

When I say that boards use their interpretive authority to work the ratchet, I do not mean that they do so consciously, or with their own bottom line in mind. Rather, these choices are a product of what could at most be called an attitude or a posture of deference to the professional point of view, especially as offered by the professional representatives that attend board meetings—like association leaders and professional school instructors. I saw boards frequently ask association reps in attendance for input before making a decision or, once, suggest that the meeting be paused for an off-the-record discussion between board and association members (this was shut down by the board's lawyer as violating the state's sunshine laws).[55]

This posture of deference is made possible by the identity of the board members as once-and-future advocates for their profession. But there is more—the posture of deference is made *necessary* by the board members' own lack of regulatory expertise, time, and resources. When it comes to working the ratchet of professional licensure, boards need to delegate. As one advocate for her profession told me, boards "rely on organizations to do their business."[56] That was not lost on the advocacy groups and for-profit companies that sought to unburden the board of its regulatory obligations.

I repeatedly saw associations offer to "rewrite" the board's own rules for them. Most of the time these revisions were described by the associations as "cleaning up" the language of the rules and promoting internal consistency.[57] But I assumed—as the board members must have—that these revisions also promoted consistency with the association's policy goals of ever-stricter licensing requirements. Private associations do not have the authority to directly change board rules, but they can propose a draft for consideration, and if the board then jumps through the formal hoops necessary to adopt the changes, the association's rules become state law. In truth, it's not uncommon for first drafts of laws or rules to be written by a private interest group—it happens all the time at the federal and state legislatures. But usually that draft is revised by the ultimate decision-maker after much debating, wordsmithing, compromising, and gnashing of teeth. What was unusual here was the way in which the associations and boards talked about it, as if the board would merely ratify the association's draft.

Another example of delegating the work of regulation to a private professional organization was the way boards made policy decisions through "taskforces," which was used as a pseudonym for the state association. I attended a meeting of the Board of Physical Therapy where the head of the association said they were nearly done with a complete rewrite of the board's rules. The chairman of the licensing board (a physical therapy assistant and former member of the association) seemed grateful for the help and offered to create a board taskforce to consider the changes. He suggested a taskforce consisting simply of himself and the Tennessee Physical Therapy Association leadership. In a similar context, I saw someone praise this structure because it skirted the state's sunshine laws, which only applied when two or more board members met.[58]

Boards can further delegate the ratchet of licensure to professional organizations by incorporating private industry standards into their regulation. Especially in smaller professions, it is common for boards to condition licensure on good standing in a national certifying organization; often, these organizations are wings of the national professional association.[59] Likewise, each profession (with the exception of law) delegates testing to a national organization, another private entity controlled by professional interests. Having one uniform exam is efficient and contributes to a sense of fairness by making everyone jump through the same hoop. But with the ability to decide what is covered on the exam and its difficulty, testing groups have the power to limit the supply of practitioners in ways that better serve the profession than the public. As a board member told me, "Tennessee is very much in bed with" her profession's testing organization.[60] As in the case of CEUs, boards' decisions about testing requirements can confer market power, and the result is monopoly pricing for entry exams. For example, the United States Medical Licensing Examination costs applicants $2,265, not including the cost of preparing for the exam.[61]

Reliance on associations and testing organizations is somewhat inevitable in a regulatory system made up of as many as fifty boards per profession, staffed with part-timers who barely have the time to make the regular meetings to discuss day-to-day issues like applications and discipline. When it comes to setting licensing standards, boards turn to quasi-regulatory groups they trust for regulatory expertise. But importantly, these organizations lack even the pretense of governmental status and neutrality, or the minimal accountability and sunshine requirements of a board. In the hands of private advocacy organizations, standards tend to change over time, and only in one direction. For example, Tennessee conditions state licensure for dietitians on certification by the Commission on Dietetic Registration. When the CDR increased its requirements from a bachelor's to a master's degree, Tennessee's rules governing dietitians changed overnight without so much as a board vote.[62]

Similarly, companies paid by boards to verify their licensees' education and credentials can work the ratchet outside of the public eye. The difficulty a recent graduate of my law school had in getting licensed in Tennessee illustrates the problem. Lawyers trained abroad may take the Tennessee bar exam if their foreign legal education is "substantially equivalent" to an American degree and they complete a one-year LLM degree in America. The Tennessee Board of Bar Examiners outsources the "substantially equivalent" determination to a private company, which had a long-standing policy of accepting most foreign law degrees, until it didn't. Maximiliano Gluzman came to Vanderbilt Law School from Argentina during the original regime, but by the time he graduated in 2015 with an impressive GPA of 3.92 (all while learning and writing in a second language) the possibility of taking the Tennessee bar exam had evaporated. It was only after an appeal (in which my dean had to get involved) that Maxi was allowed to take the exam and practice law in the state.[63]

Regulatory economies of scale are supposed to be created by federations of state licensing boards, or what I like to call a "boards of boards," but they, too, approximate professional special interest groups. These organizations bring together all state regulatory boards under one organization; the Federation of State Medical Boards (the FSMB) is the most well-known, but every profession has such an organization. Believe it or not, even these federations have a federation—the Federation of Associations of Regulatory Boards.[64] No board wants to reinvent the wheel of professional regulation, and so they rely on federations to develop policy positions, write model rules, provide training for new board members, and hold conferences where regulators from different states can meet. Unsurprisingly, federations have a lot of truck with licensing boards. The FSMB says that many of their model rules are adopted into law word for word.[65]

Likewise, federations depend on licensing boards. They survive on membership dues paid by each state board out of their licensing revenue, so federations are beholden to the boards and, by extension, the professions they represent. Unsurprisingly, federation priorities track the positions of the national professional association. At least one schedules its annual meeting at the same time and place as the national professional association's conference, as if it were a satellite group of the association instead of a regulatory body dedicated to the public.[66] Federations champion their work as contributing to interstate consistency and therefore license portability. This may be true to an extent, but it also takes the ratchet to a national level: uniformity almost always converges on the strictest state's licensure requirements.

Boards also delegate the ratchet of professional licensing to schools. The Tennessee Auctioneer Commission uses the Nashville Auction School (the alma mater of three out of the four auctioneers on the board at the time of my research) as its preferred provider for continuing education and recently awarded the school a lucrative contract (it was the only bidder) to produce the board's electronic newsletter to licensees.[67] I interviewed a professor in a professional program who told me he had taken over the role of advising licensure applicants on the board's rules, which were labyrinthine, after board staff stopped answering the phone because they didn't know the answers.[68]

In general, when schools spoke the boards listened.[69] I saw one board schedule an emergency meeting because time had run out before a school rep in attendance had a chance to say her piece.[70] Educators and students were the largest group of audience members at board meetings, even more than association representatives. The Board of Cosmetology and Barber Examiners meetings were especially packed. When I asked the beauty students sitting in the gallery with me about it, they said they got school credit toward their license for every hour they spent watching the board.[71] Influence goes beyond audience advocacy, some states even require that a seat on the board go to a school owner or representative.

It is not surprising that schools and universities occupy a special place in the hearts of professionals, as repositories of knowledge and the intellectual centers of their profession.[72] But the effect is to give regulatory authority to institutions that have a lot to gain from upward pressure on licensing requirements, particularly the requirement of an expensive professional degree.

### "Watering Down" a License: Can the Ratchet Relent?

What happens when someone tries to work the ratchet in the other direction, as Ms. Diouf did in asking the board to allow her to braid without a license? How do board members think and talk about the possibility of giving ground in their fight for high entry standards and strict practice rules? A debate I saw before the Tennessee Board of Alcohol and Drug Abuse Counselors in 2018 shined some light on these questions.

Until 2015, it had been possible to become a Licensed Alcohol and Drug Abuse Counselor (or LADAC) as long as you had a bachelor's degree in any field and 270 classroom hours of education in counseling-related topics, whether as a part of that degree or not. Under this rule, someone with an undergraduate degree in an unrelated field could go back to school for about a year, obtain the necessary hours of relevant education, and then apply for a license. But in 2015, the board had voted to limit licensure to those holding an undergraduate degree *in a behavioral-health field,* as well as requiring 270 hours of counseling courses. That meant that someone wanting to be an addiction counselor had to either know that as an undergraduate or get two different bachelor's degrees—double the time and tuition.[73] In the meetings I observed in 2018, board staff, having had to reject many otherwise qualified applicants who were now excluded from the license, were asking the board to return to the pre-2015 regime.

In these debates, no one explained how an applicant with all the required counseling coursework, but who happened to major in a different subject in college, was an incompetent or dangerous counselor. In fact, there was almost no mention of public protection at all. Instead, the debates focused on how the rule change would affect professional status, prestige, and pay. Board members characterized returning to the pre-2015 educational rules as "watering down" the license. One board member emphasized parity with other professions: "We want to be considered . . . as strong as any other license that's out there for counselors."[74] Another said, "we need to keep our license robust, otherwise the less payers will reimburse us for our services [and] the less respect [we'll get] in our community."[75] The board's lawyer tried to steer the members back toward public protection, but to no avail. Another said, "It's our responsibility to make sure we are looking out for this profession." Professional association representatives attending the meeting encouraged the board to resist the rollback. One said, "We need to have a more professional profession."[76]

In fact, alcohol and drug abuse counselors were not originally supposed to be a particularly professional profession. It was created as a way for recovering addicts to provide more formalized counseling to others than they could do as AA sponsors.[77] Creating a new profession that was more accessible than psychology or psychiatry could protect the public while addressing the shortage and high cost of addiction treatment. But over the years, under the board's watch, the profession had grown into something else. The hours of required supervised practice had doubled and redoubled. By 2018, the degree requirement had all but foreclosed anyone interested in it as a second career.

The board refused to work the ratchet in reverse. For several board members, the battle for licensure in the 1980s and 1990s was a recent memory, a hard-won fight that precluded giving any ground. "We are licensed, and Lord knows I don't want to lose that," said one board member. "Not everyone in the country has that and that gives us a leg up." Another board member put it simply: "I want to protect what we've got. When you open the door, you let the bugs fly in."[78] They voted down the change.

With all the forces of professional regulation working in one direction, it's only a matter of time before reasonable barriers to entry designed to protect the public from incompetence become something more. We should be skeptical about claims that today it takes six thousand hours of training to protect the public, when it only took fifteen hundred in 1988. By giving a profession a licensing statute and the self-regulatory board to interpret it, we put a powerful train on a one-way track. We shouldn't be surprised if, years later, it's pretty far from where it started.

In Chapter 2, I will explore more ways in which the professional perspective contributes to licensing's excesses. Boards controlled by professionals tend to take in-group / out-group politics seriously and engage in heated battles over professional turf.

# 2

## Fences and Turf

*Professional licensing is obsessed with defining who's in and who's out. Public protection can get lost in the shuffle.*

Fatou Diouf didn't get the cosmetology board to back down that day she asked them to let her braid hair without a license, but the effort was worth her while. As she was leaving the meeting, a white woman approached with a business card. "I need to talk to you," she said. "What you said is true." The woman was a cosmetology school owner in Sweetwater, TN. She said her school didn't offer braiding education; neither she nor her instructors even knew how to do it. In fact, so few beauty schools offered the instruction that very few braiding licenses had been issued at all.[1] But the school owner made Ms. Diouf an offer: "Come to my school," she said, "and I'll give you the hours for free." Ms. Diouf took her up on it and logged the three hundred hours of ostensible braiding education.

With the school hours box checked, Ms. Diouf knew she could teach herself what she needed for the licensing exam. For that, she headed to the book section of a beauty supply wholesale store. She spent three afternoons sitting cross-legged on the floor of the store, thumbing through the books on braiding, trying to figure out what an American exam on African hair braiding might ask.

She passed the exam for her natural hair styling license on the first try. A few months later her state license came in the mail. It was a license that she resented having to get, the very existence of which she would later advocate against at the state capital. But she had to admit, getting that official piece of paper from the state of Tennessee felt good. "It makes you feel proud," she said. "[It] makes you feel more professional." Ms. Diouf was finished with running out the back door of hair salons. She was now in the club.[2]

## Fences and the History of the Professions

Professions have always been cliquey; one of their defining characteristics is a sense that they are above and apart from those they serve. The way the chair of the barber and cosmetology board described unlicensed professionals like Omar Mahmoud stuck with me, as "people on your side of the fence."[3] Part of what sets professionals apart is access to specialized information—knowledge that can only be created and accessed by other professionals. The very notion of expertise requires a sharp distinction between those who have it and those who don't.

The licensing board system of self-regulation is predicated on this idea of expertise. Defenders of the status quo argue that professionals should dominate boards because only they can recognize good and safe practice; only a professional is qualified to sit in judgment of her peers. During oral argument in the Supreme Court's latest licensing case, Justice Stephen Breyer argued that brain surgeons, not bureaucrats, should decide who can perform brain surgery. Without self-regulation, he argued, "you're going to have the neurology qualification determination made by some people in the state who are not neurologists. Now, that to me spells danger."[4] Professionals agree; the president of the Tennessee Association of Trial Attorneys told me: "We understand the profession better and understand the ramifications of good and bad practice. We are by far the best judges."[5]

The notion of a regulatory fence erected to protect a chosen few evokes the concept of medieval guilds, often cited as the blueprint for modern licensed professions. Guilds were closed organizations of merchants or craftsmen that flourished during the Middle Ages in England and Europe. The guilds were hierarchical systems with internal organizational structures for deciding who could join their ranks and how. Guilds limited entry to connected, high-status individuals who learned the craft or trade through an apprenticeship—a mostly unpaid ordeal—with a master member of the guild.[6]

Medicine, the paradigmatic American profession, was an early adopter of the guild model. In America, medicine took shape as a profession during colonial times, as local medical societies (analogous to modern-day professional associations) promulgated ethics rules and practice guidelines for their members. Membership in a local society gave you an edge in the market, but societies had no formal control over nonmembers claiming to be physicians.[7]

The profession achieved closure—the ability to decide who was and who wasn't a physician—when it entered a kind of public-private partnership with state governments. Early licensing laws in New York, South Carolina, Maryland, New Jersey, and Connecticut forbade medical practice by anyone not admitted to a local medical society, while leaving the private societies free to determine their own rules of entry and ethics. At first, medical societies granted membership to anyone who passed an exam of their own design; later, they required formal medical education, as schools like Harvard began to offer medical degrees.[8]

Along with professional closure came the idea of belonging and, of course, not belonging. Professional board members are not immune to the need to belong and exclude, even as they pursue their duty to the public. We might uncharitably call it "circling the wagons," but it is only natural to see the best in one of your own and to view outsiders with skepticism. This is especially true when you have worked hard and sacrificed to attain in-group status. Stacking boards with professionals ensures that fences will play a role in regulation, and at times fairness and efficiency will take a backseat to us-versus-them considerations.

## Outside the Fence: Unlicensed Practice

Whom is the fence designed to keep out? For licensing boards, the ultimate outsider is the unlicensed practitioner—someone acting as a professional without actually being in the club. Boards are therefore especially harsh on accusations of unlicensed practice. This may sound like a good thing, since boards are supposed to enforce the laws that limit professional practice to licensees. But the frequency and severity of discipline against unlicensed practice suggests the professions benefit more from these enforcement actions than the public. I saw boards come down hard in cases where the alleged professional practice was arguably outside the profession's scope of practice, or where the matter could have been chalked up to a misunderstanding. Coupled with the overly light discipline boards reserved for their own providers (the subject of Part II), it seems that boards get discipline backward. When confronted with a licensed individual who presents a true danger to the public, they have a hard time bringing down the hammer. But they throw the book at accusations of unlicensed practice, even where public harm is hard to make out.

For example, I watched the auctioneers commission unanimously vote to open an investigation into a firefighter's unlicensed auctioneering at charity events benefitting his fire department (the decision was taken over the objections of the commission's staff).[9] Another time, I saw the Alarm System Contractors Board insist on strong medicine for a handyman who had helped his neighbor install a security camera purchased from Sam's Club. The board's attorney recommended a warning without a fine because the handyman had apologized (he was unaware that Tennessee was among the few states that licenses alarm installers) and it happened only once. "That you know of," said a board member, as they voted to assess the handyman the maximum fine for unlicensed practice.[10]

I was able to corroborate my general impression that boards were harsher on people outside the fold than their own licensees by speaking to board staff. The lawyer for the Real Estate Board told me that because her board members often felt the statutory maximum fine for unlicensed practice was too low, they would ask her to multiply it for a single licensee by as many instances that she felt she had the facts to support. The lawyer also said that more than a quarter of complaints came from other licensees, often about things like font size on "for sale" signs and which agent was listed as the principal and which as the affiliate.[11]

I wanted a more objective measure of the double standard across the fence, so I looked at a year's worth of disciplinary cases for the boards that licensed auctioneers, barbers, cosmetologists, engineers, architects, and alarm system installers. I chose these boards as a sample from the professions where an accusation of unlicensed practice is a relatively common reason for discipline—essentially, professions outside of healthcare. Confirming my hunches, the results painted a picture of board discipline that would seem to benefit incumbent professionals more than consumers.

I learned that about two-thirds of the complaints that the alarm systems contractors board considered in 2019 came from consumers, yet they took action against a licensee in only 17 percent of these cases. In contrast, when a fellow licensee filed a complaint, the board took action in about 60 percent of cases. And the board was ten times more likely to take action in a case alleging unlicensed practice than one complaining about service quality or safety. The board increased the staff-recommended penalty six times, all for allegations of unlicensed practice. Some of the consumer allegations against alarm system installers were irrelevant or unsubstantiated, but a significant amount alleged the kind of consumer harm that alarm system installers identify when you ask why licensing is necessary in the first place: scams where installers prey on security fears or make promises they don't keep. One woman complained that her elderly father was duped into signing an alarm system contract without understanding it. This, like almost all the other consumer allegations of fraud, was dismissed with no disciplinary action taken against the licensee.[12]

At the auctioneers commission, I found a similar pattern of dismissing seemingly legitimate consumer complaints while harshly punishing incumbents' allegations of unlicensed practice. In 2019, the board dismissed more than 80 percent of the consumer complaints that credibly alleged unsafe or unethical practice. The complaints again echoed the parade of horribles I had heard from professionals in defending the need for licensure: shill bidding, fraudulent descriptions of items for sale, and absconding with auction proceeds. These cases did not result in public discipline; even in the few cases about safety or quality where the board took action, the most it did was send a letter of instruction to the licensee. If the auctioneering board issued a fine in 2019, it was only for unlicensed practice.

I found the same pattern at the Board of Cosmetology and Barber Examiners, which was twice as likely to take action in a case initiated by a competitor than a consumer, and more than three times as likely to act in a case alleging unlicensed practice than one complaining about safety or quality. The Board of Architecture and Engineering showed a similar pattern, although the numbers there were less stark, perhaps because for that board, only the most meritorious complaints were presented in meetings. In 2019, the Architecture and Engineering Board took action on unlicensed complaints almost 90 percent of the time, compared with an action rate of 57 percent on allegations of incompetent practice.

At least outside the health professions, it seemed consumers were more concerned about bad service than whether their provider had a license; only about a third of the consumer complaints I collected alleged unlicensed practice. But most competitor-initiated complaints were about unwelcome competition from unlicensed providers—93 percent at the alarm system board and 100 percent at the auctioneering board. It was these cases—not consumer complaints alleging fraud, predatory sales tactics, and graft—where boards meted out the harshest punishments.

None of this data suggested that boards explicitly intended to protect the profession and not the public. Nor was it likely that the boards had any idea that this was their pattern of discipline, having no resources or incentives to systematically study their own regulatory systems. It was more likely a belief that, on the one hand, consumers exaggerate when they complain to boards and, on the other, unlicensed practice presents a clearer-cut violation. And board members may have also believed zealous policing of the regulatory fence was always good for consumers, not recognizing that over-enforcement against non-licensees—say, by broadly interpreting the scope of a profession—could deter perfectly safe unlicensed services that people might want to purchase, thereby raising price and scarcity. But whether intended or not, the end result was the same: a pattern of enforcement that gave little-to-no protection to the public while shielding incumbents from unwanted competition.

## Professional Turf

We have seen that the professions, working through licensing boards, tend to erect ever-higher fences around themselves and then sharply distinguish between the in-group and others. This raises another interesting question, one that turns out to be a major focus of licensing regulation: where, precisely, do those fences lie? Licensing laws set what are called a profession's "scope of practice" by defining who can do what. Turf, as it's more colloquially known, can be crucial to a profession's well-being. It can provide material rewards in the form of pay and lifestyle. The more services a profession can provide, the more potential streams of revenue. The fewer professions that can also provide it, the less competition there is to bid down the price. For example, if an advanced-practice nurse can do well-child exams and prescribe medications just like a doctor, that means more demand (and pay) for her services.[13] Indeed, economists have shown that "turf wars" between professions can have high financial stakes.[14]

Also at stake in defining a scope of practice are a profession's less tangible (but equally important) values like prestige and autonomy. A large scope of practice adds to public esteem by expanding a profession's perceived capacity and expertise. A nurse who can do many of the essential functions of a doctor will enjoy some of the social status traditionally reserved for doctors alone. (Of course, professions also derive prestige from specialization, so they will want to avoid attaining "jack-of-all-trades" status.) The flip side of this is that sharing turf can erode professional identity. As a medical board member told me about what he saw as the encroachment of nursing on his profession, "If you want to be a doctor, go to medical school."[15] Finally, exclusive turf contributes to professional autonomy by giving just one profession the right to define appropriate practice, so there's no second-guessing from another profession.[16]

These questions of scope of practice are rarely stable or uncontested. There are constant intrusions that can threaten a profession's turf. New technology might allow the consumer to bypass a profession's services, shrinking its footprint. Unlicensed providers may want to identify themselves to customers with words that resemble a licensed professional. A profession may want to expand its scope of practice to share turf with a neighboring profession. When professions collide, it sets off a turf war, sometimes dressed up in health and safety concerns. The turf war story has many permutations and iterations—between chiropractors and acupuncturists over "dry needling," between physicians and nurse practitioners over prescribing, between dentists and physicians over oral surgery, between veterinarians and massage therapists over animal massage, between auctioneers and automobile dealers over car auctions—the list goes on and on.[17]

Making sure a profession doesn't practice outside of what its licensees are adequately trained to do is a public safety issue. But most turf wars aren't just about keeping a profession within a safe boundary. The benefits that come from boundaries—in terms of pay, prestige, identity, and autonomy—are highest to a profession when it can exclude all other providers. Unsurprisingly, most turf wars are less about safety and more about exclusivity—about deciding whether and how professions will share a practice.[18] From a consumer perspective, fighting over exclusive turf is worse than a waste of time.

First, it makes for a lot of lobbying (what economists call "rent-seeking") and complex rules, neither of which benefit consumers or patients. Second, it deprives the public the benefit of choice, leading to scarcity, high prices, and unhappy consumers. Some women prefer an OBGYN to deliver their baby, others opt for a midwife. In economic terms, a service that can be provided by more than one profession creates more potential for competition to increase choice and quality and decrease prices.[19] A focus on turf also makes professions resistant to innovation that might shake up the old boundaries. Some conservatism in the professions may be a good thing—slow change may be better than letting the professions follow the latest fad. But if a profession is too slow, that can lead to ossification and blind adherence to the old school to the detriment of patients and consumers—not to mention hobbling professionals with a pioneering spirit.[20]

## Licensing's Cold Turf Wars

How do licensing boards react to incursions on their professional territory? Sociologists say that professions defend their turf and its exclusivity against encroachments and threats.[21] Naturally, licensing boards exhibit the same tendency. Turf battles tend to have two stages. First comes the initial clash. As the scope of one profession expands and infringes on another, the two professions fight over whether and how their jurisdictions will be shared. One way these battles sometimes start is when schools expand their offerings to include instruction in an area of practice peripheral to the core professional competency. Graduates are eager to use this new skill in their professional lives. Where licensing laws preclude it, they fight to expand the laws and rules that define their profession. The adjacent profession will fight to keep its turf exclusive by resisting these expansions.[22]

Sometimes boards or their members will get directly involved in this stage of a turf war. For example, I met a vet tech on the veterinary board who lobbied for the legislature to change her profession's title to "veterinary nurse" (the nursing lobby killed the bill).[23] But for the most part, in the open battle, it's the professional associations, not boards, that duke it out over statutory terms setting the scope of practice. To the casual observer, once those terms are set, the turf war is over, usually with casualties on both sides. In fact, the war has just begun, but the theater has changed. The bloody battle happened at the legislature. The cold war plays out at licensing board meetings.

During the cold phase of a turf war, the professions have accommodated each other in an uneasy sharing of professional jurisdiction. Interpreting the precise terms of the truce are left to a licensing board. It's a second bite at the apple for the profession who had to give ground at the legislature. Boards must interpret vague state laws defining what is (and is not) the practice of their own profession, and capacious interpretations of professional practice can neutralize competitive threats as effectively as a strongly worded statute. The questions may seem smaller in the cold war stage, but the devil of any political compromise is in its details.

One popular cold war tactic is to use the board disciplinary process to expand a profession's scope of practice. One way of doing this is to send cease-and-desist letters—essentially a threat to bring discipline—to practitioners at the margin of a board's jurisdiction.[24] I heard one board member explain his preference for this method at a national conference of licensing boards. "I support private letters," he said, "because what if you don't have any statutory authority backing up a disciplinary action? How do you let him know he's doing something you don't like?"[25] Other times a live disciplinary case presents an opportunity to relitigate a question about professional turf. A drama I saw play out at a Tennessee Board of Architectural and Engineer Examiners meeting in 2018 illustrated the importance of turf and how board decisions could effectively trump legislative compromises. And it showed that that turf could be as much about what you said as what you did.[26]

In Tennessee, professional engineers enjoyed only limited title protection: a professional could call him or herself an engineer as long as they used the word in a way that did not falsely imply that they were licensed.[27] For example, the use of the title "professional engineer" had been found to imply licensure, but something like "sandwich engineer" was probably fine for unlicensed people to use. Stronger term protection, like that enjoyed by physicians, hadn't been something the legislature had been prepared to give engineers. But a disciplinary case before the licensing board presented the profession with a second chance to gain turf.[28]

The case was against a large, multi-state building management corporation that described its unlicensed facility managers as "building engineers." A licensed engineer reported the company to the board for censure, and a board member (an engineer who also happened to be a recent recipient of the state professional association's top prize for its members), was keen to curb the use of that term. "I feel pretty strongly about this one," she said. As another board member said, "'Sandwich engineer' is one thing, "but 'building engineer' is too close to what we do."

In fact, the use of "building engineer" to describe what once were called superintendents—or, as a board member said, the guy "with a lot of keys"—was ubiquitous. As one board member observed, "every single building has somebody in it who's called an engineer who's not." With such wide usage of the term, it was a stretch to say that the company had misled the public into believing that its supers were in fact licensed professional engineers. The board members seemed to agree that this interpretation of their title act would push the envelope. "I realize this is a big task, and a big undertaking," said one board member. "If we are going to start this battle, then we need to have a game plan," said another.

The board lawyer stepped in, clearly uncomfortable with the capacious interpretation of their title protection. She reminded them of the "temperature of things" with the legislature, which had recently displayed an appetite for rolling back professional regulation in the state. One board member suggested using discipline cases, like this one, to stop the practice without raising unnecessary waves. "We just deal with it as it comes along," she suggested. So the board issued a "letter of caution" to the company, informing them that "building engineer" violated the title act. One board member asked that the letter include a threat of future fines and penalties. At the last minute, another board member suggested adding language about public protection. "I just don't want to come across as protective of the title," she said.

### When in Doubt, Shut It Down

A focus on turf can have a pernicious effect on innovation in the provision of professional services. Boards quash new business ideas or keep them at a limited scale by clinging to old boundaries of their profession's scope. For example, I saw the veterinary board kill an idea two licensed veterinary technicians had that would have brought peace of mind to pet owners afraid to travel away from their sick or high-maintenance pets. The entrepreneurs wanted to offer specialized, in-home pet-sitting services involving tasks like giving medication that were within the scope of their vet tech license. But the board (which was dominated by veterinarians) killed the business when it wouldn't budge on its rule that all vet techs needed on-site supervision by a veterinarian.[29] As bad as this problem is for small businesses like the pet-sitting service, it may be even worse for companies that seek to expand into multiple states, where they face up to fifty different battles with boards over their scope of practice.

It is also especially a problem in technologically evolving markets, where professional board members tend to cling to an outdated professional status quo. The best example I found of this problem was the case of a multi-million-dollar business idea that was stamped out when the Alarm Systems Contractors Board told its founder he would need a professional license to proceed.[30] When Adam Jackson retired from the Green Berets, he had an idea for a security system that used facial-recognition technology to distinguish legitimate guests from unwanted intruders. He called the company Edge AI and marketed it to school districts who could use the technology to keep known sex offenders off their premises. Adam told me he had developed the software with several business partners and had tens of millions of dollars in "handshake" agreements with companies and school districts intending to use the product. Edge AI's software could run on an existing camera system, but the business hit a snag when he learned that the alarm system board might see the installation of software as the installation of an alarm system. No one at the company had an installer's license, and with other competitors on their heels, they didn't have time to get one. Their only hope was a declaratory order from the board that installing the software didn't constitute alarm system installation.

The 2017 hearing before the alarm systems board was chaotic and confused.[31] The board members didn't seem to understand the technology. As if by reflex, they closed ranks, and told Adam his only options were to license his technology to an existing alarm installation company or take the time to obtain a professional license—a multi-month process. They even prohibited him from conducting any live testing of his product in public. Adam asked them to reconsider, and they did, a year later, but by then it was too late. Other competitors using facial-recognition software had overtaken Edge AI and the company was dead.

I asked Adam whether he thought the board members wanted to restrict competition in the field of alarm systems, and he said no. He pointed out that his system didn't present meaningful competition to the typical system installer. What seemed to matter most to the board members, according to Adam, was their standing within their professional community. According to him, they were protecting their regulatory legacy. Board members didn't get points for letting technology narrow their profession's scope and importance. When in doubt, shut it down.

## The Customer Is Usually Wrong

Ossified professional turf doesn't only hurt the innovators, it hurts consumers, too. As tastes change, professionals see new opportunities to meet demand, but often licensing gets in the way. Licensing rules are filled with sometimes old-fashioned rules about the consumer experience, like the cosmetology rules that mandate a waiting area in salons (and even specify its dimensions) and nametags for the stylists. Professionals who invested in the old way of doing things are unlikely to interpret their rules flexibly, even if consumers are demanding it.

Changing tastes about death rituals, for example, have ignited a turf war between funeral directors and cemetery professionals. At a board meeting of funeral directors in 2018, I met the staff of Evergreen Cemetery, located in the mountains of East Tennessee, that offered direct cremations, for which they needed a license from the funeral board. The Evergreen professionals—who identified as "cemeterians"—were at the meeting to answer for a set of accusations of mishandling client funds (which they strongly disputed). As one of them told me, "There are two things you don't do in this business. One is sexually abuse a corpse. The other is take people's money."[32]

I asked them why they were in such hot water with the board, and the patriarch, Glenn Langley, told me it was all about professional turf. "You are seeing [a] board that is mostly funeral directors," he said. "Perpetual care cemeteries [like us] sell things that conflict with what funeral homes sell." When it became clear that I didn't understand the workings of the funeral industry, he broke it down for me. "When we sell a mausoleum crypt above ground, they miss a vault sale," he said. Mr. Langley would tell his clients to buy the cheapest casket (which, until a recent constitutional lawsuit struck down the law, had to be sold by a funeral director) for the crypt. Funeral directors didn't like that, he said, but Mr. Langley didn't see the need for a lot of frills. "Jesus was wrapped in a sheet," he reminded me.[33]

Cemeteries were, as Mr. Langley told me, a "one-stop shop" for a grieving family interested in skipping the traditional formalities of a funeral. I understood the appeal when I stopped by Evergreen on my way through East Tennessee on a family vacation and observed its old-growth trees and stately marble mausoleum engraved simply with names and dates. With the current consumer trend toward cremation and memorials rather than embalmment and viewings, funeral directors with large overheads were feeling the competitive pressure from cemeteries. Of the death industry in East Tennessee, one of the Evergreen cemeterians told me, "It's the most cutthroat business I've ever seen." Compared to funeral professionals, he said, "even the old moonshiners up here get along fine."[34]

I wasn't able to assess the merits of the accusations against the professionals at Evergreen because there was no public trial where facts were presented. But it was clear that there was a lot at stake in the turf war between cemeterians and funeral directors, and only one kind of professional had a seat at the regulatory table. "If they just didn't like us, they could say we're not giving you a license," Mr. Langley's son, Chase, told me. "Where does the law begin and where does it stop in front of a board like that?"[35]

So far, I have painted a picture of regulation biased in favor of the profession. Specifically, I have implied that too much regulation in the form of high barriers to entry, strong in-group mentality, and elaborate turf battles is good for professionals and bad for consumers. Defending that point requires a full account of how consumers win and lose from licensing's tendency to exclude, which I undertake in Chapter 3.

# 3

## The Wild, Wild West

*Licensing can protect consumers in theory and to a degree. But
states take it too far, and there isn't much the law can do to stop
them.*

Fatou Diouf's in-group status didn't last long.

After getting her license, she started her own braiding practice out
of her home. She grew the business until she had a few women—mostly
African immigrants like herself—working for her. Although she had a
license, her employees didn't, having not had the luck she'd had with the
school owner from Sweetwater. As her business grew, she started looking
for a storefront to rent. "At some point, you have to make it more professional," she told me. She started renting the place on Murfreesboro
Road where I interviewed her in 2020. She called the salon "Kine," her
middle name. The little shop was perfect, except that it didn't have one
thing most salons did have: a back door.

The move to a real salon would attract more customers and, she realized, board inspectors. When the first one came, she told her employees
to stand their ground. She recalls telling the inspector: "We used to run
out the back door whenever an inspector came. But this shop has no
back door." Ms. Diouf explained that the inspector could come whenever she wanted, and that every day the braiders would be there working
without licenses. "We are not hurting anyone," she said. "Every time you
feel like coming, you can come. But we are not going to run." The inspector found Ms. Diouf's honesty refreshing, and for a while let Fatou
off with warnings.

To Ms. Diouf, standing her ground during raids by the board inspector was an act of civil disobedience. She believed the law requiring government permission to practice her heritage—one she had begrudgingly complied with years before—was morally wrong. It was equally wrong to ask her employees to bow down to the licensing system that made practicing their traditional craft illegal. To Ms. Diouf, the law was nothing more than a rapprochement in a turf war between cosmetologists and braiders. It wasn't worthy of her or her employees' respect.

The board of cosmetology and the Tennessee legislature saw it differently. In 1996, the braiding bill, like all professional licensing laws, was passed on the theory that it protected the public from dangerous or incompetent braiders. If we take the wording of the statute at face value, then the legislature saw it as a necessary step to protect the "the public welfare" of the people of Tennessee.[1]

For the cosmetology board, who had the authority to enforce it, the braiding bill was a source of revenue. When Ms. Diouf's lenient board inspector lost her job, she was replaced by an inspector who came three times a year and fined Ms. Diouf the statutory maximum penalty ($1,000) for every unlicensed braider he found working in her shop. She personally took on these costs, which quickly added up to more than she could pay. The board put her on a monthly payment plan that amounted to more than half the rent she paid for the storefront. The license, like all professional licenses, was premised on the idea that without the hundreds of hours of education and competence demonstrated in an exam, an unlicensed professional risked exposing the public to low quality, even dangerous services. If the board itself took these arguments seriously, they might have closed her shop to protect the public. Instead, they went on inspecting, fining, and collecting what they could, for years.[2]

## A World without Licensing

Licensing exists, ostensibly, to protect the public from low-quality professional service by ensuring a floor of competence below which providers cannot pass. It is therefore, on paper anyway, justifiable to the extent consumers and patients benefit from it. There is another sector of the public that is potentially helped by licensure—the professional labor force—but as we will see in Chapter 5, arguments about how licensing helps workers are made only implicitly and uneasily; consumer protection is licensing's raison d'etre.

This chapter will evaluate the claim that professional licensing leads to greater consumer welfare. The truth turns out to be complicated, because although some licensing in some professions may be good for consumers, too much licensing can keep them from accessing affordable service. And the right balance is unlikely to be struck by professionals regulating themselves.

The professional perspective on licensing and quality is often expressed in stark terms. At a meeting of the Federation of Associations of Regulatory Boards, an organization comprised of federations of professional licensing boards, an executive asked the crowd the following question: "What would happen if the government didn't regulate the professions?" The board members in the audience had a lot to say about the irreversible harm that would come to consumers and professionals alike, but one phrase dominated the discussion. It would be, they agreed, like the "Wild, Wild West."[3]

It was not the first time I had heard this expression in the course of my research; it was often repeated to invoke the merits of professional licensing, or at least the demerits of abolishing it.[4] The Wild West of the movies is a lawless place, where problems are solved by violence, life is short and brutal, and barbers pull teeth. The expression is meant to highlight the protections that licensing can offer consumers, and the promise of social order offered by rules preventing "just anyone" from practicing a trade.

This image of a world without licensing involves some unexamined assumptions. It assumes, first, that licensing unquestionably protects consumers, and second, that it does so to such a degree that we shouldn't even bother considering the downsides of licensing. In truth, experts disagree about whether licensing protects consumers by increasing service quality and safety, and no one seriously thinks the answer is the same for all licensed professions. Meanwhile, the downsides of licensing—

such as scarcity in healthcare—can be devastating. Those hit especially hard are groups who already experience prejudice and poverty.

Are the exclusionary effects of licensing—the ratchet of entry requirements, the fences, and turf wars—good for consumers? To really assess whether professional licensing is working for consumers in America (and for what professions), we need to abandon the simple view that regulation is good, and the Wild West was bad. Rather, we need a comprehensive view of how consumers and patients win—and how they lose—when professional licensing is put into play.

## Lemons and Externalities

One thing "the Wild, Wild West" image is good for is highlighting the dangers of bad professional practice, and thus the possibility that licensing benefits consumers. The risks of inadequate professional service range from disappointment (a bad haircut) to death (a botched surgery or missed diagnosis). We face similar risks all day long by using or consuming any product or service: a soda bottle might explode in your hands and injure you, a restaurant may give you food poisoning, the dry cleaner could damage your best suit.

For most consumer transactions, we rely primarily—although rarely exclusively—on market forces to protect the public. I doubt you'll go back to that restaurant again. You might tell your neighbor to avoid that dry cleaner. Knowing they may lose customers, those businesses have strong incentives to take extra care with their work. Inferior products will be sold on the cheap or not at all. The best of the best will be in high demand, raising the price. In theory, consumers could protect themselves by using a simple rule of thumb: you get what you pay for. But in all of these examples, and indeed for almost all transactions, there is some government regulation layered over those market forces to further protect consumers. Products liability law allows you to sue the soda manufacturer for causing your injury, and local governments permit and inspect restaurants and dry cleaners. For many services, the extra layer of governmental protection is professional licensing. Why is all this regulation necessary, when theoretically the market takes care of consumers?

Because markets work perfectly only in theory. Consumer markets are typically plagued by two problems that put the "you-get-what-you-pay-for" logic on shaky ground. First, consumers often don't know enough about what they are buying when they buy it. Economists call this "information asymmetry." Second, for some transactions, consumers spend their own money on the purchase, but other peoples' money when it goes bad. Economists call that the "externalities" problem. Both can result in products—and professional services—that are inferior and dangerous.

We've all been burned by "information asymmetry"—paying top dollar for an inferior product. Sometimes we find out too late that a product is bad, like when the dry cleaner ruins our suit. If enough people have a similar experience, perhaps it will make it into the online reviews, but such reputational mechanisms are imperfect. In medicine, for example, researchers have shown online reviews to be a very weak signal of quality.[5] The situation is even worse when consumers never know they have been swindled, such as when they have been sold an insurance policy they didn't need, or have gotten sick but can't pinpoint the restaurant that's caused it.

As if these problems aren't bad enough, economists have shown that information asymmetry can also have a systemic effect on markets. In 1970, economist George Akerlof identified the "lemons problem," a theory often invoked as a reason for professional licensing. The theory explains that if consumers can't tell which products are good (peaches) or bad (lemons), then high-quality providers—who usually also have high costs in providing great products—won't be able to command top dollar to cover their costs. Consumers won't pay extra for a peach that might be a lemon. Taken to the extreme, nobody will offer high-quality products and consumers won't even have the option of splurging for something nice.[6] The theory is usually illustrated with used cars, but it applies equally well to any market, like that for professional services, where consumers aren't sure what they are getting.[7]

The problem of market externalities, another justification for licensing, is also intuitive. Imagine that the builder of an apartment building needs to purchase engineering services to design it. He might be tempted to cut costs on those services, figuring that the building is unlikely to fall, and if it does, the full social costs of such an accident won't be borne by the builder alone. Without a government-granted right to sue for injuries, the builder will bear only the cost of replacing the apartment building, probably a fraction of the total social harm: from lost wages, to pain and suffering, to grief and fear, the list goes on.

Economists say that the full costs of this transaction for cheap, shoddy engineering services are "external" to the transaction between builder and engineer. Under these circumstances consumers (the builder) have an incentive to cheap out and expect someone else to pay the cost if it goes wrong, resulting in more low-quality transactions than is socially optimal, especially if building codes (another form of government regulation) are ambiguous or easily skirted. Again, the apartment building is just an example; it's easy to think of lots of transactions, including bad or dangerous professional services, where the full cost of consumer harm goes beyond buyer and seller.

Government regulation, including professional licensing, can protect consumers in markets with information asymmetry and externalities. Permitting and inspections for restaurants address the information asymmetry problem by providing diners some assurance that a restaurant has met some minimum standard of food safety; asking restaurants to post their cleanliness score goes a step further. Requiring manufacturers to pay for accidents caused by their products both compensates victims and addresses the externalities problem by making companies *internalize* the costs of shoddy manufacture. Finally, and most importantly for our purposes, professional licensing for engineers assures the builder—and the public—that buildings will meet some minimum level of safety, which reduces accidents and the ripples of harm they create.

The market for many professional services would seem to suffer from information asymmetries, externalities, or both. One of the defining features of a profession—at least the traditional "learned professions"—is its opacity to the public. Medicine and law comprise vast systems of knowledge and complex logical machinery that outside observers cannot easily assess. The main reason why we seek out a professional service in the first place is because we cannot do it for ourselves. How, then, are we to assess whether we have received good legal advice or the correct diagnosis? Externalities also plague traditionally licensed professions, especially in health care. Bad health outcomes are visited not only on the patient, but on his family, his employer, and his community as a whole.

Professional licensing addresses information asymmetry and externalities by seeking to ensure a minimum level of quality of professional services. It does this indirectly—for most professions, the government can't directly evaluate the quality of services any more than consumers can. Rather, licensing systems impose education, experiential, and examination requirements on anyone wanting to practice. Licensing requirements assume that by barring any provider who has not completed the requisite professional training and passed an exam will eliminate the bottom sector of providers. This eases the information asymmetry problem, because now consumers know that there is a floor to the quality of service they purchase; it eliminates the "lemons" from the market, leaving consumers confident they are purchasing a "peach." And it addresses the externalities problem by removing (at least theoretically—more on that in the second half of this book) the dangerous and incompetent providers that may create wide-spread social harm. Practitioners also theorize that licensing benefits consumers by creating a higher standard of living for professionals, which prevents burnout and makes for happier, more effective (and therefore better and safer) practitioners.

## Quality or Scarcity?

One puzzle, then, is why researchers have struggled to show definitively that licensing actually improves service quality and safety. Some studies suggest that licensing modestly increases service quality, but a lot show no effect at all.[8] A few even conclude that licensing actually *decreases* the quality of professional services, or at least decreases health outcomes for consumers as a whole.[9] As we shall see in the Chapter 4, the American experience with COVID may help explain the apparent paradox of worse health outcomes associated with stricter licensing laws.

Part of the variability of the results of these studies, and perhaps why they should be taken with a grain of salt, is that it is difficult to measure service quality and safety in an objective way. Economists have come up with some ways to indirectly measure outcomes—such as by measuring how licensing midwives affects infant and maternal mortality, or how licensing rules affect malpractice premiums for professionals—but each study has its flaws.[10] Another weakness in this research is that these studies must exploit differences in licensing laws between states, or over time, to see if they have an effect on service quality. That means that most of the studies focus on professions that are not universally licensed, or that only recently have become licensed.[11] It's probably a mistake to use research on new or marginal licensed professions to make claims about licensing's effect on quality in professions like medicine or law.

Because of all these flaws, we shouldn't be too troubled by the fact that some studies are unable to show that licensing improves service quality or safety. We should not abandon the commonsense idea that by requiring education and training designed to increase practitioner competence, licensing actually will increase practitioner competence, at least to some extent, and for some professions. But the equivocal nature of the data on licensing and quality also means that it is far from obvious that *all* licensing restrictions *always* lead to better and safer service.

Even if licensing does result in improved professional service, that does not mean that it benefits consumers in the final analysis. Licensing requirements create provider scarcity by erecting barriers to entry into a profession; economists have estimated that licensing reduces the number of providers in a profession by somewhere between 17 percent and 27 percent.[12] Professionals are capacity constrained; there are only so many hours in the day. Limited availability drives the prices of professional services up. And licensing rules that limit what professionals can do further depress competition and increase consumer prices. Economists estimate that the 10 percent premium from licensure costs consumers almost $250 billion a year.[13] Of course, some of this premium is attributable to higher quality services, but scarcity probably plays a large role.

Higher prices are only part of the problem. For some consumers—especially those with low income or no insurance—licensing places professional services out of reach.[14] The problem is well-documented in the healthcare sector, where lack of access to affordable medical and dental care has created a public health crisis in rural and inner-city communities. Access to services is also a concern outside of healthcare. For example, one scholar blames the current licensure system for the deplorable level of representation in most noncriminal legal proceedings, observing that 95 percent of people facing evictions can't afford a lawyer.[15]

It's also possible that licensing regimes actually make for *less* enforcement of health and safety standards through a phenomenon few people recognize—regulatory crowding out. If licensing is in place, other regulators may assume the regime is doing its job and not pursue their own enforcement actions against professionals. Sometimes the presence of a state licensing regime doesn't just discourage but precludes other regulatory efforts. For example, some states exempt the "learned professions" from consumer fraud laws, apparently relying on the licensing system to catch bad actors (reliance that is not justified, as we shall see later).[16]

Another example of regulatory crowding out involves preemption of local efforts to protect consumers and the public. In an effort to crack down on sex trafficking at massage parlors that the Massachusetts state massage board was unwilling to shut down, the town of Oxford passed ordinances requiring background checks and inspections for the town's massage therapists. But the state licensing law preempted these local enforcement efforts, according to a cease-and-desist letter sent by the state's Division of Professional Licensure. The Oxford police chief told the *Boston Globe*: "We went to do the inspections and we were trumped by the state licenses. We couldn't do anything."[17]

### A Constitutional Right to Reasonable Regulation?

The idea that professional licensing can be a bad deal for consumers—offering them little in the way of enhanced quality in exchange for higher prices and less access to services—has become a familiar criticism in some reform-minded policy circles. In 2015, the Obama White House issued a report describing the American licensing system as creating "substantial costs" for consumers that too often go unrecognized by policymakers.[18] That same year, the Supreme Court decided a case against a licensing board and described the licensing system as creating an inherent risk that professional interests will dominate policy goals.[19]

This criticism—that states' regulation of the professions is illegitimate when it provides little benefit to the public—is also the animating principle behind a movement to recognize a constitutional right to lighter professional licensing. The architect of this movement is the Institute for Justice (IJ), a nonprofit law firm whose mission is to "end widespread abuses of government power and secure the constitutional rights that allow all Americans to pursue their dreams."[20] At the center of the IJ's reform strategy are its high-profile lawsuits against state governments alleging that the fit between a licensing law and public protection is so poor as to render it unconstitutional. The IJ's rhetoric—abuse of governmental power versus the American Dream—is reflected in the cases it chooses for litigation. For example, the IJ has recently represented someone who fought California wildfires while in prison who now cannot be a firefighter on the outside because of his criminal record, and a Georgia lactation consultant whose decades-long career was halted by a new law requiring professional licensure for anyone helping new moms adjust to breastfeeding.[21]

These lawsuits are extremely hard to win. The Constitution makes unlawful any state regulation that is not "rationally related" to a "legitimate state interest."[22] Theoretically, that asks courts to decide whether the trade-offs of licensing are worth it for consumers—whether the benefit to the consumer is worth the inevitably higher prices and increased scarcity. Yet over the years, both conservative interests (in states' rights) and liberal political pressures (in favor of regulation) have led to a very narrow reading of this constitutional rule.

Today, rationality review of a licensing law boils down to one question: Did the restriction serve, even indirectly or inefficiently, some state interest? The rational basis of the regulation can be extremely thin, it can be hypothetical, and it need not be a part of the record of why the law was created; indeed, it can even be invented after the fact during the course of litigation. In some federal circuits, the state need not make *any* arguments about public welfare, because some courts have held that protecting a profession from unwanted competition can itself be a "legitimate state interest."[23]

Despite these long odds, the Institute for Justice and its affiliated law firms have succeeded in rolling back some of the worst professional licensing rules using constitutional theories about a poor fit between licensing and its ostensible benefit to the public.[24] The IJ and its partner firms have convinced courts to throw out hair-braiding laws, tour guide licenses, and "good moral character" requirements that arbitrarily keep ex-offenders out of the professions. Every time the IJ convinces a court to invalidate a state licensing law that has no grounding in public protection, consumers potentially win. As we shall see in Chapter 5, each successful case opens a door for workers throughout the state who would have otherwise been locked out.

Yet the payoff from these suits should not be overstated. Very few of the cases challenging a regulation's "rational basis" have been successful. Perhaps part of the problem is explained by the "Wild, Wild West" concept. This metaphor plays into the idea that licensing exists as a dichotomy, where the only two options are licensing exactly as it exists now or nothing at all. For the libertarian lawyers attacking licensing using the Constitution, the highly deferential "rational basis" test means they are most likely to win cases involving professions that shouldn't be regulated at all (tour guides, for example).

This is part of the "free pass" that I said motivated me to start my research with the medical board. Very few of the Institute for Justice's cases featured on its website involved a healthcare profession, despite the fact that about two-thirds of all licensed professionals work in the medical field.[25] Likewise, the legal profession gets a free pass in the libertarian case against licensing. An attorney for the IJ told me he believed licensing for lawyers goes too far, but he pointed out convincing a judge, as a lifelong member of that profession, of that would be "an uphill battle," to say the least.[26]

One of the major contributions of these suits is that, win or lose, they put pressure on state governments to rein in their licensing rules. Lawsuits have a way of bringing attention to some of the worst of professional licensing and making boards look ridiculous in court, as when the state of Louisiana was forced to argue that licensing florists helped prevent infection from misplaced floral wires and potentially disease-carrying soil.[27] Sometimes that's enough political pressure to pave the way for legislative repeals of licensing laws, a topic we will return to in the Conclusion.

Whether consumers benefit from licensing turns out to be a far more complicated question than whether you'd rather have a toothache in Montana in 1875 or in Manhattan today. What we can say is that licensing has the *potential* to benefit consumers. For some professions, the optimal level of government regulation probably does involve licensing restrictions. But even for those professions, there is a delicate balance to be struck between two equally important features of public safety: quality of service and access to care. Instead of engaging with questions about how much is enough, we rely on a regulatory system set up to ignore all the ways in which too much licensing hurts consumers and patients.

Chapter 4 explores what happens when a healthcare workforce shaped by decades of licensing board regulation is put to the test. The American experience of COVID revealed that provider scarcity is more than a theoretical result of licensing gone too far. It's a recipe for disaster on a national scale.

# 4

# Stress Test

*Heading into 2020, the United States was already short on nurses and doctors. COVID made the problem hard to ignore.*

In early March 2020, signs were showing that New York City was poised to become the epicenter of the first major American outbreak of a new coronavirus strain. Each day, the *New York Times* reported the number of confirmed cases in the city: at first a handful, then dozens, then hundreds.[1] By the end of the month, thousands of New Yorkers were diagnosed with the virus on a daily basis. Epidemiologists said the city's outbreak was just ten days behind that in Lombardy, Italy. Out of Italy were coming harrowing stories of New York's seemingly inevitable future: patients crowded into hospital hallways, ventilator shortages, and doctors forced to decide who would receive treatment and who would die.[2]

If countries like Italy couldn't cope—with more hospital beds, physicians, and ventilators per capita than the United States—how would our nation's densest and most populous city? One New York City doctor put it bluntly on March 14, "We are not prepared."[3] Andrew Cuomo, governor of New York, began to make increasingly desperate pleas in the press for help reinforcing his state's healthcare capacity. He pled for ventilators from President Trump, saying the state would be "be thousands short. Thousands."[4] The stories from Italy hit Governor Cuomo hard. "This is where Italy got into trouble," he said. "They didn't have enough ICU beds to handle the number of patients who needed intensive care."[5]

Governor Cuomo was right to link overwhelmed hospitals to COVID deaths. The mortality rate of the disease spiked in hotspots around the world when infections pushed healthcare systems to their breaking points. Around this time a graph went viral, illustrating how "flattening the curve" could keep help keep COVID infections within our healthcare system's capacity and reduce deaths.[6] "Social distancing" became words to live by.

Governor Cuomo was wrong about one thing, however. It wasn't the lack of ventilators that would bring New York's healthcare system to its knees. It was the lack of professionals to work them.[7]

In late March, as the virus ravaged the city, as accounts of wartime conditions in hospitals filled the newspapers, and as President Trump told Governor Cuomo of emergency equipment needed to battle COVID, "try getting it yourself," the narrative changed.[8] A city once desperate for beds and ventilators became desperate for doctors and nurses. On March 23, Cuomo did what in normal times would be unthinkable—he swept aside the state's entire licensing system for healthcare professionals. His order said that any nurse or doctor licensed in any state could practice in New York.[9]

Cuomo held yet another press conference begging for help. This time he appealed not to the president, but to the national professional community. "I am asking health care professionals across the country, if you don't have a health care crisis in your community, please come help us in New York right now," he said in front of a makeshift hospital running out of the Javits Convention Center. "We need relief."[10] This call didn't go unheeded; in a single day ten thousand out-of-state doctors and nurses signed up through New York's registration system.[11]

That was good, but not enough. By April 8, twenty-five thousand out-of-state licensees had answered Cuomo's call, but only about nine hundred had been put to work.[12] Part of the problem was the bureaucratic maze the out-of-state workers had to navigate before getting to the front lines. Cuomo called on a team of 175 lawyers and other staff to individually verify each volunteer's state license and screen out those with significant disciplinary actions against them.[13] As a public health expert would later say: "You can always add more beds. It's much more difficult to add more workforce."[14] Cuomo did what he could to expand the healthcare capacity of New York City, but even in a crisis, you can't turn a professional system on a dime.

The wave crested, and then hit. New York's hospital system was overrun by the virus. Stories of overworked and overwhelmed professionals filled the headlines. Nurses who usually cared for two ICU patients at a time had to care for as many as eight.[15] Doctors worked twelve-hour shifts, broke down in tears at the nonstop death around them, and came back the next day to do it all over again.[16] Healthcare professionals lived in fear of bringing COVID home to their loved ones. Professionals fell ill. Many died.[17]

The emotional and physical toll the disease took on tapped-out providers was one thing. The toll it took on their patients was another. You can lengthen shifts and increase patient ratios, but it all comes at a cost. New York lived out the Italian experience: working hospitals at overcapacity spiked the death rate. I interviewed a physician in New York City whose twelve-bed ICU was turned into a seventy-bed operation in the spring of 2020, and he explained the effect this way: "The sickest patients you've ever seen in a five-to-one ratio, with non-ICU nurses and non-ICU attendings? Yeah, you're going to have worse outcomes."[18] COVID fatalities were two, perhaps three times as high at hospitals that lacked the resources—including staff—of their counterparts.[19] In New York City, the death rate for patients hospitalized with COVID in the first three months of the outbreak was more than 50 percent higher than the national average.[20] In the end, it was the hospitals in the city's poorest neighborhoods that lost the highest percentage of COVID patients.[21] But no hospital was spared. In a single month, ten thousand New Yorkers died.[22]


## Not Enough to Go Around

No reasonably designed healthcare system could effortlessly adapt to a pandemic on the scale of the COVID-19 crisis. But some countries did better than others, and most countries did better than us. America was uniquely susceptible to hospitals becoming overwhelmed. Even before the crisis, we simply didn't have enough doctors and nurses to go around.

Licensing had a lot to do with that. And when politicians tried to repair our broken regulatory structure on the fly, we learned just how entrenched—and dysfunctional—our state-by-state system of professional regulation really was.

In 2019, the same year the federal government ran a simulation of a pandemic flu originating in China (in which the American healthcare system did not rise to the challenge), we were about thirty thousand doctors short of what a well-functioning system should have. That number was expected to grow to more than one hundred thousand by 2032.[23] A 2018 study described an even more dire problem in nursing, where we faced a shortage of more than 150,000 nurses that was expected to grow to half a million by 2030.[24] The problem remains especially acute in rural areas, where physician-to-population ratios are roughly half the national average. The numbers are so low, in fact, that three quarters of all rural counties in the country are Healthcare Provider Shortage Areas, qualifying them for special federal programs and funding.[25]

Lack of access has serious consequences. A recent study found that a hospital closing in a rural area meaningfully increased that population's risk of death from time-sensitive emergencies like heart attack, stroke, sepsis, and asthma; while urban hospital closings had no effect. The hardest hit were Medicaid patients and racial minorities. In addition to their lack of access to emergency care, rural communities struggle to receive adequate primary care, which has serious consequences for both health outcomes and healthcare expenditures.[26]

People explain the shortages in rural areas by focusing on the personal choices of medical and nursing school graduates. Nursing, and especially medical schools, are expensive; students often graduate with significant debt. Unless the graduate has a connection to a particular rural community, she's more likely to settle down in a city where salaries are higher and opportunities more diverse, especially if she has a spouse with professional aspirations as well.[27] Governments and professional schools have both tried to influence these choices by creating incentives and opportunities to learn about benefits of rural practice.[28] But these personal choices of where to practice are partially—and, in the aggregate, significantly—driven by supply and demand. The bottom line is that we just do not train and qualify enough doctors and nurses to meet demand. Licensing plays a significant role in creating that scarcity.

Doctors have been working the ratchet of ever-increasing barriers to licensure longer than anyone, and that has had a serious impact on provider scarcity. Medicine is by far the hardest profession to enter, requiring an undergraduate degree with specific and difficult prerequisites, a medical degree that leaves students with an average of $200,000 of debt, and a four-part exam followed by a four-year residency at an approved program.[29] The residency requirement operates as an additional bottleneck: there are fewer residency slots in teaching hospitals than graduating medical students, partly because of lobbying by the American Medical Association and other organizations that fear physician surpluses.[30] Foreign-trained doctors, thought to be essential to closing the gap in rural medicine, face an even higher set of barriers—some erected by the federal government in the form of visas, and some by state licensing boards that condition licensure on completion of an American residency program, regardless of whether the applicant has completed a substantially similar one abroad.[31]

Nurses, too, have been working the ratchet for a long time. Forty years ago, a typical nurse had a two-year associate's degree, while today most have a bachelor's or master's. But the evolution of nursing into a more highly trained, specialized field has also introduced an easier, less burdensome path to becoming a primary care provider. The advent of the "advanced practice registered nurse" (commonly known as an APRN, or nurse practitioner) has had the effect of *reversing* the ratchet effect for some kinds of healthcare. A similar effect has been achieved by the rise of physician assistants (PAs), practitioners who are trained to perform a subset of what doctors can do.

Again, state licensing regulation plays a crucial role in deploying nurse practitioners and PAs to increase access to care. Nurse practitioners and PAs (collectively called "mid-levels," though those professions resist that term for obvious reasons) can perform well-child exams, diagnose common illnesses in adults, write prescriptions, and refer patients to specialists.[32] The rise of this kind of provider—someone who could perform most of the functions of a primary care physician—kicked off turf wars with doctors in every state. The various truces and standoffs in that war have left us with a patchwork of regulation that, in most cases, keeps mid-levels from practicing to the full extent of their training.[33]

Some states—mostly in the more rural West—allow nurse practitioners full independent practice and prescribing authority. At the other extreme, states like Tennessee require physician supervision over all practice and prescribing. "Supervision" is defined by medical boards, and usually involves an agreement between the providers spelling out protocols for care, periodic site visits, and chart reviews. It also usually involves a hefty payment (up to $3,000 a month) from nurses to doctors for the supervision.[34]

Burdensome supervision rules impact scarcity in several ways. First, fewer people want to be a nurse practitioner or PA when they know they will be under a doctor's thumb (and will have to pay for the privilege). Second, supervision reduces the overall output of mid-level providers by limiting what they can do and cutting into their productivity with administrative tasks related to it.[35] Finally, different regulations in different states further hinder the mid-level labor market by reducing worker mobility.

Even with all this regulation keeping mid-levels from practicing to the full scope of their expertise, they are essential to our healthcare system. There are almost five hundred thousand physicians' assistants and nurse practitioners working in the United States today.[36] For the care they are trained to provide, most research shows that they are just as safe as physicians; some studies show that mid-levels actually provide *better* care for some services.[37] Most are primary care providers (in fact, as much as a third of all primary care providers are mid-levels), but—importantly for COVID—mid-levels are also crucial to running a safe and organized ICU.[38] In what turned out to be a timely study published in 2019, researchers found that the use of mid-levels in intensive care decreased the length of patients' stays, contributed to higher physician and nurse satisfaction, led to faster discharges, and decreased hospital readmissions.[39]

Not only does the research show that mid-levels are at least as safe as physicians, studies have shown that the greatest public health benefits accrue when mid-levels are able to work without physician supervision.

For example, one study found that in states allowing certified nurse-midwives to practice independently, there are healthier newborns and fewer inductions and c-sections.[40] It also seems that allowing independent practice for mid-levels affects *physician* behavior. One study showed that greater independence for mid-levels correlated with physicians spending more time with patients.[41] It was not clear whether that was because doctors had more time without the administrative burdens of supervision, or because their bedside manner got a healthy dose of competition from nurses and PAs.

The data also show that unsupervised mid-level practice can be a bastion of hope for rural and other underserved communities. Liberal scope-of-practice laws increase the supply of rural providers and meaningfully reduce the likelihood that a county will be designated a Healthcare Provider Shortage Area.[42] Nurse practitioners are just as likely as doctors to take Medicaid and other forms of public insurance.[43]

All this data about the benefits of using mid-levels co-exists with another reality. America spends far more of its GDP on healthcare than any developed country—and one fifth of those expenditures goes to physician salaries.[44] Mid-levels make good money, but not nearly as much as doctors, and their services cost less. Simply put, using nurse practitioners and PAs to their full potential could save patients and taxpayers a lot. With the signs pointing to a safe, cheaper alternative that could bring relief to the millions of Americans without adequate access to healthcare, broadening mid-levels' scope of practice should be a no-brainer.[45] But doctors in every state have fought the expansion of mid-levels' authority. Not even COVID could change that.

### States React, California Resists

On March 24, the day after Governor Cuomo suspended the in-state licensing requirement for health care workers in New York, the Secretary of the US Department of Health and Human Services (HHS) Alex Azar wrote an open letter to all American governors. Azar implored them to take emergency measures to alleviate what was rapidly emerging as America's weakness in fighting the novel coronavirus: a too-small and too-fractured healthcare workforce. In the letter, he begged governors to override state medical and nursing board licensing rules that prohibited practice from out-of-state licensees, and that kept mid-levels, who were seen as crucial for the kind of intensive care demanded by COVID patients, from practicing to the extent of their training. He also asked governors to suspend limitations on telemedicine, traditionally another area of resistance among professional associations. His letter captured the emotional tenor of the moment, saying of healthcare essential workers, "They need backup." "Your help is needed to ensure health professionals maximize their scopes of practice and are able to travel across state lines," he went on. "We are all in this together."[46]

Chastened by stories from New York and urged on by the pleadings of HHS, every state enacted measures that loosened access to telemedicine or allowed for immediate interstate practice.[47] The latter change was particularly breathtaking, because it stripped state medical boards of most of their authority. In a matter of days, the national system of state-by-state licensing, long defended by the American Medical Association and the Federation of State Medical Boards, was swept aside for a de facto national system for doctors and nurses in which anyone licensed anywhere could now practice everywhere. It was a move that under any other circumstances would have been blocked by the physician advocacy groups. But when it came to temporary interstate practice, the medical professional lobby saw the writing on the wall. Desperate times called for desperate measures.

In contrast, when it came to the rest of HHS's request—that states should allow providers to practice to the extent of their training and to reduce restrictions on supervision—the doctors chose to fight. The call to action from Washington sent states back into the battlefield of a bitter turf war between nurses and doctors. More than twenty states waived all or part of their PA supervision requirements, at least temporarily.[48] But in many states, physician groups' efforts at obstruction were successful.

One of those states was California. The California Medical Association (CMA) had a history of winning its battles with the nursing profession. It was one of twenty-two states, along with Tennessee, that required physician supervision over nurse practitioners. And it was one of a small handful of states that limited how many nurses one doctor could supervise, effectively placing a quota on the number of nurse practitioners who could practice in the state.[49]

Just the year before, the CMA had spent $6 million defending their "physician-led" model of medical care against the latest incursion from the nursing profession: a bill allowing limited independent practice for some highly experienced nurse practitioners.[50] The CMA's rhetoric acknowledged the state's healthcare shortages, but advocated for increasing pay and opportunities for physicians to incentivize rural and primary care practice.[51]

In early 2020, just before COVID, the CMA's winning streak came to an end. The reality of California's healthcare situation—too few providers in both urban and rural areas coupled with negative health outcomes for its most vulnerable communities—overcame physicians' resistance and the bill passed. While the law would not come into effect until January 2023, nor would it cover all nurse practitioners, it was a powerful symbolic victory for scope-of-practice expansion, with up to thirty-two thousand nurse practitioners expected to apply for certification under the new regime.[52]

Stinging from this defeat and gearing up to fight the implementation of the new law, the California Medical Association was not prepared to compromise, even in the face of COVID. In March 2020, the CMA pressured California's governor, Gavin Newsom, to keep the supervision requirements in place, while most of the other states lifted or lightened their supervision rules.[53] In the end, Newsom gave the doctors what they wanted, for a small price: he temporarily suspended the four-to-one ratio of nurse practitioners to doctors.[54] But the ratio had been in effect for years, which had kept California's supply of nurse practitioners artificially low. For Newsom's emergency order to have any real impact in responding to COVID, those nurses would have to come from out of the state. That would require slack in the rest of the country's supply if California ever became a hot spot.

The CMA praised Newsom's move in early April, explaining that increasing physician employment was a better way to expand the healthcare system's capacity. "In a world where you have primary care physicians and literally thousands of other physicians out of work, I'm not sure what eliminating supervision of nurse practitioners gets you," said a CMA spokesperson. He noted that California's emergency rooms were operating under capacity at the time anyway, unlike hotspots like New York that were experiencing elevated death rates.[55]

That, of course, would change.

## From Supervision to Collaboration: Tennessee Turf Wars

Back in Tennessee, the medical board met (virtually, for the first time) on March 25, 2020. In the weeks before, Governor Bill Lee had suspended much of the board's regulation, including the basic requirement that physicians and nurses hold a Tennessee license to practice in the state.[56] Lee had also relaxed the physician supervision requirements for mid-level providers like nurse practitioners and PAs.[57] As the unusually short meeting concluded, a board member asked the staff whether the board had any role to play in licensing under the COVID emergency orders, "or we're just, like, out of that loop?" The staff member gave a diplomatic response.[58]

It was quite a reversal of fortune in the medical board's ongoing dispute with advanced practice nurses in Tennessee. Just two months before, in January 2020, the board had considered a rule change that would have further entrenched physician control over nurse practitioners in my state. In fact, it was the very rule—the four-to-one ratio of nurses to supervising physicians—that in California had held down the supply of providers.

To understand the context of the Tennessee board's proposed four-to-one rule, we have to go back to the most recent battle in the Tennessee turf war between physicians and nurses. In 2015, the Tennessee Nursing Association (TNA) had backed a bill providing for full, unsupervised practice authority for nurse practitioners.[59] When it failed on the hill, lawmakers convened a taskforce comprising representatives from each association and charged them with developing a compromise position that could be presented for the 2017–2018 legislative session.[60] In other words, the Tennessee General Assembly asked them to play nice.

The TNA wanted full practice authority—to be out from under physicians' supervision which they found both expensive and belittling. On their side, they had the research showing that primary care provided by nurses was as safe as that from physicians, but it cost less and increased access to care. That was an especially important fact in Tennessee, where we have a significant access-to-care problem, especially in rural parts of the state.[61]

The Tennessee Medical Association (TMA) saw things differently. Dr. John Hale, then president of the TMA, was on the taskforce and during his service he published an op-ed that portended stalemate. "APRNs on the task force," he wrote, "were direct and unwavering in their efforts to modify or remove mandatory collaboration laws so they can practice beyond the scope of their education and training." He said his own view was that the existing supervision laws needed to be more strongly enforced, not relaxed. "What we cannot do, however, is allow APRNs to practice without a collaborative relationship with a physician."[62]

Indeed, the taskforce was a bust. In some ways, it was doomed from the start. Doctors on the taskforce outnumbered nurses and nurse practitioners.[63] Among them was physician and state senator Joey Hensley, who would in 2019 face professional disciplinary charges for prescribing opioids to himself, his wife, his son, and his employee—who was also his romantic partner and his second cousin.[64] (Despite a finding that the drugs were prescribed outside of the legitimate practice of medicine, the board declined to suspend or revoke Senator Hensley's license, in part because he served a rural part of the state with inadequate healthcare provider coverage.)[65]

In the end, the taskforce recommended a legislative change that would pay lip service to the idea of expanded APRN practice but make no substantive changes to the law whatsoever. In 2017, the legislature adopted the taskforce's modest recommendation that the word "supervision" be substituted with "collaboration" wherever it appeared in the practice act.[66] Although the nurses couldn't have been happy to get "collaboration" in name only, at least the word change would prompt the medical board to revise their supervision rules for the first time in fifteen years. The nurses were hoping for more meaningful changes that might expand their scope of practice. After all, Tennessee had some of the most onerous supervision requirements of any state.

Instead, in January 2020, the Tennessee Board of Medical Examiners—which now included Dr. John Hale, the taskforce member so outspoken about resisting independent practice for APRNs—proposed the opposite: a cap on how many advanced practice nurses a single physician could supervise. The proposed rule would, like in California, make it unethical for a doctor to "collaborate" with more than four nurses, effectively placing a ceiling on the number of primary care practitioners in a state that already had a devastating shortage of providers. The doctors on the board focused on the role that inadequate supervision of nurse practitioners played in the over-prescribing crisis—a problem that the medical board had showed little interest in confronting in other contexts, as we shall see in Part II. Whatever merit this public safety argument had, the other public health considerations—that a broader scope of practice could mean more and better healthcare for our state's most vulnerable residents—weren't discussed.[67]

Instead, the debate drifted away from public health to a topic familiar to Dr. Hale and his colleagues: turf. The physicians on the board agreed that the biggest problem with the proposed cap was getting it past the "very aggressive" nursing lobby. Noting the failure of the 2016 taskforce, one board member said the two groups "could not be further apart" on agreeing about collaboration rules. The trick, then, was to convince the lawmakers of the need for the change. One physician board member had an idea: frame the issue in terms of child safety. Suggesting that pediatricians had significant lobbying power, the board member felt it would "be harder for [nurses] to dispute."[68]

The medical board never got the chance to formally propose the rule and defend it in the court of public opinion. By the time the next board meeting came around, COVID had indeed pushed them out of the loop.

## "There Are No Hotspots"

March and April 2020 were busy months for travel nursing agencies. With the in-state licensing requirements suspended across the country, the labor force moved more freely. This allowed nurses around the country to "answer the call of duty" according to Alexi Nazem, CEO of

Nomad Health, a travel nursing staffing agency.[69] Hospitals that didn't typically use just-in-time staffing solutions to meet their provider needs, like Vanderbilt University Medical Center, put in orders for extra ICU and hospital floor nurses.[70] Prices for travel nurses soared to the point that agencies would later be accused of price gouging.[71] Hospitals counted their ventilators and waited.

The summer months of 2020 were a "fallow period" for nursing orders, according to Nazem.[72] With infection rates declining, many states lifted their social-distancing measures, leading to a second wave that started in the late summer. By now, COVID was in every state and every city, hitting the south and the West particularly hard. On a single day in July, Texas reported more than fifteen thousand new cases, three thousand more than New York on its worst day in April.[73] This time, there was no one to call. I spoke to John Henderson, CEO of the Texas Organization of Rural & Community Hospitals, about that moment. He said in the first wave, nurses and doctors from Texas had rushed to New York to help. "But it seemed like when Texas was having its moment everyone else was too," he said. He told me, "When everybody's in a bind you can't shuffle everyone around. There's nobody to send."[74]

As the surges mounted, the weather grew cooler and socializing moved indoors. Cases continued to rise. "Orders are coming from everywhere," Nazem was quoted in an article on December 15, 2020. "There are no hot spots."[75] There was good news about a vaccine, but it wouldn't be available in time to make Thanksgiving or Christmas gatherings safe. And it would be nearly summer of the following year before it would be available to everyone who wanted a shot. During that second wave, it became commonplace to double an ICU nurse's patient load. In normal times, critically ill patients require so much attention that one nurse can only manage two of them, at most. Now four was the norm, and that was in cities experiencing only moderate surges. Some places reported assigning eight critically ill COVID patients to one nurse. At that level of overwhelm, "medical care grows disorganized," explained a *New Yorker* article—titled "America Is Running Out of Nurses"—from December 2020.[76]

Even at a hospital like Vanderbilt University Medical Center, which never came close to using all its ventilators, patient ratios went up. A critical care pulmonologist and director of Vanderbilt's COVID intensive care unit told me the combination of overworking existing staff and relying on travel nurses unfamiliar with the hospital's systems and procedures impacted care. "There is a real value in the ICU in attention to detail," he explained. Referring to New York's first wave, he told me, "the real reason the fatality rate in New York was so high was that when you overwhelm a system . . . you undoubtedly have worse outcomes."[77]

If it was hard to find a trained ICU nurse in Tennessee in the autumn of 2020, it was even harder to find a nurse practitioner. Nurse practitioners are "ordering providers," meaning that they can decide on a course of care that can be executed by registered nurses. Without enough ordering providers, even the best ICU nurse couldn't do much for a COVID patient. To meet this need, Vanderbilt pulled residents from other areas of practice and searched for additional APRNs to hire. The travel nursing agencies were overwhelmed, and even in normal times they don't tend to deal in advanced practice nurses, in part because of the difficulty of navigating the patchwork of licensing rules and scopes of practice for nurse practitioners.[78] Instead, Vanderbilt asked its existing APRNs to work "a truckload of overtime." "We are paying for that now because they are all burned out," the director of its COVID response told me in May 2021.[79]

The COVID staffing crisis, and particularly the toll it took on the country's too few APRNs, was felt well beyond the ICU. I spoke to Sanjay Basu, the director of research at the Harvard Medical School Center for Primary Care. He told me that while everyone had been focused on the death toll from inadequate hospital and critical care coverage, he'd been more worried about the lives lost in "the in-between spaces." In a year when patients—particularly the elderly and vulnerable—felt unsafe going to the hospital, chronic illnesses like hypertension and heart failure went untreated. There, independently practicing APRNs could have made a big difference, Dr. Basu said.[80] Indeed, a recent study of overall mortality rates in 2020 (not just from COVID) suggested that states with independent practice for nurse practitioners fared better than states that required supervision.[81]

In late 2020, the existing supply of healthcare workers was like a too-small blanket, with every state trying to pull its own corner over itself.

The flexibility given by the licensing system in March—the near-universal instant reciprocity among states—couldn't address the fundamental problem with our healthcare workforce. As COVID-19 became a part of our social fabric, promising signs of progress on supervision requirements for mid-levels faded.[82] Emergency orders ran out. Thanks in part to the broken licensing system, we don't have enough providers in normal times, let alone in a public-health crisis. The irony is that COVID—even as it forced us to confront the reality of provider shortages—may have left us worse off in that department. As the director of an ICU in New Orleans told me, COVID patients "die at a higher rate than almost any other ICU diagnosis. Day after day, month after month, humans were never meant to see that."[83] We took what few providers we had and burned them out. "We asked people to do ten years of work in one year," Nazem told me. "People are leaving the profession because of this."[84]

California was one of the last states to surge before the vaccine was widely available. In November 2020, as cases were creeping up in Los Angeles County, Governor Gavin Newsom was photographed having a maskless, indoor dinner with California Medical Association lobbyists at the French Laundry in Napa.[85] His emergency orders authorizing interstate medical practice and suspending the four-to-one ratio were still in place, as was his California Health Corps, which he had touted in the spring as attracting ninety-three thousand volunteers (by year's end, only twenty-eight professionals were participating).[86] But he had continued to resist a measure that didn't depend on an influx of personnel into the state: expanding nurse practitioners' scope of practice.

Los Angeles became the first city to report one million cases in December of that year. By this time, the national pool of providers had been depleted. As Marc Futernick, an ER doctor involved in setting up a surge hospital in Los Angeles in the spring told a reporter: "There's no cavalry coming."[87] Conditions in Los Angeles's hospitals deteriorated as staff ran short. "We are working in a complete battlefield," said an ICU nurse. Travel nurses worked fourteen-hour shifts with high caseloads. One said of her patients, "I expect them to die. They die, I put them in body bags, the room gets cleaned, and then another patient comes."[88] Yet the surge hospital Dr. Futernick had set up remained shuttered. "There would be no way to staff it," he explained.[89]

A healthcare workforce—diminished and fractured by a dysfunctional licensing system designed to be more attentive to turf and red tape than patient health—was once again overwhelmed. New York's COVID crisis happened all over again in Los Angeles, where, by mid-January, one person was dying every six minutes of the disease.[90]


The COVID pandemic helped us see that the "Wild West" logic—in which more licensing is always better for consumers—can be tragically wrong. But before we conclude that licensing's tendency to go too far in locking out providers is a bad thing, we should consider its effect on another group whose welfare is important. Does licensing help workers? As we shall see in Chapter 5, the answer is, again, equivocal: it helps some, while hurting others. One thing is clear, however. Licensing's benefits and costs are not distributed equally.

# 5

# American Dreams

*Having a license can make or break you in the labor market. The stakes are especially high for workers who typically experience discrimination.*

When the Board of Cosmetology and Barber Examiners fined Fatou Diouf $11,000 in a single year, she knew something had to give.

If she was going to push back against the braiding license, she knew better, by now, than to go to the board. If she had a hope, it was with the state legislature. And she would need allies from outside the braiding community. That came in the form of Braden Boucek, an attorney for the Beacon Center, a Tennessee libertarian litigation firm and think tank affiliated with the Institute for Justice. Braden had made his career at Beacon Center fighting licensing laws using the IJ's "lawfare" tactic— bringing individual suits as a way of pressuring legislatures to change the law. I met Braden through a mutual friend who knew I was writing a book on licensing, and it was through Braden that I met Ms. Diouf.

I first saw her in the hallway outside of the chamber where the House Government Operations committee was set to debate H.B. 1809, a bill that would deregulate hair braiding and legalize Ms. Diouf's shop.[1] She was standing with a cavalcade of about a dozen hair braiders, many in traditional African dress. Ms. Diouf rallied her troops, briefing them on how to act when they sat in the audience and listened to the testimony and debate. Her campaign that year would take her and her crew up the capitol steps sometimes several times a week, as the legislature entertained no fewer than nine bills about licensing for hair professionals. Braden and the Beacon Center were behind several of them, including H.B. 1809. The turf war between cosmetologists and braiders was back on.

## It's Good to Be Licensed

So far, we have assumed that licensing regulation that protects professionals without protecting the public is illegitimate. But if we take a broader view of the costs and benefits of regulation, beyond the platitudes about public protection found in the preamble of statutes and incanted in board meetings, we see that there is another group besides consumers whose fortunes are tied up in licensing laws: workers. Should a system that provides meaningful benefits to workers be rejected just because it was created in the name of the consumer? After all, a great deal of regulation is dedicated to improving the working lives of Americans. Perhaps we need a full accounting of how licensing affects workers—licensed and unlicensed—before we decide whether, and for whom, the system is working.

This chapter considers the benefits of licensing to various categories of workers—licensed and unlicensed professionals, female workers, racial minorities, immigrants, and people with criminal records. The upshot is that licensing laws benefit those who can jump through the hoops of licensure and hurt workers who are for various reasons unable to do so. Most of the time, this benefits people who already have advantages in life. As an intervention in the labor market, it's regressive. There are some important qualifications, however, to that observation. For groups that are often discriminated against: women, African Americans, and immigrants, having a license is an even bigger boost within the job market than it is for their white, male, nonimmigrant counterparts. In other words, licensing creates a system of haves and have-nots within groups of marginalized workers: it's especially good for those who can jump through the hoops, and especially bad for those who can't.

As should be clear by now, having a license makes a worker better off, and not just because without one he couldn't work at all in the professional field. Economists have shown that workers in a jurisdiction that licenses a profession are better off than workers in a jurisdiction that allows you to practice without government permission—*even controlling for things like education and experience.* Wages are higher in licensed professions; on average studies find the wage premium to be about 10 percent.[2] This is the flip side of the price premium consumers pay—higher prices for services and higher wages for providers go hand in hand. The 10 percent figure is about in line with the wage premium workers get by being in a trade union, but remember that there are many more licensed workers than unionized ones.[3]

Other benefits of licensure are less measurable but equally important; many have already been discussed. State licensure symbolizes fully professionalized work, and it stands for exclusivity—"not just anyone" can perform this service. It suggests that the practice is specialized and expert, adding to its mystique. It bears the imprimatur of government, with all its officiality. For a profession, licensure is the ultimate status symbol.[4] And for a professional, her license is a badge of honor. I have few things on the wall at my office, but I do have my certificate of admission to practice law in Tennessee. Licensing confers this prestige and pay by locking certain workers out. The ways in which licensing acts as a barrier to income and professional identity for this latter set of individuals should be counted when we add up the effect of licensing on workers.

The barriers raised by professional licensing are high. Many professions require advanced degrees, potentially saddling workers with hundreds of thousands of dollars of student loans before they even enter the profession. Even professions that would seem to involve little in the way of classroom learning can demand large investments in education. In Tennessee, which is typical of many states, you must complete fifteen hundred hours of training to be a cosmetologist, more hours of instruction than law school. This can cost a student anywhere from $10,000 to $20,000, and a year of lost wages.[5] A barber school owner told me her students often put tuition on their credit cards, if they don't have a family member who can lend them the cash.[6] (Another barber school, one that accepts student loans, reports that about half of its graduates default on those loans.)[7] On top of the time and financial cost of education, professionals must sit for an exam (or four, in the case of accountants).[8] Review courses, mandatory professional membership dues, books, exam fees, and license application fees add up to a hefty price tag.

One overlooked barrier raised by licensing is the bureaucratic thicket that must be traversed to get a license. An applicant has to learn all the rules and deadlines in her state, obtain official documents from testing companies, educational institutions, and sometimes courts, all in the proper notarized format and by the sometimes draconian deadlines. Each state has slightly different requirements and procedures for application, and in some professions even the board members don't understand them.

For some, the barriers to professional entry created by licensing aren't just high, they are insurmountable because of facts they cannot change about themselves. Many licensing regimes limit professional entry to people with clean criminal records, either by explicitly barring certain ex-offenders or by requiring "good moral character" that's assessed by asking invasive questions about the applicant's criminal history.

Who are the people who manage to navigate the licensure process? People who have access to education and money, a clean criminal record, and the time to make it all happen. That leaves out a lot of workers who lack these advantages, but who may still have the raw ability and ambition to succeed as a professional. Perhaps unsurprisingly, white workers are especially likely to have a license and all its benefits: 23 percent of white workers hold a license, compared to 20 percent of Black and 14 percent of Hispanic workers.[9]

So, while licensing is probably always good for a profession abstractly because it confers prestige and status, it's less clear that its good for the people who want to work in it. There are winners and losers: those who can navigate the process and get a license win; those that can't—and not always because they aren't good at what they do—lose.

## Two Views of Equality

Braden's experience with the Beacon Center as an advocate for licensure reform gave him an up-close view of the workers that licensing leaves behind. In 2017, he found himself in the audience of a meeting of the board of barbers and cosmetology watching a series of disciplinary cases where a handful of unlicensed barbers—almost all without lawyers—would lose their livelihoods. Though he was there representing someone else, the case of an unlicensed barber from Memphis stuck out to him. Braden watched as Elias Zarate told the board he was sorry that he cut hair without the state's approval, but he was grateful for the board's invitation to the hearing to help him get a license, especially since his barber shop in Memphis was the only means he had of supporting himself and his family.

Braden knew where this was going. The board explained: there would be no help with a license, and Mr. Zarate owed $2,100 in fines, including a charge for the board lawyer's time. The hearing, which lasted all of five minutes, fit with what Braden knew was the pattern in licensing board hearings: if you had a lawyer, you won; if you didn't, you lost. Barbers make around $30,000 a year and can't afford lawyers.[10]

What was interesting to Braden about Zarate's case was a detail the barber shared when explaining his story: he had never graduated from high school.[11] As Braden would learn later, Mr. Zarate had come to barbering from desperate circumstances. His mother was killed in a car accident when Zarate was ten; three years later his father was deported. He spent his teen years essentially homeless, bouncing among friends' houses and working nights while attending high school during the day. His performance in school was abysmal, and in his senior year, he dropped out entirely to take over the care of his two younger siblings. Mr. Zarate worked a mix of jobs that involved cutting hair under the radar of the licensing board. He was good at it; people from the neighborhood came to him and the money helped him get by. But in his early twenties, when he started working in a legit barber shop, the licensing board caught up with him. By then he had seen his siblings through high school and was now supporting his own family—a partner and a baby daughter—by cutting hair. The board's enforcement action put an end to this revenue stream.[12]

After the hearing, Braden watched Mr. Zarate approach a board staff member to ask about how to pay the fee and what, if anything, he could do to legally pursue his profession. When the staff member explained that Mr. Zarate should enroll in barber school, Braden could not remain silent. He approached the barber, introduced himself and explained that Mr. Zarate could spend more than a year in school, go more than ten thousand dollars in debt, and still not be allowed to cut hair. Tennessee law barred anyone who had not graduated from high school from barbering, a restriction they did not impose on cosmetologists.[13]

Braden's motives in approaching Mr. Zarate were mixed. He did it in part because he didn't feel right sitting by and watching the barber be bullied by a licensing system rigged to benefit existing license-holders. He also did it because he believed the high-school requirement was unconstitutional and had been looking for the right plaintiff to challenge it in court. A suit about an American Dream denied could turn up the heat on legislators as they worked through the slate of licensing reform bills he had put on their desks.

In debating those bills, however, the General Assembly would hear another side to the story about licensing and the American Dream. In fact, the fight Braden picked with the Tennessee legislature over the law of hair in 2018 could have been a case study in licensing's disparate impact on underprivileged workers—for better and worse. Lined up on both sides of the fight were Black entrepreneurs who saw their profession as their ticket into the middle class. For every Fatou Diouf or Elias Zarate who saw licensure as a barrier to a rewarding career and comfortable living, there was a stylist who saw deregulation as taking away the one thing that set her apart from her peers, gave her an exit strategy from poverty, and the chance to be seen not just as a laborer but as a professional. It turns out that these conflicting views of equality and opportunity aren't just a product of the political climate of Tennessee. It is an inherent tension in what sociologists and economists know to be effects of licensing on workers.

## Licensing and Discrimination

How does licensing affect racial, gender, and other kinds of equality among workers? The answer turns out to be surprisingly complex; the statistic cited above—that a higher percentage of white men hold licenses than any other group—isn't the end of the story.

Legal scholars have pointed out that licensing has been used throughout American history to disadvantage and exclude minorities and women from the professions. During the early twentieth century, southern states in particular passed a series of licensing laws designed to exclude African Americans from the professions. And during World War II, when our country was facing a mass immigration of highly skilled Jews fleeing the Nazis, medical boards rushed to establish residency and citizenship requirements to keep them out. Critics of licensing cite this history as a reason to roll back licensing laws in the name of equality.[14]

But some economists have recently advanced a counterintuitive argument challenging this narrative. They say that even if the intent behind these laws was exclusionary, their effect was the opposite. Looking at the data, these researchers argue that licensing and its barriers to entry have actually *helped* women and minorities enter a profession. Whatever disparity there is now between white men and other categories of professional workers, it would have been worse without licensing.

For example, a study that looked at data from the late nineteenth and early twentieth centuries suggests that government-run licensing regimes made it easier for women and minorities to enter the professions than the good-old-boy networks that came before.[15] Licensing has the advantage of (relatively) clear requirements that, once met, formally entitle you to a license regardless of your gender or the color of your skin. As one researcher put it: "it is easier to overcome a series of known obstacles than tilt at a series of shadowy specters."[16] This dynamic is also reflected in data from contemporary labor markets. For example, one study showed that the licensing premium for Black men is more than three times as high as for white men.[17] And while studies usually show that licensing reduces the supply of workers, a study examining licensing's effect on Black men in particular was unable to show any significant reduction in labor market participation.[18]

Licensing's effect on workers with criminal histories is more straightforward than its effect on women and minorities in the sense that there is little doubt that licensing regimes systematically exclude individuals with a criminal history. In this sense licensing "discriminates" against those who have been in trouble with the law. But whether licensing rules disadvantage people with a criminal history in a way that we should be concerned about depends on whether you think it's fair to use a criminal history as a proxy for competence to practice. Where there is a nexus between someone's criminal history and likelihood of professional success, there is an argument that the disparate treatment of ex-offenders is rational and protects the public.

But where it bars people from a profession arbitrarily, such as when very old or unrelated crimes are held against applicants, it's unfairly discriminatory. For example, Jose Salcedo, who grew up in juvenile detention, recently told PBS that he now wants to work in the system, to be for kids today "that person I needed when I was younger, because I never had nobody else tell me that I could do better." But his criminal record, which is more than a decade old, has so far prevented him from becoming a licensed correctional officer.[19] It's also problematic to use the criminal justice system as a gatekeeper to the professions because it compounds the consequences of what many view as a racist system; Black individuals, for example, are five times more likely to be imprisoned than white individuals.[20]

Nearly every profession in every state has a rule that allows a board to take into consideration whether an applicant has a criminal history, but the blanket ban on all felons, common a generation ago, is less prevalent than it once was.[21] Felony bans became unpopular because they were arbitrary and unfair, but also for practical reasons. Research shows that employment is an important determinant for whether someone will reoffend, and licensing reduces employment opportunities significantly among ex-offenders. One study showed that states with relatively onerous licensure laws saw a 9 percent increase in recidivism over a ten-year period, while in states with the lowest licensure burdens, recidivism went down 2.5 percent.[22]

Some states reformed their ex-offender policies to disqualify only those convicted of crimes of moral turpitude or violent felonies. Others introduced requirements that the offense be related to the profession and left that determination up to the board.[23] But it's not clear that these changes have done much to increase access to the professions for people with criminal histories, because uncertainty and bias still play huge roles in the process. In most cases, people with criminal histories would have to invest thousands of dollars and several years in a professional education before they could even get to the stage where a board would consider whether their past disqualified them from the profession. The deterrent effect of that uncertainty is made even worse by application questions that imply the barrier for people with criminal records is higher than it really is. For example, some applications ask about arrests when by law only non-expungable felony convictions can lawfully be used as a bar to licensure.[24]

In the end, most people with criminal histories who take all these risks *do* get a license, but not before a humiliating and anxiety-inducing hearing where the applicant must appear before the board—typically whiter and more privileged than the profession overall—to publicly answer for past transgressions. I watched a dentist interrogate a Black applicant for a dental assistant license about her driver's license charges, saying that when it came to the licenses, "what applies to one . . . applies to the other." He asked her probing questions about the financial, family, and work circumstances that gave rise to the criminal charges. Although he implied that he didn't trust her with a professional license, the board eventually voted in her favor.[25] These hearings impose a real cost to applicants' dignity, perhaps accounting for the low representation of ex-offenders in licensed professions even in states that have relaxed their felony bans.[26]

Some recent state reform efforts have promised to smooth the path to licensure for applicants with criminal histories. In 2018, for example, Tennessee limited boards to consider only convictions for recent and relevant crimes.[27] Similarly, Tennessee followed other states in creating a prequalification review process where ex-offenders could obtain a declaration from a licensing board that their history would not be a barrier to licensure *before* they invested in the education and experience necessary to obtain a license.[28] Reforms like these are important, although it's not clear how many people know about the prequalified review process; I didn't see a single case before a licensing board during my research. More fundamentally, streamlining the licensure process for people with criminal histories will only do so much to get people coming out of jails and prisons into the workforce. The biggest problem people face when they leave custody is poverty and isolation, hardly a good position from which to embark on a costly professional education. A more meaningful way to increase professional access for people with criminal records would be to eliminate professional licensing altogether for jobs that don't need it.

Licensing can also have a disparate impact on immigrant professionals. The Supreme Court has held that states cannot explicitly condition licensure on citizenship, but that hasn't meant that noncitizens have an easy path to licensure in the United States. States may, and many do, limit licensure to citizens and lawful permanent residents, precluding a large category of workers—typically highly skilled and in great demand—who wish to work temporarily in the United States or enjoy a career that spans international borders.[29] In the medical professions, this has contributed to our national shortage of healthcare practitioners.[30]

Even where immigration status does not present a formal bar to licensure, there are other rules that erect barriers to immigrants becoming licensed. Many states require licensure applicants to pass an exam written in English. There are a few exceptions to this; Florida and California, for example, offer many of their licensing exams in Spanish, and others allow the use of interpreters or dictionaries.[31] But the fact remains that for many immigrants wishing to join a profession, they must pass an exam in a language they don't speak and won't necessarily need to use in their work, either because oral communication isn't paramount or because they will be working primarily with people who speak their native tongue. One empirical study showed that states that demanded English-language exams for manicurists had significantly fewer Vietnamese immigrants working in that profession. The authors observed that this form of discrimination impeded assimilation by keeping these workers out of a profession where they might learn English, and in fact could earn higher wages if they did.[32]

Why don't boards take a more internationally inclusive perspective on their profession? I never heard a board member express hostility toward immigrants or voice a protectionist view about American professional jobs. Yet implicit bias cannot be discounted as part of the explanation, nor the intuition that your profession is and therefore should be made up of people like yourself. Further, many board members probably don't realize that the system they oversee is withholding a valuable credential in a discriminatory manner. As expert as they may be in medicine, massage, and auctioneering, labor market issues like these just aren't on their radar.

## The New Closed Shop?

In 2013, labor economist Morris Kleiner published an article with a graph that I get asked about a lot. It shows what percentage of the workforce was unionized from 1950 to the present. It has a declining line starting at 30 percent in the 1950s and ending at about 10 percent today. Also on the graph is the percentage of the workforce that holds an occupational license. The lines are mirror images of each other: the line representing licensed workers starts around 5 percent in the 1950s and slopes upward to about 30 percent today.[33] It would appear that licensing has "taken over" for unionization as the dominant labor institution in the country. But has it taken over for unionization as a force that protects workers? The graph can't answer that, but it has inspired some to push an analogy between unions and licensing that doesn't stand up to scrutiny.

Both unions and licensing increase wages—and by approximately the same amount.[34] Both have the potential to create scarcity; licensing by eliminating unlicensed practice, and unionization by limiting who employers can hire and obliging them to provide better working conditions for their employees. And both have the potential to increase provider quality—licensing by requiring education and testing, and unions by providing training and other important skills to members. Licensing and unionization both increase wages for workers who make the cut. And both leave some workers out, who are probably made worse off than if the credential didn't exist in the first place.

There are also major differences between the two labor interventions. Although some of the wage premium of unionization may come from higher-skilled workers, much of it comes from solving the asymmetry of bargaining power between workers and employers. Unions prevent employers from using their power—of size and sophistication—over workers who need collective action to get a fair deal. This probably does not describe the typical licensed professional. Often, licensed professionals are self-employed, or work in small practices where the asymmetry of bargaining power is less acute than, say, in a factory. Professionals like doctors and lawyers have especially strong bargaining power, given their social status and the high demand for their services. Others, like nurses, already have unions to look out for their interests.

Another reason to resist the idea that licensing ought to be seen as a replacement for unionization is that unions and collective bargaining agreements are subject to significantly more government oversight than licensing regimes. The National Labor Review Board, a federal agency, enforces laws that require both sides of the table to bargain in good faith over the terms of employment, whereas consumers of professional services have no voice in professional regulation. Perhaps all these differences are why licensing seems to increase wage inequality while unionization reduces it.[35] Thus, when it comes to their effect on the fair treatment of workers, licensing and unions should not be painted with the same brush.[36]

## Black Hair, White Money

The room where the Government Operations Committee of the Tennessee State Senate debated H.B. 1809, the bill that would roll back the braiding license, was packed and split into two factions, like a groom's side and a bride's side at a wedding. Diouf and her crew sat with Braden and some officials from the Department of Commerce and Insurance, the agency that oversaw the braiding license. The presence of the executive director of the cosmetology and barber board on that side of the isle was seen by defenders of the status quo as a betrayal. A barber school owner later told me, "When you're sitting there right next to the Beacon Center, instead of looking out for our industry, are you really there to protect us?"[37] Besides Diouf and her braiders, the rest of the supporters of licensing reform were white. Across from her were dozens of cosmetologists, mostly from Memphis, and mostly African American. It got loud. It got rowdy. At one point the representative running the hearing told the crowd to pipe down. "We're not at a baseball game!" he said.[38]

The substance of the debates that year over H.B. 1809 had two layers. On the surface were arguments about what the bill was supposed to be about—the efficient regulation of health and safety. Here, Ms. Diouf's side had the upper hand. In her testimony, Ms. Diouf emphasized the harmlessness of braiding and pointed out the threat these raids posed to her small business. "We are poor and take care of our families with this money," she said. To back up her claim about the safety of braiding, a state official presented data about their enforcement of the "natural hair" licensing requirement. He said that in the history of the license, approximately two consumer complaints had come to investigators' attention about dangerous or inept practice. Yet the state had opened two *hundred* cases against unlicensed braiders and levied more than $100,000 in fines.[39]

Against this data, the arguments made by the other side about the health and safety risks from unlicensed braiding seemed particularly thin. Yet the cosmetologists at the hearing made them anyway, and with their backs against the wall they made them stridently. A member of the cosmetology board testified that traction alopecia caused by overly tight braiding was an "epidemic in the African American community." A state representative from Memphis opposing the bill circulated a gruesome photograph of someone he said had been injured by a braider.[40] A beauty school owner testified that without proper sanitation, braiding could spread diseases, including HIV.[41]

If this had been the only layer of the debate, it was clear to me that H.B. 1809 and its bid to deregulate braiding would have succeeded. The safety arguments were overcooked, and the enforcement data was damning. But underneath this debate was another one, with higher stakes, where the hair professionals from west Tennessee had the political advantage. To the Black salon owners and cosmetologists who showed up to stop H.B. 1809, the bid to deregulate the beauty industry wasn't a costless way to cut red tape or a win-win for consumers and entrepreneurs like Ms. Diouf. It was an act of aggression against their license—not just their livelihood but their toehold in the middle class.

Over and over, African American witnesses made this point, in various ways, at hearings about H.B. 1809. A fifty-year veteran of the beauty industry and former licensing board member testified that the profession brought young people up out of poverty. She noted the pride that her stylists took in that piece of paper that let them cut hair. "Every one of my operators displayed on the wall a license from the state of Tennessee," she said. Another witness—a high school track coach with no personal stake in the beauty industry—implored the legislature to keep the licensing scheme in place because it inspired her students to be more than "a cashier at the local grocery store or . . . a fry cook at McDonald's." The bill, witnesses argued, would shutter African American-run beauty schools and reduce the state technical college system's budget by almost half a million dollars.[42]

On these terms, Ms. Diouf and the braiders lost the debate. H.B. 1809 failed, although it wasn't the end of her fight against the braiding license on the hill. And Braden was still very much in the game. There were still eight other bills about hair professionals pending before the legislature that term, including one that would eliminate the high-school requirement for barbers that was keeping Mr. Zarate out of the profession.[43]

In evaluating the arguments made by the cosmetologists from Memphis, we should be mindful that the advantage given to professionals in the form of a license comes from exclusion of people like Elias Zarate and Fatou Diouf. We should not embrace a regulatory system that makes some members of a marginalized group worse off merely because it also makes others in that same group better off. Yet the racial politics of Braden's 2018 legislative campaign got me thinking about whether, in the movement to roll back professional licensing, it was fair to start with the hair industry.

To the African American beauty professionals defending their license, the debate may have looked like a new chapter in an old story. There is a long history of Black entrepreneurs finding new ways to make money off Black hair, and white people either shutting them down or getting in on the game. Understanding this backstory puts Tennessee's hair wars and the economic research about race and licensing in context.

The Black hair business has always been big. Sarah McWilliams, better known as Madame C.J. Walker, was the first self-made female millionaire in America (Black or white). In the early twentieth century, she marketed a haircare system that earned her Black female salespeople fifteen dollars a day at a time when an unskilled white woman earned eleven.

Later in the century, other Black-owned companies marketed creams and treatments with similar financial success. Today Black hair is a multi-billion-dollar industry, and not all the people who profit from it are Black. Jheri Redding, inventor of the Jheri Curl, is white. White-owned Revlon built a beauty empire by buying up independent Black-owned hair product companies.[44]

Sometimes these white entrepreneurs haven't played fair. For example, Brooklyn-based, white-owned "African Pride" encouraged consumers to believe that its hair grease was by and for African Americans. It blew its cover, however, when it sued the Black-owned maker of "African Natural" for trademark infringement. And when the Federal Trade Commission (FTC) required a Black-owned producer of a lye-based hair product to include a warning label, Revlon took advantage of the FTC's lax enforcement against white-controlled companies to place a "better and safer" label on their chemically similar product.[45]

Around the time I was researching the complexities of how licensing affects workers, I met someone who knew more than the average professional about the advantages of licensure for underprivileged workers. And she had some strong opinions about white attempts to deregulate Black hair. Danika Keyes taught for years at a cosmetology school that goes back four decades. It's a typical school: ten stations and sinks. The only difference is it's housed in Tennessee's women's prison, and all the students are inmates.

The schooling is offered for free to anyone who is considered low-risk, which Danika points out is a $22,000 value for students who can complete the whole eighteen-month program. That's a challenge for many inmates who move in and out of custody, but she says the benefit of any professional education while in prison is significant. She says training to be a hair professional gives the inmates self-respect and independence. "It takes away stigma, the stigma of checking that box, reliving their crime," she told me. She said it gives them discipline to work toward a goal, and the school is a place to learn conflict resolution as she models how to handle a disgruntled client. "This is your training ground," she tells them. Even before heading up this cosmetology program, Danika was no stranger to prisons. Her brother was executed on death row.

To Danika, it's not just the training but the fact that they are working toward a state license that gives her students pride and hope. "I consider myself to be a professional," she says. "My license looks the same as a doctor's," she told me. "I take it just as seriously as my PCP." To her students, she says "your knowledge is what's going to set you apart . . . you have to make people respect your license."

As for H.B. 1809 and the push to deregulate braiding in Tennessee, Danika saw it as yet another episode in the history of whites attacking economic advantages Black workers have made for themselves. Braiding, she pointed out, is a huge business for Black salons, most of which are operated by fully licensed cosmetologists. When the legislature created an easier path to braiding with the three-hundred-hour license, that cut into the bottom line for Black salons, but it was better than no licensing at all for braiders. By returning for more, she said, the reformers "are coming after the African American dollar," while keeping the economic protections of licensure in place for white cosmetologists. "If you want to deregulate it, deregulate it all," she told me.[46]

## A Change in Luck

But that's not the way politics works, and it's not the way that hair licensing reform went down in Tennessee. The idea that only the lower-income professions—not doctors or lawyers—have to show up to defend themselves against deregulation applies within a profession as well. When it comes to reforming licensing in the beauty industry, it is the most marginalized who have to fight for the economic protections they enjoy.

Just like the cosmetologists, the barbers showed up on the hill that term to fight hair deregulation. Again, the health and safety arguments were only the surface layer of the debates; underneath were arguments about the personal dignity and financial opportunity offered by licensed professional work. One barber implored the legislature to "preserve my master barber's license." He said, "I've raised generations—I've got kids that are barbers."[47] A senator later explained the political economy of licensure reform to me like this: "I don't want to spend every haircut this year trying to explain to my barber why I messed with his license."[48] And just like Ms. Diouf's braiding bill, the bill that would let high-school dropouts become barbers died in committee.

Relief for Mr. Zarate would have to come from somewhere else. A few weeks after the 2018 legislative session closed, Braden and Mr. Zarate filed suit against the Tennessee Board of Cosmetology and Barber Examiners, alleging that their enforcement of the high-school requirement was unconstitutional.[49] Because they had to meet the extremely high bar of rationality review, their suit was, legally speaking, a long shot. But the barbering bill, while technically a failure, gave them an edge. It had highlighted the unfairness and irrationality of the requirement, and underscored that the democratic process was stacked against people like Mr. Zarate.

It also forced the state into publicly making a strained justification for the requirement: that it promoted the overall high-school graduation rate in the state.[50] In court, the state doubled down on this argument, and added another—that requiring high school for barbers "shield[s] the public against the untrustworthy, the incompetent, or the irresponsible."[51] The judge didn't buy it. In August 2020, she handed down a win for Mr. Zarate, finding that "the generic aspiration that Tennessee students finish twelve years of school has no particular relation to the barbering profession," and the law otherwise had no rational basis in public protection.[52] In the meantime, Ms. Diouf also had a change in her luck. She and Braden had introduced yet another bill rolling back the regulation of hair braiding, this time offering a compromise—require braiders to attend a two-day course on safety and sanitation. It passed.[53] By late 2020, Ms. Diouf's salon was fully legit, and Mr. Zarate was eligible to attend barber school.

At the time of this writing, Mr. Zarate is still saving up the money he'll need to attend.

When we add up how all workers are affected by the "locked out" phenomenon of professional regulation, the answer is, at best, ambiguous—more likely the losers lose more than the winners win. And licensing is regressive, not progressive, because it gives advantages to those who already have the time and money to invest in an education.

For all professionals, it is a powerful thing to have a license. For women, racial minorities, workers with criminal histories, and immigrants, the advantage is especially profound. But so is the sting of being locked out. The licensing system in general, and boards in particular, have the power to make or break the fates of marginalized workers. Boards should know and care about the labor dynamics of their decisions, and their membership should reflect the diversity of their profession. That's not remotely the board system we have today.

Advocates and politicians, too, should recognize these complexities before going after the low-hanging fruit of reform, especially if it means giving a free pass to professions where health and safety is on the line. As we shall see in the next part, the problem with licensing in America isn't always that we have too much regulation. Sometimes, we don't have nearly enough.

# Part II

---

# Locked In

# 6

## Licensed to Ill

> The licensing system is supposed to hold the line against incompetent or dangerous providers. In truth, licensing boards put very bad actors back to work.

On a hot day in Nashville in the summer of 2019, Dr. Michael LaPaglia could be seen outside of the Tennessee Department of Health building pacing and smoking with his lawyer. It was not the first time the Tennessee Board of Medical Examiners had considered a disciplinary case involving the forty-seven-year-old ER physician from Knoxville, but the fourth.

His first brush with the board was in 2014, after he was arrested by law enforcement for dealing opioids, benzodiazepines, and marijuana out of his home. When the state board learned that he'd pled "no contest" to the charges in that criminal case, it placed his license on suspension, and then probation, and ordered the doctor to attend weekly Narcotics Anonymous meetings.[1] He also lost his Drug Enforcement Agency registration (informally called a "DEA number") and thus his ability to legally prescribe controlled substances.

His second encounter with the licensing board came in January 2019, when the board took the unusual step of summarily suspending Dr. LaPaglia, in absentia, from practicing medicine after learning what he had done while his license was on probation. In early 2018, he met a doctor named Charles Brooks at one of his board-mandated NA meetings. Both doctors had restricted licenses, in Brooks's case because of an incident where he gave a patient a sedative before having sex with her (he said it was to calm her nerves over their clandestine affair). But, Dr. Brooks had something Dr. LaPaglia did not—a valid DEA number.[2]

Later that year, the two doctors teamed up to form L&B Healthcare, a clinic with no brick-and-mortar presence, just a prescription pad with Dr. Brooks's DEA number and Dr. LaPaglia's phone number. Dr. LaPaglia used that pad to prescribe dangerous combinations of benzodiazepines and the addiction medication Suboxone—an opioid with significant street value. Dr. LaPaglia sold the prescriptions for $300 cash out of his house, at patients' homes, and, once, in a McDonald's parking lot. When federal law enforcement officers found out about L&B Healthcare, they charged Dr. LaPaglia with trafficking narcotics and fraud. He pled guilty to both felonies in late 2018, but would go on to wait more than two years before being sentenced.[3]

Dr. LaPaglia's third brush with the Tennessee medical board was a few months later, when he testified at Dr. Brooks's disciplinary hearing and admitted to using Dr. Brooks's DEA number to circumvent his own inability to prescribe narcotics. The board members found that the pre-scriptions were "transactions" and not the practice of medicine, but they allowed Dr. Brooks to keep his license.[4]

Finally, Dr. LaPaglia was subject to board proceedings that fourth time, when I saw his contested case hearing about L&B Healthcare and his federal plea. He again admitted to the essential facts—the forgeries and pre-signed scripts, the co-prescribing of benzos and Suboxone, even the McDonald's parking lot. The attorney prosecuting the disciplinary case put both drug dealing pleas into evidence, but seemed to pursue the case with a faint heart. "Dr. LaPaglia did something that was dumb," he argued. LaPaglia agreed. He said that while he and Dr. Brooks might have cut corners, their hearts were in the right place. L&B Healthcare was a good-faith effort to help addicts who, if they had been forced to go cold turkey, would have relapsed hard. The house calls and parking lot meetups were for the patients' convenience. He spoke about his own struggle with addiction and the resolve it gave him to help others in his community.[5]

The newest board member led deliberations after hearing the proof. "My duty is to protect the health, safety, and welfare of the citizens of

Tennessee," he began. "Do I think taking [Dr. LaPaglia's] license protects the people of Tennessee? I do not," the board member said. "I hope I'm a good judge of a heart. I saw someone who has a good heart." In the end, the board reinstated Dr. LaPaglia's license with fewer restrictions than when he formed L&B Healthcare in the first place.[6]

## Unethical, Dangerous, and Licensed

Every profession has its bad apples. They are few and far between, and it wouldn't be fair to judge a profession by the acts of its worst members. But it is fair to judge a system of professional regulation by how it deals with problem providers. And the licensing board system, where professionals truly face a jury of their peers, fails to meet even the most modest standard of public protection.

I began attending licensing board meetings believing that if I, as a lawyer, abused or stole from a client, and my licensing board found out about it, my professional career would be over. Most lawyers and doctors facing ethical dilemmas, even when it's a close call, tend to think, "I could lose my license." That belief, it turns out, comes not from reality, but from a combination of mythology (professions like to perpetuate the idea that they are tough disciplinarians) and the tendency among conscientious providers to internalize professional norms to the point where they seem ironclad and inviolable.

Ninety-eight percent of professionals never have the occasion to learn the truth. But for the approximately two percent who have faced discipline with their professional licensing board, they encounter a system full of second, third, and even fifth chances.[7] The fact that you hold a license to practice law or medicine is perfectly consistent with the fact that you have also been adjudged by your licensing board to be an incompetent, predatory, or abusive provider. And it would seem that the higher a profession's status, the more lax the discipline, which is a problem considering the social harm bad doctors and lawyers can inflict.

When I began attending board meetings in Tennessee in 2018, the state government was in crisis-response mode to address the opioid epidemic. That year also saw the rise of the #MeToo movement, when the country was experiencing a newfound intolerance of sexual abuse and predation. Yet at the first board meeting I ever attended, the medical board relicensed Dr. Edward Owens, the OBGYN discussed in the Introduction whose professional misconduct—a sex-for-drugs arrangement with eleven of his patients—combined both of these hot-button issues. Dr. Owens's case prompted two questions: First, was lax discipline the norm, or was this case an aberration? Second, if it was the norm, how could a system run by high-integrity professionals result in such plainly inappropriate decisions?

Indeed, Dr. Owens's case was not an anomaly, and medicine isn't unique in the grace it gives its bad apples (other professions do it, too). Likewise, Tennessee isn't an outlier—the problem of lenient professional discipline exists on the national level. And discipline that's too light has the same roots as the other dysfunctionalities of the board system: board members given too little time, resources, and regulatory savvy to do anything but go with their instincts as seasoned advocates for their profession and its members.

## Too Little, Too Light

The leniency in Dr. Owens's case was reflected broadly through the cases I collected while watching the medical board. There was the case of Robert Windsor, who had recently pled guilty to a federal felony for a $1.1 million healthcare fraud scheme. He received a reprimand.[8] Then there was Gregory Sullivan, a neurosurgeon and recently sober alcoholic with a visible hand tremor, who was given a path back to licensure (albeit a circuitous one) after retiring ten years prior in order to avoid professional discipline for his alcoholism.[9] Then there was Anand Rajan, who survived three rounds of discipline—once for poor record keeping, then for sexually touching his patients, and finally for improperly prescribing opioids at his clinic—before having his license fully restored to unrestricted status in 2021.[10]

In terms of empirical data, the medical board's decisions from 2016 to 2020 also showed a policy of light discipline. During that period, the

Board of Medical Examiners revoked a doctor's license in just 33 percent of cases where they found sexual misconduct. (In Tennessee, the standard revocation allows a physician to reapply for a license after a year; in some states they may do so in as little as six months.[11]) Doctors received a similar rate of leniency in cases where the board concluded that the doctor had engaged in fraud. And at the height of the opioid crisis, during a period in which ten thousand Tennesseans died of drug overdoses, the board kept in practice almost two-thirds of the doctors they found to have improperly prescribed.[12] I was unable to find any cases where the board permanently revoked a license in an over-prescribing case where the doctor did not consent to it.

Outside of Tennessee, the picture of leniency for egregious physician misconduct is similar. Reporters for the *Atlanta Journal-Constitution* gathered years of data on medical discipline nationwide and found that an alarming number of doctors who engaged in sexual misconduct kept their license. Reporters gathered 2,400 licensing board cases of sexual misconduct involving patients, finding that state boards kept half these physicians in practice. Among the doctors still practicing were ones who had performed oral sex on patients during pelvic exams, and assaulted patients under anesthesia. They included doctors who had been arrested and convicted for their misconduct.[13]

It's not just second chances for doctors, but often third or fourth. A national study of medical board discipline showed that a high rate of discipline was taken against repeat offenders, suggesting that disciplinary actions were not having their desired effect. The study looked at all medical board sanctions nationwide during a twelve-year period and found that physicians receiving a moderate or severe sanction were *thirty times* more likely to get serious discipline again than their colleagues without a disciplinary history were likely to get their first infraction.[14] That was consistent with what I observed in Tennessee in cases of repeat offenders like Dr. Rajan and Dr. LaPaglia. It was also consistent with comments I heard from board members about their expectation that disciplined providers "will be back."[15]

Boards in other states seem to take the same attitude. A doctor in Virginia lost his license three times—first for sexually touching patients, then for over-prescribing opioids, and finally for federal drug dealing charges for which he is serving seven years in prison.[16] The Missouri medical board put back into practice a physician who had violated their board orders five different times, including by fraudulently prescribing pain killers.[17] There was the doctor who removed a healthy kidney during colon surgery and, on another patient, a fallopian tube believing it to be an appendix. He lost his license in three states over these and other botched surgeries, but the Ohio board gave him a fresh start with a clean license which he holds today.[18]

How big of a problem is this outside of medical boards? It is tempting to say that when it comes to shockingly light discipline, doctors present an isolated case. They work in an extremely safety-sensitive area where patients are uniquely vulnerable to predatory or incompetent practice. A doctor's ability to prescribe controlled substances gives them tremendous power in an age of pill addiction, and the bodily nature of medical practice creates a special risk of sexual abuse. Combine this potential for extreme misconduct with the power and prestige of the profession, which allows medical boards to get away with lighter discipline than, say, a midwifery counsel or massage board, and we may expect medicine to be an outlier in terms of egregiously light discipline. Professionals regulating in the shadow of medicine certainly think so. A member of the nursing board told me that when it comes to over-prescribing cases, "the medical board does this," and lightly slapped my wrist. The nursing board, she insisted, was different.[19]

Although there may be a kernel of truth to this story, there is evidence that at least to some degree other professions struggle to come down on their own. For example, a few weeks after the Owens case, the physician assistants board gave Walter Blankenship a new license after he pled guilty to trafficking narcotics through one of the most infamous pill mills in East Tennessee. The professional members of the board advocated for relicensure (against the holdout nonprofessional board member) by pointing out that if Blankenship were a doctor, the medical board wouldn't hesitate to give him a second chance.[20]

Despite what the nursing board member told me about her profession being harsher than doctors, nurses also struggle to maintain a safe level of professional discipline. A national study of nursing board cases alleging sexual abuse found that states only discipline an average of one or two nurses a year for this offense despite the likelihood that abuse is relatively common.[21] When they do decide cases it would seem that they, too, have a tendency to slap wrists. For example, in 2018, the Tennessee Board of Nursing decided the case of Christina Collins, whom prosecutors said was the top prescriber of controlled substances in the state.[22] She prescribed one patient so many controlled substances that he would have to have taken fifty-one pills a day. She tripled another patient's morphine prescription after he was hospitalized for an overdose. Citing controversy over how much was too much when it came to opioids, the nursing board kept her in practice and left her prescribing unrestricted.[23]

Similar stories have come to light about other health professional boards. The Iowa chiropractic board landed in the news for relicensing a practitioner who had already been through two rounds of discipline for repeatedly touching patients' breasts without clinical justification.[24] The *Las Vegas Review-Journal* reported that the Nevada Board of Dental Examiners kept in practice at least a dozen dentists with repeated lawsuits and board actions in Clark County alone, prompting the governor to demand additional ethics training for the board.[25] And at a conference for licensing boards I heard a funeral board staff member describe inspecting a mortuary where unrefrigerated bodies were piled up on banquet tables at various stages of decomposition. She was not able to get the board to do more than fine the establishment, an outcome she partially attributed to board members' conflicts of interest in disciplining fellow funeral professionals.[26]

Since the regulation of lawyers is more secretive, it's harder to directly measure the inadequacy of board discipline in law, but there is reason to think there's a problem there, too.[27] The nationwide rate of state board discipline is probably similar to what it is in medicine—about 3 percent of licensed lawyers have a history of discipline.[28] It is not uncommon for boards to ignore repeated complaints from indigent defendants about their appointed counsel's refusal to communicate, or to give minimal discipline to lawyers who steal from their clients. An example of the latter is Wesley Becker, who was allowed to return to practice after stealing $5,454 from a nonprofit providing legal aid and other services to the homeless, for which he acted as treasurer. The board voted to give him a reprimand (although on appeal the chancery court imposed a brief suspension "to protect the integrity of the profession"). He was allowed to return to practice in 2020.[29]

Recidivism is a big problem in attorney discipline, too, where some states have had to implement a "three strikes" rule.[30] Without such rules, lawyer discipline is a revolving door. For example, Tennessee attorney Carlos Mitchell Hayes's license was censured in 1992, placed on probation in 1995, suspended that same year, reinstated in 2001, placed on probation again in 2004, and censured in 2007. Over the next five years the board petitioned for discipline against the attorney five more times before revoking his license (though he is eligible to reapply).[31] Becker, who stole from the nonprofit, went on to reoffend, too. There is conflicting evidence about how often disbarred attorneys seek reinstatement, but research suggests that a high percentage of those who try succeed, and of those, about 44 percent go on to receive more discipline.[32]

Lawyers, like doctors, can be forgiving of colleagues who use their privilege and power to extort sex. For example, Iowa attorney Gerald Moothart was arrested in 2011 for sexually assaulting his client, but the state board of professional responsibility didn't decide his disciplinary case until 2015. By then four other women, two of them clients, had come forward with stories of sex-for-services and nonconsensual sexual encounters. The board opted for suspension over revocation, leaving him eligible to return to practice in 2017.[33]

Licensing boards can seem blind to the fact that when an attorney sexually abuses a client, almost invariably it involves a power dynamic that goes beyond the typical attorney-client relationship. When an attorney is appointed to represent an indigent client, that client cannot walk away. Appointed attorneys often represent clients facing dire personal consequences, like losing their children or freedom. It is often in this context that attorneys engage in sex with their clients, yet board members see consent where others would see coercion. For example, in the case of Tennessee attorney Christopher Scott Warner, the board found that his addicted client facing criminal drug charges eventually submitted to his sexual advances because he "held her future in his hands." The opinion says both that she was a "reluctant participant" and that the sex was "consensual." As in the Moothart case, the board declined to revoke his license.[34]

Indeed, attorney-dominated disciplinary panels in sex-abuse cases often struggle to empathize with those they are supposed to protect.[35] For example, after Ohio attorney Jason Allen Sarver was criminally charged with repeatedly coercing sex from a defendant he was appointed to represent, the board imposed professional discipline. But because the victim / client had received a plea deal in her own criminal case in exchange for testifying against Sarver in his case, the panel declined to revoke his license. The board's order stated: "[N]ot only was there no harm to the client but the client leveraged her relationship with [Sarver] to get a better plea deal."[36] A recent study of attorney discipline finds that cases like Moothart's, Warner's, and Sarver's are not aberrations: "Too many attorneys have sexually abused and harassed their clients with relative impunity and returned to the profession with little to no additional oversight, limitations, or safeguards against future abuses."[37]

## The Iceberg

It's important to recognize that these cases of too-light discipline reflect only the cases that boards *do* pursue. Patients and colleagues rarely file complaints with licensing boards, and when they do, they are mostly dismissed. An audit of Georgia's medical board found that about two percent of complaints against physicians result in formal discipline; 17 percent are resolved with a private letter of warning to doctors, and 81 percent are dismissed.[38] And states have disturbingly disparate rates of discipline against medical providers; Kentucky's board disciplines doctors at seven times the rate of New Hampshire's.[39] A national patient advocacy group concludes: "There is no reason to believe that even the highest rate currently observed is adequate for protecting the public from dangerous physicians."[40]

In the legal profession, these numbers are higher; somewhere between three percent and six percent of complaints against lawyers result in public sanction, and only about forty percent of discipline is handled privately (as opposed to almost 90 percent in medicine).[41] But to the extent that lawyers are slightly harsher on their own than are healthcare providers, it tends to be in reaction to criminal conduct outside of professional practice (such as a DUI or domestic abuse). Overall, Harvard Law professor David Wilkins says the American Bar Association's claim "that a properly functioning disciplinary process can effectively control lawyer misconduct" is not plausible.[42]

What lies beneath the tip of the iceberg of professional discipline? It's hard to observe the disciplinary cases that a board *doesn't* decide—complaints are confidential and, for the most part, we cannot observe investigations that do not result in public discipline. But academic researchers have found a way to use malpractice settlement data to measure board inaction, and their findings suggest that board discipline is seriously inadequate.[43] In Illinois, a physician who pays out on ten major malpractice claims still only faces a 33 percent chance of board discipline.[44] Using national data, researchers have shown the same is true of doctors who face disciplinary actions by their hospitals—most of them face no board sanction.[45]

Using malpractice suits and hospital actions to identify professionals who slip through the cracks of our licensing system tell only part of the story, because not all professional misconduct can be captured by these measures. In this category we may put pill mills—prescribers selling prescriptions for cash, who tend to operate outside of hospitals, and serve patients who are unlikely to sue for malpractice. These cases, too, are in the iceberg of inaction.

Take, for example, Samson Orusa, a pill mill prescriber whose story illustrates licensing's "false negatives"—the cases that never get brought but should have been. I first read about Dr. Orusa in early 2019 after he was indicted by the feds for drug trafficking. His license, at the time, was clean. I later learned from court filings in his civil and criminal cases that medical board investigators knew essentially everything the feds knew about his practice. In fact, they had known about it for more than six years.

In December 2012, investigators for the Department of Health received a complaint from a state law enforcement officer about a doctor overprescribing controlled substances at his clinic in Clarksville, a military town about an hour outside of Nashville. Nine months later, board investigators inspected Dr. Orusa's clinic and found violations of nineteen pain clinic rules and noted that the clinic "smelled of mold; was not in a safe, clean, and sanitary condition; and there were no handwashing supplies or latex gloves in the exam rooms." The licensing board enforcers filed the report and waited.[46]

A year passed, during which time 1,263 Tennesseans died from drug overdoses, surpassing the number of people killed in car accidents.[47] Local law enforcement prodded the board again with another complaint in 2014, and again investigators inspected the clinic. They found the same nineteen violations and added few more: Dr. Orusa wasn't checking the state database to see if his patients were doctor shopping, he had no aseptic techniques nor systems for controlling infections, he kept opioid pills on the premises, and took cash for services. Still, the board enforcers waited.[48]

Board investigators let two more years go by, during which time overdose deaths had taken so many young lives around the country that the overall life expectancy of Americans declined for the first time in one hundred years.[49] By 2016, Orusa had become the fourth top prescriber in the state among family practitioners. On this third inspection, board investigators noted all the previous ongoing violations and added that the doctor simply "failed to comply with patient safety standards."[50]

Although it's not clear from the report what the licensing investigators meant by "patient safety," evidence adduced at Dr. Orusa's 2021 criminal trial completes the picture. Federal prosecutors said that during this time, Dr. Orusa wrote 66,353 prescriptions for controlled substances.[51] They produced undercover video of "cattle call" appointments at the chaotic, crowded clinic. They said that Dr. Orusa cut and pasted chart entries, ignored drug test results, and fraudulently billed public insurance programs—sometimes claiming he performed more than twenty-four hours of work in one day.[52] On at least two occasions a patient overdosed in the clinic.[53] Each time, an ambulance was called and then Dr. Orusa turned back to finish his day's work of writing scripts.[54]

Another year went by before the licensing authorities opened negotiations with Orusa and his lawyer about professional discipline. His criminal case had gone federal, but he had not yet been indicted. Feeling the heat, the doctor accelerated his prescribing. That year, he topped the charts as the number one prescriber among family practitioners. The feds say he sent millions of dollars away to offshore accounts.[55]

He appears to have taken a defiant stance with the licensing board attorneys, and it worked. Years of dealing drugs out of his clinic would go on to land him a forty-five-count indictment and conviction with the potential for a decades-long prison sentence. But with the licensing boards in 2018, it merely cost him his official designation as a pain clinic operator, making it technically unlawful for him to see mostly pain patients. Both his medical license and his ability to prescribe controlled substances remained unscathed. On the day he lost his pain clinic license, he wrote 164 controlled substance prescriptions for a total of more than twelve thousand pills.[56]

## Just a Few Bad Apples?

It's tempting to dismiss cases like Dr. Orusa's as outliers and point out that even a disciplinary system that has a blind spot for the worst of the worst might still function well for the other disciplinary cases. But there are several flaws to this argument.

First, the data suggest that dealing with outlying professionals is, for better or worse, all the board disciplinary system really does (other than imposing sanctions for failing to complete continuing education). This conclusion is supported by the very low rate of professional discipline, by the fact that most cases I have encountered involve what anyone would consider extreme misconduct, and by the fact that there seems to be little overlap between malpractice payouts and board discipline. Licensing boards simply don't concern themselves with ordinary cases of poor professional performance.[57]

Second, even if boards were concerned with more mundane cases of neglect or incompetence, light discipline for extreme malfeasance limits what you can do with the rest of disciplinary cases. If the sex-abusing drug dealer gets a slap on the wrist, there's little room to step down for lesser offenses. A related point is that light discipline for extreme misconduct sends a message to the rest of the profession: You'll have to do a lot more than cut a few corners to get in trouble with the board.

Finally, there is evidence that the worst of the worst have an outsized impact on the public's welfare. This is especially true in the context of the opioid crisis, where unethical prescribing has accounted for a disproportionate share of opioids dispensed in the United States.[58] When it comes to sexual abuse at the hands of a professional, just one instance can cause devastating harm.[59] Yet some particularly predatory professionals can count their victims of sexual abuse in the dozens or even thousands.

One notable example is Dr. George Tyndall, who served as the OBGYN at University of Southern California's student health center for twenty-seven years.[60] He abused so many women and girls during that time that their claims were resolved through a class action—a procedural mechanism used to aggregate legal claims where there are too many victims to each bring suit individually. Between the class action and other lawsuits, USC has settled with sixteen thousand victims of Dr. Tyndall for a total of $1.1 billion.[61]

Indeed, how a profession deals with its bad apples matters a lot.

## Set Up for Failure

What accounts for this extraordinarily forgiving disciplinary system? To fully understand the dysfunction of professional discipline, it's important to understand its legal procedure.[62]

First, board staff members receive a complaint that they typically review with a professional (acting as a consultant) to determine if it warrants investigation. In Tennessee, staff members and investigators are employees of a state agency, but they work for the board in the sense that they act at its behest and charge the board fees for their time. In other states, these investigators work for the licensing board more directly.[63] Complaints deemed worthy of investigation are worked up. Investigating authorities can ask providers for documents and interview witnesses in response to complaints.[64] After the investigation, another go / no-go decision is made in consultation with a professional about whether to pursue discipline.[65]

If discipline is in order, an attorney—typically a state employee—prosecutes the case and begins a negotiation process with the license holder. If they work out a deal, the prosecutor presents a consent order to the licensing board, which is like a plea bargain in the criminal system. The board members must vote to accept or reject the consent order; in my observation, this is usually a rubber stamp. If negotiations fail, the case proceeds to a contested case hearing, where board members hear from a board prosecutor, the license holder, and, if he has one, his attorney.

The biggest procedural variation among states is in who hears the cases. For most states, including Tennessee, the professional licensing board itself, or a panel of its members, presides over disciplinary trials.[66] There is an informal policy in Tennessee that two out of the three panelists must be members of the profession. Administrative law judges (again, state employees) attend these trial-like proceedings to keep the presentation of evidence and arguments organized, and to rule on legal technicalities like the admissibility of evidence. But as in most states, it's board members that decide everything that really matters: what happened, whether it violated their profession's practice act, and what penalties to impose. A few states try cases directly to an administrative law judge, which is preferable to using panels dominated by professionals. But even in these states, the administrative law judge's opinion is merely advisory—the licensing board must vote to adopt or reject it, undercutting the independence of the judge.[67] In either case, once a board has made its decision, disciplined professionals can then appeal disciplinary decisions in state court, but all that court can do is affirm or remand the case back to the board because state courts lack the authority to make disciplinary decisions in their own right.[68]

So how does it all go so wrong? Part of the answer should be familiar by now: boards are seriously under-resourced. Remember that most boards are funded only by licensing fees (some don't even get to keep all of these), and the average board regulates only a few thousand providers so their total budgets are small. At every step of a disciplinary case—from investigation to prosecution—boards lack the funding, personnel, and expertise to get it right. That makes for a system that's reactive, slow, and bogged down by due process. Empirical research supports this link between scarce board resources and lax discipline.[69]

When you confront members of a profession about inadequacies in discipline, the first thing you will hear is that the board disciplinary system is "reactive."[70] What they mean by this is that there is little-to-no proactive investigation of questionable providers, which they blame on budgetary and staff constraints. Instead, disciplinary cases are opened only when someone files a complaint with a board.

Typically anyone can file a complaint—even someone who isn't a patient or a client of the provider (a staff member of the medical board told me she once opened a complaint about a doctor whose misconduct she heard about on the radio while driving to work).[71] Sometimes colleagues will turn a provider in to the board, and indeed many professions impose an ethical duty on its members to rat out their colleagues. But feelings of loyalty and collegiality prevent this from being a large or reliable source of disciplinary complaints.[72] Hospitals, too, have the obligation to report misconduct, but often fail to meet this requirement.[73] Law enforcement agencies may refer cases to boards, but they are not obligated to do so, and it happens less than one might expect.[74] Federal law enforcement officers I spoke to about opioid disciplinary cases explained that the criminal system likes to stay in its own lane.[75]

So most often complaints must come from patients and clients. There are major drawbacks to such a system. First, a consumer or patient must know that he has received bad or unethical service, yet the licensure system is predicated on the idea that consumers do not know what they are getting—that they can't tell the peaches from the lemons.[76] Second, they must actually feel harmed by the conduct. For large classes of cases—from doctors selling scripts to lawyers helping clients commit fraud—consumers will have no complaints about the unethical services they received.[77] Third, the aggrieved consumer must have enough confidence in the licensing board system to think it's worth the effort; the fact that 98 percent of all complaints result in no public discipline hardly provides that.

Finally, the complainant must be willing to confront a powerful social force that is hierarchical and patriarchal. Sometimes complainants are explicitly reminded of this, as when the online form to file a complaint against a lawyer says that clients often misunderstand what constitutes acceptable practice of law and warns that complaints may expose the complainant to a lawsuit.[78] Some boards refuse to investigate at all unless the complainant identifies themselves.[79] A former investigator for New York's Office of Professional Medical Conduct, the office that investigates disciplinary cases against the state's medical professionals, told a reporter asking about the complaint process, "[i]f I were a person who was violated and I knew that system, I would never go in and tell my story. Never, never."[80]

Victims of sexual misconduct are especially unlikely to come forward, when the best-case scenario is a public, adversarial dissection of their experience. Many don't even know where to go. I interviewed someone who had been touched and photographed inappropriately by a physician. She told me that, at the time, "I wanted someone to know about it, but I didn't know who." Years later, when she filed a complaint with the California Medical Board, they told her it was too late—the statute of limitations had run. She asked if they would at least keep her complaint on file for context in the event others complained about the same doctor. In response, she received a two-sentence email: "Due to retention process your complaint will be maintained in the Central Complaint Unit for one year. After a year, your complaint will be purged."[81]

It's easy to imagine a more proactive system. Massage licensing boards could prioritize inspections of operations that are easily identified on the internet as brothels (the Louisiana Massage Therapy board was recently criticized by its state legislature for not doing this).[82] Boards could use public information about controlled substance prescribing, malpractice suits, or hospital discipline to initiate investigations into problematic physicians. Boards could access public criminal records or develop stronger relationships with local law enforcement that might encourage information sharing. Some of these measures may cost more money and require extra manpower, which are things boards don't always have. But often, a simple internet search would reveal red flags worth pursuing. I saw several cases involving providers whose misdeeds were plain from internet searches and supported by publicly available evidence like criminal convictions, sworn testimony, and—perhaps most damningly—other states' licensing databases. One example is the case of Dr. Windsor, the doctor whose $1.1 million fraud conviction was the basis of a reprimand; in fact, he defrauded insurers of $20 million, according to a separate civil suit he settled with the federal government over the same scheme.[83]

The board disciplinary process is also notoriously slow. It took the Iowa attorney licensing board four years to put Gerald Moothart's law license on probation after his arrest for sexually assaulting a client. The Tennessee medical board first learned about Dr. Owens trading scripts for sex with his patients in 2013; they allowed him to stay in practice without restrictions or any discipline until 2017.

Even when a provider's case involved patient deaths, boards can drag their feet. Board prosecutors accused Darrel Rinehart of contributing to the overdose deaths of three of his patients in a single year by prescribing them deadly combinations of high-dose opioids and benzodiazepines. (Two other patients died under similar circumstances but neither were autopsied because Dr. Rinehart himself ruled them deaths by natural causes.) It took the board three years to decide his disciplinary case, during which time he held a clean license in Tennessee and practiced in Illinois. Ultimately, the board decided not to revoke his license but let it expire so as not to jeopardize his practice in Illinois.[84] "If he's not coming back [to Tennessee]," said one board member, "then that's a good thing."[85]

One terrible irony is that the more serious cases tend to take especially long. The proof in Darrel Rinehart's case was immense; in addition to the five deaths there were six non-fatal overdoses, and a total of thirty-two charts with dangerous prescribing. Proof and deliberation took three trial days, but because Tennessee's medical board meets only every two months when its members from all over the state convene in Nashville, the proceeding was spread over a period of almost four months.[86] I followed one trial that took sixteen months from opening arguments to deliberations.[87]

Systematic studies of professional discipline suggest that it's slow everywhere. A law professor who read five years' worth of disciplinary decisions against lawyers in New York found the length of time between when misconduct came to light and when the board acted "unconscionably long." He said, "it mocks the professed goal of protecting the public and the administration of justice if a lawyer who will be (and should be) suspended or disbarred is left to practice for years until the day of sanction."[88] An investigative journalist in Florida found that it took the medical board an average of 434 days to resolve a case. (He studied a two-year period during which the Florida legislature had cut the health department's budget by $55.6 million.)[89]

Another factor that adds sand to the gears of the disciplinary process is whether the provider is represented by an attorney, a situation most likely to occur in high-status professions (doctors and lawyers are almost always represented) and in cases with serious charges. In all states, a license to practice is considered a property right and it cannot be taken away without due process.[90] Due process in the administrative context means you have the right to know about the charges and evidence against you, the evidence must be reliable and relevant, and you must be afforded a hearing. Due process also means you have the right to be represented by an attorney throughout the process, if you can afford one.[91]

Marshalling and presenting all that evidence, usually done by a board prosecutor who works either for or under the aegis of the board, is costly as it is. Defense lawyers have a way of making it even more so. I interviewed a former member of Tennessee's massage therapy board who said that when an accused provider made noise about hiring counsel, the board would back off. "We don't have the funds to have to fool with that," she told me.[92] Even when board lawyers (who tend to be paid less than private practitioners) are prepared to go toe-to-toe with private defense attorneys, they must worry that the provider might appeal the board's disciplinary decision in state court, where state law says discipline that's "arbitrary and capricious" must be thrown out.[93] Board decisions—made by members who are inexpert in regulation, busy, and underinformed—can be all over the map. "Arbitrary and capricious" may actually describe most board disciplinary decisions.

Board prosecutors are therefore keen to work out negotiated settlements with providers and save the expense and hassle of a trial. Providers, for their part, are motivated to keep the case as quiet and private as possible, and so favor plea deals, too. Another advantage of an agreed order is that the professional can negotiate what is included in the board's findings of fact. For example, the fact section of Orusa's negotiated settlement revoking his pain clinic license failed to mention the 66,353 prescriptions he had written, his fraudulent practices, or the in-clinic overdoses. Rather, it focused on his lack of documentation, his failure to check the state prescription database, and the fact that he did not offer his employees a flu vaccine, as required by the pain clinic guidelines.[94]

This emphasis on compromise between prosecutor and provider can lead to chumminess between parties that should be adversarial. Even contested case hearings have the casual air of a joint presentation by prosecutor and defense, for the board's consideration. Some states even allow the same lawyer to represent the board and to prosecute cases before them. As the attorney for Dr. Owens and Dr. Orusa told me, the process is "not quite adversarial."[95] At the same time, professionals have lobbied for all the procedural protections afforded to defendants in fully adversarial legal proceedings. The most successful, of course, have been the lawyers.[96]

## Stopping the Buck

These are the features of the disciplinary system that board members from around the country cited when I confronted them with cases where too little was done, too late. The system is reactive—we cannot learn about misconduct without a complaint. The system is slow—by the time we learn about the misconduct during a contested case hearing, sometimes it's been going on for years. We're hamstrung by legal technicalities—we can't revoke a license without a lot of evidence and due process. We only really see the trials—a lot of wrist-slaps are negotiated by our staff.

From what I observed, these answers were factually accurate descriptions of *how* the system fails to protect patients and consumers. But they did not answer the question of *why* such a broken system is tolerated—by the public and, importantly, by the board itself. Each of these defects is procedural and could be fixed by a better allocation of resources and more zealous advocacy for patient and public protection. And all of it operates in the shadow of the board's authority.

If faster and safer discipline was a priority for the board members, every one of these problems could be addressed. Although it is conventional to use consumer complaints to drive professional discipline, there is no hard-and-fast legal impediment to using a more proactive system (and empirical evidence suggests it might be a lot safer).[97] Delays in bringing cases need not be tolerated by the board. Of course, better funding would also be required for the system to move faster and in a more directed manner. But again, licensing boards could advocate for more funding to do their work—and there are plenty of stories of disciplinary failure to raise political capital at the statehouse. It's true that there are legal requirements that must be satisfied to restrict or revoke a license, but that's also true in every area of law enforcement. Not all of them are as slow or lenient as the professional licensing system.

The bottom line is that for the disciplinary process to work well, there must be a realistic threat that a hammer will come down at the end of it. If the board is unwilling to put their foot down at the end of the process, there is little incentive for their staff to hurry, for professionals to comply with investigations, and for both sides to agree to plea deals that actually protect the public. Even if the board hears only 1 percent of cases, what they do in those cases defines the terms of the other 99 percent. As the executive director for the medical board in South Carolina told me, "The medical board has to realize that the buck stops there."[98] For reasons discussed in the next section, licensing board members seem to find themselves unable to be the bad guys they need to be for the rest of the system to work.

So now we know that boards aren't stopping the bad actors. We also know a bit about *how* the disciplinary system goes wrong. But we still need to understand why. Chapter 7 will explore why boards have such a hard time bringing down the hammer, and how their impulse to forgive, rehabilitate, and redeem drives disciplinary decisions.

# 7

# Recover and Repair

*Board members see the humanity in the colleagues they discipline, a tendency encouraged by private interest groups with their own motives for leniency.*

The day before Dr. Stephen Loyd decided Dr. LaPaglia's case, he arrived at the Tennessee Department of Health building in a nondescript office park in north Nashville. It was his first day as a member of the Tennessee Board of Medical Examiners. He had been told that the first half of the two-day meeting would be devoted to approving applicants and discussing rules and policy. The next day would be contested case hearings, and he might be put on a panel to consider disciplinary charges against a doctor.

He was nervous. In his professional realm, he was an expert and totally confident. Like most of his colleagues on the licensing board, he measured his medical career not in years but decades. He was the medical director for a drug recovery treatment program with five locations. He had just finished a stint as the outgoing governor's "Opioid Czar," advising on state policy responses to the addiction crisis that was ravaging the state.[1] Dr. Loyd believed that it was this experience that led to his appointment to the medical board.

His work on the opioid crisis was not only professional but personal. Years ago, he confronted his own pill addiction when he hit rock bottom. As he explained to me on his first day of board service, it was a matter of life or death. "I was going to bed every night, half the nights afraid to die and half praying I would," he said. He turned to the state's program for physicians struggling with substance abuse for help, and he credits his ongoing relationship with that organization with his recovery and for inspiring his career shift into addiction medicine.[2]

But despite all this experience, there was a way in which Dr. Loyd felt out of his depth. He had been given a two-hour orientation on the basics of board service and the procedure for recusal in the case of a direct conflict of interest. He hadn't been briefed on, or even given a copy of, the rules or statutes that he was now in charge of interpreting and applying. He hadn't been given guidance about how to decide contested cases or about the goals of physician discipline. He hadn't even been told what remedial and punitive measures the board had at its disposal.[3]

The next day, he would decide Dr. LaPaglia's contested case.

## "We Expect Disciplinary Action"

Of all the instances I observed of boards going too easy on dangerous providers, it was the licensing boards' decisions in opioid cases that surprised me the most. They also provided the most fertile ground for understanding how a disciplinary system comprised of such high-integrity professionals could yield such inappropriately lenient results. Licensing board discipline is too light to keep the public safe because of a mix of two forces: a little psychology from board members prone to seeing things from the professional perspective; and a lot of opportunism from organized groups with skin in the game of professional discipline.

On March 14, 2018, one week before the medical board would relicense Dr. Owens after taking his license for trading opioids for sex with eleven patients, the Tennessee State Senate held a hearing about professional discipline in opioid cases. Senator Farrell Haile, a pharmacist, was fed up. He had been reporting physicians who overprescribed to the medical board for years, to no avail. "You pull in the parking lot, and you can tell by the license plates," he said of the pill mills. "You walk in the office, you can tell what's going on." He was backing a bill that purported to override board discretion and impose mandatory minimums in discipline cases for overprescribing, a law styled after criminal sentencing minimums.

The senator's anger was understandable. It was impossible to live in Tennessee during the time of my research—much less attend governmental meetings and hearings—without knowing that the state was in an all-hands-on-deck response mode to the opioid crisis. Annual overdose deaths, driven by opioids, were climbing toward two thousand. The crisis of opioid addiction was taking its toll not only on Tennessee's communities, but on the state's budget. The number of babies born with neonatal abstinence syndrome had grown sixfold since 2005; each case cost the state nearly ten times as much as a healthy delivery. Emergency room visits and hospitalizations for overdoses placed a financial burden on the state's public health care spending, too.[4]

Tennessee's governmental response began in 2012, with a new "pain clinic" designation that imposed additional regulatory requirements for prescribers seeing more than half their patients for pain treatment. Two years later, the state mandated adherence to its "Chronic Pain Treatment Guidelines," that steered doctors away from the prescribing patterns most likely to lead to addiction and abuse.[5] In 2016, Tennessee passed a law requiring that all opioid prescriptions be reported to a Controlled Substance Monitoring Database so that pharmacies and prescribing professionals could track doctor shopping and prescription drug abuse.[6]

By 2018, it was clear these measures were not enough. That year, the state general assembly passed "Tennessee Together," an omnibus opioid bill that allocated millions of state funds to addiction treatment and other harm reduction measures.[7] Dr. Loyd, who would go on to decide Dr. LaPaglia's case, advised on the bill.[8] Governor Haslam signed the bill at a ceremony in Maryville, Tennessee, in the Appalachian part of the state hit so hard by the crisis.[9] Maryville was home to Breakthrough Pain Center, a notorious pill mill raided by the feds in 2010 leading to nine indictments against prescribers (among them Walter Blankenship, the physician assistant I saw get his license back in Chapter 6).[10] Maryville was also the mailing address for Brooks's and LaPaglia's L&B Healthcare, which was in full swing at the time of the ceremony.

The same month that Tennessee Together was signed into law, the state sued Purdue Pharmaceuticals for its role in the opioid crisis. Some of Purdue's misconduct was ancient history. As early as 2003, it was clear that Purdue had promoted its blockbuster drug OxyContin, released in 1996, through a fraudulent marketing scheme designed to counter the commonsense notion, in place among health professionals for one hundred years, that opioids are addictive, dangerous, and appropriate only to treat acute pain or pain in dying patients. Purdue called this "opioiphobia" and used professional continuing education courses to reeducate prescribers about its miracle drug. Purdue told professionals that the alarming drug-seeking behavior prescribers saw in their pain patients was "psuedoaddiction," and the cure was more OxyContin. That particular house of cards came down in 2007, when Purdue executives pled guilty to federal crimes for misbranding and the company promised states, including Tennessee, to stop fraudulently marketing its opioids to prescribers.[11]

Tennessee's 2018 suit against Purdue alleged more recent misconduct by the pharmaceutical company. The state attorney general claimed that since 2007, the company had continued to contribute to the financial and personal devastation of the people of Tennessee by running the state's prescribers like street-level dealers of OxyContin. The lawsuit asked the company and the family of billionaires who owned it to pay—literally—for shifting its sales strategy for OxyContin from well-meaning doctors (who by then knew better) to professionals who Purdue knew were operating pill mills.[12]

The lawsuit and "Tennessee Together" were splashy, and both were the subject of presentations by state officials at licensing board meetings. Yet, that year, the boards decided case after case in ways that were plainly at odds with the rest of the state government's attitude toward overprescribing. That was the year the nursing board decided the case of Christina Collins, the nurse practitioner from Chapter 6 who prescribed so many opioids and other controlled substances that one of her patients would have to have taken fifty-one pills a day.[13] It was also the year when the PA board relicensed Breakthrough's Blankenship, citing a philosophy of "recover and repair."[14] And it was the year the medical board preserved full prescribing authority for Dr. Thomas Ballard, despite having found that his prescribing was "unprofessional, dishonorable, or unethical." The feds later claimed Dr. Ballard had moved 4.2 million opioid pills through his clinic, traded sex for prescriptions, and prescribed to a pregnant woman who later died of an overdose. He pled guilty in 2021.[15]

This disconnect between a state government panicked about the opioid crisis and its licensing boards sitting on their hands was palpable at the legislative hearing about minimum discipline for opioid prescribers. It didn't help that the licensing boards' refusal to impose discipline had rendered the legislature's own efforts to combat the crisis ineffective: the primary consequence for doctors failing to adhere to the state's Chronic Pain Guidelines, or the requirement that they consult the Controlled Substance Monitoring Database, was licensing board discipline, which was not forthcoming. It was time to get tough on licensing boards. "We are expecting the boards to begin acting in good faith," Senator Haile said in the hearing about his minimum discipline bill. "If you want to serve on these boards, we expect disciplinary action. That's what you're there for."[16]

If the bill was designed to rein in licensing boards' tendency toward forgiveness in disciplinary cases, it had a fatal flaw. Although the bill set a default mandatory minimum for overprescribers—loss of controlled substance prescribing for five years—it appointed a taskforce with the authority to change it. The taskforce was to be comprised almost entirely of sitting licensing board members, with representatives from each prescribing profession. Thus, the taskforce's composition doubled-down on the state's strategy of letting the professions govern themselves—the very strategy that had created the crisis of lax discipline in the first place. By the time the taskforce was done with its work, the legislature's five-year time-out from prescribing for disciplined prescribers was down to six months.[17]

## Always Save a Doctor

Why would professionals sitting on licensing boards protect pill mill prescribers? Why, years after every responsible prescriber knew opioids shouldn't be handed out like candy, when a public health crisis unlike any other (albeit one that would soon be eclipsed—or perhaps the better word would be amplified—by another), would boards give second chances to those who had turned their prescription pad into a cash machine?

Tennessee Board of Medical Examiners member Thomas Richter is an award-winning pathologist, medical school professor, and, from my observations, an outspoken advocate for rehabilitation over revocation in disciplinary cases. A public member of the board told me that Dr. Richter's philosophy was to "always save a doctor" when that could be accomplished without compromising public health and safety.

We met for dinner on a rainy summer evening after one of the board meetings. He was nearing retirement age, having served for many years in the leadership of the Tennessee Medical Association, our state's professional association for physicians. He told me that's why the governor asked him to serve on the medical board. I picked Dr. Richter up at the hotel in Nashville where he stayed when he was in town for the bi-monthly board meetings, and we headed to dinner. Dr. Richter reminded me of my father-in-law: tall, soft-spoken, warm, and very, very smart. He was the kind of man who was self-confident without being smug, who—in his own low-key way—was in complete control in any professional or social situation. He was quick with a turn of phrase, framed in his Memphis drawl.

When the conversation turned to second chances for doctors like Dr. Owens, he clarified that the board was there to protect the public, not the profession. "We do a good job," he said. "We do not miss that objective." He said that in most cases rehabilitation, and not license revocation, better protected the citizens of Tennessee. He told me it took $1.5 million of public funds to train a physician. His duty was to protect the public, which included protecting its investment in medical training. He put it this way: "If you had a one-point-five million dollar piece of equipment with a broken belt, would you dump it in a ditch?"[18]

### "None of Us Is Perfect"

There are two parts to the save-a-doctor mentality (or, because I heard it across many professions, the "save-a-professional" mentality). Part of it is logical, as Dr. Richter's math illustrates. But that logic would be far less compelling without the emotional identification board members feel with their peers—even ones facing discipline, and even ones who have apparently acted predatorily or in bad faith. Professional board members deciding disciplinary cases are presented with a colleague who started out a lot like them, before they went off the rails. How does it feel to be pulled in two directions—one way by how your profession rationalizes misconduct, and another by the outrage the public would probably feel about keeping a dangerous or predatory provider in the profession?

No one knows the sacrifices and hard work it takes to be a professional better than someone who's been through it herself. Board members have this in mind when they consider what to do with an accused colleague. "I know how hard it is to go to med school, I know the sacrifices I've made for my license," a medical board member told me. "When you impede that, put sanctions on that, I know it's a big deal to somebody," she said.[19] Her fellow board member agreed. "We all are aware of what it takes to make it through pre-med, medical school, to go through a residency, and to do the day in and day out of practice."[20] Lawyers representing professionals facing discipline play on this theme; I saw one open argument in a disciplinary case by telling the board, "We all know how hard it was for all of you to get licensed."[21]

As Dr. Richter pointed out, that investment and its potential returns aren't just personal. Every trained professional represents a wellspring of care and services for society, created at great cost, sometimes to taxpayers (although not all of the $1.5 million it takes to train a doctor are public funds, as Dr. Richter suggested).[22] Revoking a license leaves not only a professional out of work, but his patients and clients unserved. Here, board members consider access to care paramount, unlike when they work the ratchet or engage in turf wars. This logic creates some disturbing distortions in the market for professional services, as explored in Chapter 8. But it also allows board members to reconcile their instinct to protect the profession with their mandate to protect the public.

It's not just the investment that board members seem keen to salvage, but the professional himself. Another medical board member told me it was hard not to be a "softie" in disciplinary hearings when you hear the professional's side and they raise doubts about what on paper looks like bad intent.[23] This was reinforced by the fact that victims only rarely testify before licensing boards. The president of the medical board explained it to me this way: "It's head versus heart: how does your heart feel? That's where you might think 'God, that could have been me.'"[24]

Board members reminded me that wayward providers didn't start out that way; when they graduated from professional school, they were full of promise and hope. One pointed out that this kind of identification could cut in favor of harsh discipline. He said that sometimes when he heard discipline cases, he thought, "You should be held to a higher standard. You had a talent. What happened?"[25] Professionals also assured me that they were especially strict on their wayward providers, because their behavior reflected badly on their profession. A former member of the chiropractic board said, of predatory providers, "I don't want these guys in my profession. They make us look bad."[26]

Every profession has an ostensible line in the sand. In the medical context, board members told me sexual predation and trafficking in controlled substances were unforgivable. In law it's stealing from a client, in funeral services it's sex with a corpse. But I saw boards offer second chances to providers who had engaged in each of these "unforgivable" sins (and during my research, I saw the funeral directors' board change the disciplinary consequences for a licensee found to have sexually abused a corpse from "will" lose their license to "may" lose their license).[27] In finding ways to forgive the unforgivable, board members seemed to reach for an earlier version of the respondent they could relate to—before it all went so wrong—and give them a path back into the fold.

This tendency to identify with accused colleagues is closely related to another reason for leniency: a professional culture of not second-guessing colleagues. It's the same culture that makes it hard to find experts to testify against doctors and lawyers in malpractice suits. A medical board member told me that, as a doctor, you can sometimes find yourself treating a patient who was seen first by someone else, and it seems like a mistake was made. "But I wasn't there," he said, "so you're not quick to judge." Disciplinary cases can feel the same way. "You can't tear a fence down until you know why they put it there in the first place," he told me.[28] Or, as another board member said, "In the practice of medicine, none of us is perfect. We all make mistakes."[29]

Relatedly, professionals may feel the need to protect their profession, as a general matter, from second-guessing by outside voices, even (or especially) if those voices are patients or clients. A professor reading a sample of disciplinary decisions against attorneys concluded that the system evinced an "institutional hostility to both [the lawyers prosecuting disciplinary cases] and victims of lawyer misconduct."[30] Sociologists emphasize the importance of autonomy in establishing professional identity; governmental incursions on that, in the form of a disciplinary action, may be viewed as encroachments on the professional domain.

## No Bad Men

For all I heard about professional identification, I still struggled to accept it as the only explanation for what I was seeing. Did this highly respected and successful board member, and former president of his professional association, really believe that but-for-the-grace-of-God he would be selling prescriptions out of his car? Did this OBGYN with fifty years of medical experience, the first woman to serve as chief of staff at her hospital, truly believe that writing 164 opioid prescriptions in one day was an honest mistake?

Remember that who board members are—colleagues of the accused—is only half of why they are problematic regulators. Licensing board members get it wrong also because of who they *are not*. They are not experts in the adversarial system of law enforcement. They do not know, as law students are told, that the law exists not for the good man who will follow norms out of social pressure, altruism, or habit. It exists for the "bad man" who will walk right up to the line society draws to circumscribe acceptable behavior.[31] Draw the line and hold it not for the kind of professional sitting on a licensing board, but for the kind who needs legal consequences to keep from inflicting harm. Board members are also not given the time or information necessary to develop disciplinary policy to control these bad actors. That has to come from somewhere, and most of the time the gap is filled by associations and other organizations with the explicit mission of protecting the profession and its members.

Medicine provides a good example. In 1982, the American Medical Association published an article that sent licensing board members a message that was easy for them to swallow: there was a tidy model for understanding physicians who improperly prescribed, and for the most part it justified a disciplinary philosophy based on second chances. The "4D" model explained that physicians misprescribe because their education was "dated," they were "duped" by their patients, they were "disabled" by their own addiction, or they were simply "dishonest." The model deflected blame away from prescribers in all but the "dishonest" category, which was dismissed anyway as being rare and better handled by the criminal system.[32] By shifting the focus to external (or, in the case of a physician's own addiction, quasi-external) causes of overprescribing, the 4D model pointed toward discipline that would remove a physician from his unfortunate circumstances, not from the profession itself.

Since the early 1980s, this "tough love" philosophy of professional discipline has been dominant—well beyond prescribing cases and well beyond medicine. Specifically, board disciplinary orders throughout the professions have tended to focus on continuing education (even in cases where the provider could not possibly have mistaken his conduct as meeting the professional standard), sometimes bizarrely specific limitations on practice (even where the facts suggested a general lack of judgement, boundaries, and competency), and addiction treatment (even for conditions very likely to relapse, or even after multiple relapses).

No doubt a significant number of mistakes made by professionals can be chalked up to ignorance or a dated education. Most professions require providers to engage in continuing education for every licensure cycle, but critics point out that participation in a CEU course can be very casual and the substance very light (and I can confirm that with my own personal experience).[33] In theory, it can make sense for boards to require intensive and directed educational courses as a way to remediate imperfect professional practice. In practice, boards impose continuing education in disciplinary cases where it is probably falling on deaf ears.

Christina Collins, for example, seemed more than just misinformed about controlled substance prescribing. The state said she was the top opioid prescriber in Tennessee, among all the prescribing professions. She worked at a clinic with five other providers who went on to be indicted on federal drug trafficking charges. She prescribed opioids, benzos, and muscle relaxants in combination, known to abusers as the "holy trinity." In response, the nursing board asked her to attend a continuing education course about safe opioid prescribing.[34] Likewise, Dr. John Popescu may not have learned much from his board-ordered continuing education class, which was imposed after he got in trouble for prescribing controlled substances to his girlfriend and, after she ended the relationship, breaking into her house and sexually assaulting her. He faced criminal prosecution over the incident and pled no contest to aggravated trespassing and stalking.[35] In response, the licensing board asked Dr. Popescu to attend a course about maintaining proper patient boundaries.[36]

I did encounter one story where a doctor credited a board-ordered continuing education course with a dramatic change in his practice. As reported in the *Atlanta Journal-Constitution,* Dr. William Almon was allowed to resign from the army early in his career as a psychiatric resident when it came to light that he had had sex with a patient at an army medical center. He then worked as a physician at a jail, where he faced criminal charges for sexually assaulting three inmates. Those charges were dropped, but at his next job, at a primary care clinic, he was accused of molesting a fourteen-year-old patient and a schizophrenic adult (he pled no contest to those charges in 2006). In 2008, the Georgia medical board placed his license on probation and, among other restrictions, required that he attend a course on maintaining proper professional boundaries. In 2011, all restrictions on his license were lifted by the board, and when the *Atlanta Journal-Constitution* reporters interviewed him that year, he told them he had so fully embraced the lessons from the course that he was now teaching a similar one at Professional Boundaries, Inc., a company offering continuing medical education to troubled physicians.[37]

In addition to education, the 4D model has also put an emphasis on board-ordered practice restrictions as a disciplinary tool. If the overarching goal is to preserve the expertise and professional contributions of a provider (a win-win for society and the professional), then the task of discipline becomes to prevent the specific misconduct from happening again. To save the patient, the bad behavior must be surgically removed.

One common tool is practice monitoring, which can mean different things to different boards—from a volunteer within the professional community meeting weekly with the provider, to rigorous practice review conducted at great expense to the licensee.[38] In Tennessee, the medical board usually demanded that disciplined physicians use Affiliated Monitors, a national firm that charges about a thousand dollars a month to supervise a physician.[39] Those fees must come out of the physician's salary or be passed through to the patient. In addition to the problem of cost, outsourcing board regulatory work to a private entity creates a problem of watching the watchmen. It was not clear to me that the members of the board knew or cared about how Affiliated Monitors worked or even what they did. And on at least one occasion, I saw the board lift licensure restrictions despite Affiliated Monitors' lingering concerns.[40]

In cases of sexual misconduct, boards will sometimes demand that a chaperone be present for patient encounters. But while chaperones are widely used in gynecological practice as a matter of course, they are a controversial tool in professional rehabilitation. Like practice monitors, chaperones can run the gamut in terms of rigor, independence, and cost to the licensee. Some chaperone orders are written so broadly as to permit a doctor to use any third party who happens to be present, including someone like a receptionist, who may have no training or independence from the provider. Even a chaperone from a third-party service is usually paid by the licensee or his practice, leading to the possibility of conflicting interests.[41] I saw the medical board grant an order of compliance to a physician who used his own medical assistant as a chaperone, despite concerns among board staff about whether the chaperone was "objective."[42]

Indeed, there is strong evidence that chaperones are ineffective. A study on the effectiveness of chaperones found that 19 percent of cases where physicians sodomized a patient took place in the presence of a chaperone.[43] Dr. Larry Nassar, who abused more than one hundred girls while serving as doctor for the US gymnastics team, abused several children while their parents were in the room.[44] As Dr. John Hall, the former executive director of the Mississippi Board of Medicine told me, "chaperones won't keep you safe. . . . [They] just don't work."[45]

There is also the compelling logic that says a professional who needs a chaperone because of a history of sexual misconduct with patients probably shouldn't be in practice at all. At the very least, the use of chaperones undermines public confidence in the medical profession and its regulators; the general public expects something more than a chaperone to protect them from a provider known to have engaged in sexual misconduct.[46] Board members understand this—in Dr. Owens's case (for trading drugs for sex with eleven of his gynecological patients), the medical board took pains to design a chaperone requirement that would ensure that his patients wouldn't know why it was in place.[47]

When it comes to cutting out misconduct, specificity is key; as in surgery, less is more. Boards craft oddly specific restrictions designed to prevent the exact scam or abuse from happening again, seemingly failing to recognize the fundamental lack of judgment revealed by the misconduct in the first place. Many of these providers do not deserve the trust and power a license to practice—in any form, on anybody—bestows.

Overprescribing cases illustrate the problem. Take the case of Dr. Christopher Lockwood, who ran a cash-for-Suboxone practice in East Tennessee, not unlike L&B (he also sold scripts in a McDonald's parking lot). In his 2017 consent order with the medical board, he admitted to trafficking Suboxone for non-medical purposes and to having a sexual relationship with one of his addicted patients (whom he hired, gave an allowance, and bought a car). The board asked him to surrender his federal certification that allowed him to prescribe Suboxone but left in place his ability to prescribe other addictive drugs like opioids and benzos.[48] Another provider lost his ability to prescribe high-dose opioids in a board order but retained his ability to prescribe other controlled substances with street value like Klonopin and phentermine (and continued to do so, even while under federal investigation for trafficking drugs).[49]

In sex abuse cases it is likewise common to craft discipline that prevents an exact repeat of the offense but fails to address underlying pathologies. In Washington, DC, a psychologist who had sex with a client was put under a disciplinary order disallowing him from seeing women under fifty.[50] Boards often order sexual predators to see only male patients; at least one is known to have continued the abuse.[51]

## Hate the Sin . . .

"Dated" and "duped" play important roles in professional discipline, but the real workhorse of the 4D model is "disabled"—the idea that professionals err because of their own issues with addiction. Here, association-driven narratives about substance abuse meet a receptive audience in board members, especially within the health professions, who are primed to attribute misconduct not to incompetence or sociopathy but to sickness—to see an errant provider as worthy of empathy and receptive to treatment.

In theory, it makes sense for boards to focus on a provider's substance abuse. Addiction can lead to poor decision-making, a lack of boundaries, and mental or physical incapacitation.[52] Professionals are particularly susceptible to addiction and other mental health problems; rates of chemical dependence, depression, and suicide tend to be higher than average for doctors and lawyers.[53] It's also true that many mental health problems, especially addiction, can be treated and managed, leaving the professional a happier and safer provider.[54] The logic of "save a doctor" works here, too: if a provider's misconduct stems from mental health, treating the underlying cause of the misconduct would seem to be the most effective way to stop it at minimal cost to the provider and the public.

In practice, boards so fully endorse the "illness" model of professional misconduct that they lose sight of public protection. A laser focus on the provider's story of recovery, relapse, and redemption ignores how that process victimizes the public. The board presented its decision to relicense Dr. Owens more as a reward for his recovery than as a way to keep the public safe. Later, I heard a board member explain his chances of relapse this way: "he won't make it two years."[55]

Perhaps the biggest problem with the "illness" model of professional discipline is that it has provided yet another opportunity for a group dedicated to professional interests to insert themselves into licensing regulation. When a board determines that mental health is in play in a disciplinary case, the case gets diverted to a "professional health program" (PHP), essentially a shadow disciplinary system run by a private entity that operates explicitly for the benefit of professionals and without any of the accountability (such as it is) of a licensing board.

Originally called "physician health programs," PHPs were started in the 1990s by state medical associations, conceived as a resource for professionals seeking treatment and support from within his or her professional community. The programs could help connect doctors with mental health treatment and monitor compliance. They were considered so successful in addressing physician addiction, burnout, and depression that the model quickly spread to other high-pressure jobs (like law) and other safety-sensitive workers (like nurses). Today, lawyers and virtually every health profession has a professional health program (which also use the acronym "PHP").[56]

Participation in a PHP is expensive, and the professional must foot the bill himself. An initial multi-day evaluation can cost anywhere from $6,000 to $10,000.[57] If ongoing treatment and monitoring is recommended, that can add up to about $1,200 a month.[58] Professionals "contract" with PHPs for monitoring for two to five years, an expense felt especially acutely by lower-income professionals like licensed practical nurses, according to the head of Tennessee's PHP for nurses, physical therapists, massage therapists, and other health care providers.[59]

Participation is not entirely voluntary. PHPs—originally creatures of professional associations—began as an optional resource for struggling professionals, and some still use them this way. (Dr. Loyd, the member of the Tennessee Board of Medical Examiners, is a good example; when he confronted his pill problem he turned to his professional community for help, in the form of the Tennessee Medical Foundation [TMF], and its president Matthew Archer.) But over the years PHPs have become entangled with the licensure system in ways that can make participation heavily coerced. At the same time that PHPs grafted themselves on to the ostensibly governmental licensure process, they sought to formally distance themselves from professional associations, but their roots run deep; most PHPs retain financial ties to professional associations.[60] Their missions are similar; someone who works closely with Tennessee's PHP for doctors told me, "[T]he physician's health program is there to protect the physicians."[61]

Today, the power that PHPs have in the licensing disciplinary system cannot be overstated. Many PHPs can refer a participating professional for state board discipline, and the relationship works in reverse; boards often condition licensure on "advocacy" from a PHP. A PHP will advocate for a professional when, according to the judgment of someone at the PHP, the professional is compliant with their monitoring contract. In addition to donations from professionals, PHPs survive off large grants from licensing boards; the physician PHP in Florida receives $7.4 million annually from the medical board.[62] Luke Steinbach, a lawyer who specializes in licensing board disciplinary defense, told me that the medical and nursing PHPs were more powerful than the licensing boards they contract with. "I can tell you two people [who run the licensing system]," he said, and named the heads of the PHPs for doctors and nurses, respectively.[63]

That gives a private entity—essentially one person—the make-or-break decision for a large percentage of professionals under discipline. Boards, lacking either the capacity to oversee professionals in drug recovery or the bandwidth to stay involved with disciplinary issues in general, welcome the opportunity to outsource these responsibilities. I saw the board send doctors to TMF for a pricey evaluation with only very modest evidence of substance abuse, and once without any, just for good measure.[64]

Public criticism of PHPs has focused mainly on issues of fairness in such a coercive and opaque system.[65] I spoke to a psychiatrist whose bipolar disorder was well-controlled with medication, and who had no documented issues with patient care stemming from her illness. She opted for full disclosure on a licensing application, which asked, point blank, whether she had bipolar disorder. The result was a mandated (and expensive) relationship with her state's PHP and the constant threat of losing her license over an unfavorable evaluation. She explained the feeling this way: "Your whole livelihood is dependent on the pontification of someone who doesn't know you."[66]

Accused providers are afforded no due process rights to be heard or to present counter evidence when a PHP determines they have a disabling mental health issue. One doctor reported being sent to his state's PHP for an evaluation based on a joke he made about misusing pain medication. When his drug tests came up negative, the PHP "listed all the ways [he] could have cheated the system" and insisted he receive a $9,000 inpatient evaluation.[67] There have also been allegations of financial conflicts of interest between PHPs and the mental health facilities to which they refer professionals.[68] One critic says PHPs have "taken on the role of what is more akin to 'diagnosing for dollars.'"[69]

In addition to these concerns about fairness and due process for professionals in the PHP system, one could add a concern about public safety. There is little data about the rate of relapse of professionals in PHPs, and although there are differences across states, many provide professionals in their care with a troubling degree of confidentiality.[70] The head of the PHP for psychologists in Tennessee told me that he was barred from telling the licensing board about any self-reporting psychologist, even if he had a concern about public safety.[71] And the American Bar Association's model rules for law licensing boards provide an exception to an attorney's duty to report a colleague's misconduct if the lawyer in question is under a contract with a state professional assistance program.[72]

As eager as licensing boards are to hand off troubled professionals to a PHP, they are equally happy to welcome them back into practice whenever a PHP is willing to attest to their compliance. I spoke to Matthew Archer (the director of TMF who was also a former medical board member) about his role in board decisions, and he said that his advocacy in licensing cases was narrow. He said he would only opine about the sobriety of the physician and his compliance with the TMF program, not about other issues, like clinical competency, ethics, or professional judgment.[73] But from what I observed in meetings and learned in interviews with board members, Dr. Archer underestimated his influence. In case after case, advocacy from a PHP seemed to make all the difference. One public member explained his decision to vote in favor of relicensure in the Owens case: "We all trust Matthew Archer a lot."[74] And at one point in Dr. LaPaglia's hearing, Dr. Loyd said to the doctor, "whatever Matt Archer says you can do is what you can do."[75]

Sobriety, in the eyes of one man, stands in for professional competence, even in cases of extreme misconduct. Take Dr. Lockwood, who ran the cash- (and sometimes sex-) for-Suboxone practice in East Tennessee. The board's 2017 consent order in his case asked him to enter a contract with TMF and attend continuing education courses. Now that his term of probation has run, he can have his license restored to its full, unrestricted status, so long as he secures the blessing of Matthew Archer.[76]

## A Model Policy for Pain

Given the inevitable conflict of interest between the profession and the public, it's problematic to hand over regulatory policy to groups like the American Medical Association and state professional health programs that are likely to play into board members' forgiving nature. But licensing boards' lack of regulatory expertise, resources, and time make them vulnerable not only to influence from professional groups, but also from entities even less likely to put patients and the general public first. The story of how Purdue Pharmaceuticals, maker of OxyContin, exploited the inexpert, self-regulatory nature of physician licensing shows how vulnerable the professional regulatory system is to interests far afield of public health and welfare.

Tennessee's 2018 complaint alleging that Purdue was still marketing OxyContin to pill mills was big news, and the allegations against the drug company damning. To me, it also implicated the state itself by highlighting what was already evident from the failed minimum discipline taskforce: its own licensing boards were not under state governmental control. The complaint said that a prescriber's history of board discipline (it described Samson Orusa's and Christine Collins's clinics, among others, as examples) was evidence that Purdue knew, or should have known, that a provider was running a pill mill. But Purdue didn't have any information the state didn't already have in the form of its own licensing board's fact findings about over-prescribing. And for each disciplined prescriber listed in the suit, the board had preserved his or her ability to practice and prescribe opioids.[77] The logic of Tennessee's claims thus forced the state into a striking admission: its own boards weren't stopping known pill mill prescribers. And at that point, Tennessee was relying on Purdue's salesforce as an unlikely regulator of its prescribing professionals, reliance that turned out to be misplaced.

Not in the news in 2018 was the fact that Purdue not only capitalized on the licensing boards' lax disciplinary policy when it came to prescribing opioids. They helped create it.

With little expertise in regulation and no economies of scale to develop their own rules, boards often turn to their federations for model rules and policy statements. This solves the economies of scale problem, but as I said in Chapter 1, it tends to contribute to the ratchet effect of ever-increasing requirements for licensure. It also presents a unique lobbying opportunity for companies who have a stake in board regulation. In 1997, Purdue Pharmaceuticals, which had just launched OxyContin, began providing funding to the Federation of State Medical Boards (FSMB) and lent them one of their employees—the one who had coined the term "pseudoaddiction"—to act as a consulting expert.[78] According to a 2012 US Senate inquiry, the FSMB received almost $2 million from Purdue and other opioid makers over the ensuing years.[79]

One product of the collaboration was a model policy of opioid-prescribing discipline.[80] The first edition of the FSMB's model discipline rules, published in 1998, stated that "[f]ears of investigation or sanction by federal, state and local regulatory agencies may also result in inappropriate or inadequate treatment of chronic pain patients." To that end, the model policy assured physicians that they "should not fear disciplinary action from the Board . . . for prescribing, dispensing or administering controlled substances, including opioid analgesics, for a legitimate medical purpose and in the usual course of professional practice." The legitimacy of prescribing, in turn, would be evaluated "based on the physician's treatment of the patient and on available documentation, rather than on the quantity and chronicity of prescribing."[81] Medical boards in twenty states, including Tennessee, substantially adopted these model rules into their regulations.[82] Six years later, the federation, again with financial support from Purdue, revised the model policy. This version said that the "undertreatment of pain" was "a departure from an acceptable standard of practice" and therefore grounds for discipline.[83]

These policies achieved what was probably Purdue's desired result. Assessing data from the early 2000s, researchers have found that "[t]he actual risk of an American physician being disciplined by a state medical board for treating a real patient with opioids for a painful medical condition is virtually nonexistent."[84] That forbearance has persisted through two decades of an accelerating opioid crisis.

Purdue Pharmaceuticals has taken a lot of blame for the opioid crisis, and rightly so. But it could not have set in motion an epidemic that would take more than one million American lives (and counting) without a dysfunctional licensing system that could be manipulated in its favor.[85] Purdue's confidence game would not have worked as well as it did if we had had functional agencies to regulate doctors and prescribing nurses that didn't need to take money and advice from the pharmaceutical industry itself. And Purdue would have had a harder time pushing its pills through unethical doctors if we had had a disciplinary process that wasn't designed to give prescribers every benefit of the doubt, and second, third, and fifth chances. As it was, the company found a broken system of licensing made up of professionals who were too inexpert in regulatory policy, too busy to learn it, and too naïve about the "bad men" in their profession. And it played them to the beat.

## Second Chances

I met Dr. Loyd for coffee about a month after Dr. LaPaglia's July hearing before the medical board.[86] Dr. Loyd was dressed in jeans and sneakers, wearing a purple "overdose awareness" pin on his T-shirt. The conversation began with his telling me about his work to promote understanding and reduce stigma about opioid addiction in Tennessee. He told me he was grateful for the second chance he'd received from the Tennessee Medical Foundation and his professional community when he'd confronted his addiction and sought treatment. "You don't always get a second chance," he said.

When I asked him about Dr. LaPaglia's case, he said that as soon as he and the other panel members had handed down the decision, he'd regretted it. He told me that it was immediately after the hearing, when

Dr. LaPaglia shook his hand in thanks, that Dr. Loyd first considered the idea that Dr. LaPaglia was something other than a well-intentioned, but troubled, practitioner. Dr. Loyd told me he'd since lost sleep over the idea that he had been conned by the doctor.

As Dr. Loyd suspected, there was more to Dr. LaPaglia's story than what he was presented with in that July 2019 hearing. On at least two occasions, while Dr. LaPaglia was working as an ER doctor in 2010, he medically paralyzed arrestees brought in by police and, against their will, penetrated their rectums looking for drugs. In one of the cases, the patient had to be intubated because the paralysis stopped his breathing.[87] One search turned up nothing, but another turned up drugs that led to a criminal conviction.[88] A federal court reversed the conviction on appeal because Dr. LaPaglia's search violated the defendant's Fourth Amendment rights. It was, the judge said, "so unreasonable as to shock the conscience."[89] These searches, which led to two civil lawsuits that Dr. LaPaglia settled, were never mentioned in any of his proceedings before the medical board.[90]

Going back further in his career—to his residency at a University of North Carolina hospital—revealed yet more red flags. The North Carolina medical board charged him with misconduct after they learned that he had an inappropriate relationship with a sixteen-year-old hospitalized psychiatric patient during his training. He allegedly shared personal information with her, got her phone number, and kept in touch after her release.[91] It appears that he lost his residency spot over the incident, but Dr. LaPaglia was able to forestall a decision in his disciplinary case by entering a contract with the state's PHP and leaving the state.[92] Later, he abandoned a licensure application in Pennsylvania when that board raised the issue.[93] Like the rectal searches, the inappropriate patient relationship was never discussed in any of Dr. LaPaglia's disciplinary proceedings before the Tennessee board, though all of it was easily found searching the internet and accessing public databases.

When I told Dr. Loyd the full story of Dr. LaPaglia's past, he grew quiet. When he finally spoke, there was a catch in his voice: "How come I don't know that?"

Like most board disciplinary cases, Dr. LaPaglia's trial was low-information and non-adversarial. When the board prosecutor mentioned the doctor's 2013 arrest and subsequent criminal plea, the prosecutor did not mention that the police said they had found forty-five quart-sized jars of marijuana, two guns, and formulary of paralytic and sedative agents that, outside of the hospital, were more appropriate as weapons than for recreation.[94] Rather, he referred obliquely to "some criminal charges related to [Dr. LaPaglia's] own personal use of drugs." The prosecutor did hand Dr. Loyd and the other board members a copy of LaPaglia's 2018 federal plea for drug dealing through L&B, but failed to correct the doctor's claim, later in the hearing, that he had never even been accused of trafficking narcotics.[95]

But that doesn't fully explain why Dr. Loyd made the decision he did. He was presented with enough facts in the hearing to see that Dr. LaPaglia was a doctor undeserving of further chances at a medical career. He was handed copies of two criminal judgments against the doctor for using his medical license to deal prescription drugs. He knew the latest scheme was hatched while the doctor was under a board disciplinary order. And he knew the prescriptions were forged.

The rest of the answer can be found by understanding who Dr. Loyd is, and who he is not. He is a physician who believes that the sick can get better. Dr. LaPaglia fit his troubles with pill addiction into the "disabled" narrative supplied by the AMA by speaking about his own recovery with apparent vulnerability. He steered the narrative away from the lapse in ethics and judgment evident in the L&B scheme and toward something Dr. LaPaglia and Dr. Loyd had in common: support in their recovery from the Tennessee Medical Foundation.

And when it suited him, Dr. LaPaglia lied. That worked because of who Dr. Loyd is not. He is not a regulator who knows the bad man will walk the line, nor is he a judge who is used to being lied to. It was his very first board meeting; he had been given no training on contested cases. "I have experience in being a doctor," he told me. "It'd be like me bringing you into my clinic and . . . you're a lawyer, you don't know anything about what I'm doing."

Dr. Loyd has regrets about the case, to say the least. "I was appointed by the governor to protect the health safety and welfare of the people of Tennessee," he told me. "I didn't do that." But not all the blame for the relicensure of Dr. LaPaglia rests with Dr. Loyd. Some blame must be placed on the system that asks an addiction doctor, given far too little information about the case, to give up on yet another pill addict in Tennessee.

When I confronted board members about light discipline that kept dangerous and unethical providers in practice, they often pointed out that any public discipline can ruin a professional's career. From their perspective, a reprimand or probation *was* throwing the book. "He'll never work again," was a common refrain I heard about disciplined professionals.

What board members may not realize is that in many cases that's not quite true. Board discipline may take problem providers out of the mainstream, but they tend to resurface in the less prestigious underbellies of law and medicine, where they serve society's most vulnerable. Chapter 8 explores this phenomenon and reveals that it's the poor, incarcerated, and addicted who pay the steepest price for a dysfunctional disciplinary system.

# 8

# The Fallen Professional

*What does a professional do after board discipline? Often his or her only option is to serve as doctor or lawyer to the poor, incarcerated, or addicted.*

When LaPaglia got the first round of discipline on his Tennessee medical license—his 2014 order placing his license on probation based on his state charges for dealing prescription drugs out of his home—it made working in the mainstream of medical practice impossible. At his disciplinary hearing in July 2019, where I first met Dr. LaPaglia, his lawyer told the board that it was difficult for doctors under disciplinary orders to find employment. "It's a trap, it's a conundrum," he said. Dr. LaPaglia, he explained, "can't get onto the insurance panels, no employer will touch him."[1]

That wasn't quite true, but it was close. The probation order probably did preclude his participation in private insurance programs, although he might have had more luck taking public insurance like TennCare (my state's Medicaid program). His disciplinary record likely would have prevented him from getting a job at a hospital—he was fired from his emergency department job the day after his 2013 arrest.[2] His options were to work for an institution with lower standards for their providers—like a prison or a rural clinic—or to turn to the underbelly of American medicine: the cash clinic. Cash-based clinics range from surgeons to the elite, to the country doctor who provides affordable care to his uninsured neighbors, to the pill mill selling scripts for $300 cash at a rate of fifteen patients an hour. (The line between these latter two kinds of practices can be surprisingly fine.) Cash-based medicine also includes cosmetic surgery, medical weight loss, and, because it is inadequately covered by health insurance, addiction treatment like Suboxone.[3]

Dr. LaPaglia needed to take one of these options. He had a mortgage on an expensive house and was still paying off his student loans. He also probably owed settlement money to the men on whom he performed forcible rectal searches in the ER. By the time he filed for bankruptcy in 2016, he also owed $530,000 in unpaid taxes.[4] In the end, it was a Suboxone clinic that took on Dr. LaPaglia. EHC was located in a small nondescript office in a strip mall, located a mile off I-40 in the heart of the Appalachian region of Tennessee hardest-hit by the opioid crisis. Suboxone is the state-of-the-art "medication-assisted treatment" for opioid addiction and can be a lifesaving drug when prescribed responsibly.[5] But as an opioid itself, it can be abused.[6]

He testified to the board at his disciplinary hearing in July 2019 about how his work at EHC gave him the idea for L&B. Most opioid addicts are also addicted to benzodiazepines, the class of drugs that includes Valium and Xanax.[7] But EHC was restricted by state law in its ability to prescribe patients benzos because mixing opioids—even the relatively safe Suboxone—and benzos significantly increases the risk of an overdose.[8] Dr. LaPaglia saw an unmet demand in the patients coming to EHC, one that could be filled by providing them Xanax and Valium prescriptions for $300 cash on the side. And so, L&B was born.[9]

L&B stopped being a going concern when the feds arrested Dr. LaPaglia in the fall of 2018. Then things got even worse for Dr. LaPaglia's revenue streams when the board suspended his license on an emergency basis in January 2019.[10] His only hope of getting back to work was catching a break from the medical board, which is exactly what he got when Dr. Loyd and the rest of the panel reinstated his license at the hearing I saw later the same year. After the hearing, I spoke with Dr. LaPaglia. He was pleased with the result. "All I really wanted today was to get my license off suspension," he said, "so I could go make some money."[11]

## The Invisible Hand

Board members aren't wrong when they point out that any disciplinary measure can have serious consequences for a provider's career. It doesn't look good with potential employers or clients to have a dent in your record, and there are ways someone might find out if they knew where to look. Individual states and boards have varying degrees of transparency; for the health-related boards in Tennessee, you can search a state-maintained database for a provider's name and learn about public discipline.[12] Tennessee maintains a similar website for lawyers, but not for professionals like accountants, funeral directors, and real estate agents.[13]

But even the most transparent of online databases are useful only to patients and clients who know about them and think to look up a provider. Many consumers believe that the licensing system obviates this kind of research—if you can practice legally, you must be relatively clean. As my spreadsheet of lightly disciplined bad actors grew, I realized this wasn't true. Still, few consumers know to look up a provider's disciplinary history. Of course, patients and clients aren't the only ones interested in a professional's history; employers want to know about licensure issues and are more savvy than consumers about doing their due diligence. But, with potentially fifty different state records to search, even large organizations can struggle to learn the relevant licensure information. Professionals with disciplinary records can take advantage of these gaps of information by practicing in another state on a clean license, or even seeking a new license from a board who may not know—or doesn't care to learn—about the professional's disciplinary history. This problem is especially well-documented in medicine, and it was a phenomenon I observed frequently in Tennessee.[14]

In the healthcare professions, this problem has been partially solved by the National Practitioner Data Bank (commonly known as the Data

Bank), which was created by Congress in 1986.[15] The Data Bank lists public state board discipline for the nation's healthcare practitioners along with hospital discipline and major malpractice lawsuits the provider has lost or settled.[16] It's an indispensable tool for hospitals in making employment decisions and for insurance companies in deciding whom to include as covered providers. In theory, licensing boards can use it—for a fee—to keep tabs on their licensees' malpractice activity and out-of-state board discipline, but very few use it more than sporadically (only three boards pay the extra $2 per licensee for the Data Bank's "continuous query" feature that proactively informs subscribers of new information).[17] Provider-level information from the Data Bank is inaccessible to anyone else, including patients, journalists, and observers like me.[18] When Congress tried to open the database to the public, the AMA "crushed it like a bug."[19]

The transparency (such as it is) afforded by board discipline databases like the Data Bank creates a sorting mechanism where practitioners with serious disciplinary histories sift down to the bottom of professional practice. This is how free-market capitalism works: buyers (in this case, employers), with reasonably adequate information (thanks to the Data Bank), find sellers (professionals) offering something fitting their budget. The better employers offering higher salaries and more prestigious gigs get the best professionals, while employers that are budget-constrained, rural, or are otherwise less attractive places to work, get the rest.

Adam Smith called this the "invisible hand" of capitalism—the force that, as if by magic, matches buyers and sellers and sorts everything according to quality and willingness to pay.[20] But licensing is meant to soften the harsher effects of a capitalistic market for professional services. The disciplinary process is supposed to take out the lemons and leave the peaches—to place a floor on professional practice so that everyone, even the poorest client or patient, gets someone who meets a minimum competency and ethical threshold. As I describe how the invisible hand works on the market for professionals, ask yourself whether licensing's promise to protect the public is fulfilled by a system that doesn't remove the most problematic providers, but rather shuffles them to the bottom of the barrel of professional practice.

# Down but Not Out

Different hospitals react differently to learning that a professional has a record in the Data Bank; the invisible hand works at the hospital level, too. Healthcare economist David Hyman and his co-authors studied the link between board discipline and hospital employment in Illinois and found that there were a handful of hospitals that had very high percentages of disciplined doctors, suggesting that they "either ignore [Data Bank] information or may even target [disciplined] physicians for recruitment."[21] Professor Hyman told me that one likely explanation was that these may be "hospitals of last resort . . . the last stop on the line" for problematic doctors.[22] Even if a doctor manages to hold on to his hospital job, he may have trouble staying on an insurance panel. Insurance companies, too, track Data Bank activity, and most retain the contractual right to remove disciplined doctors from their rolls. Whether they do so comes down to how large a stream of revenue they provide to the insurance company and whether they are seen as being replaceable.[23]

Losing the ability to take private insurance or work at a hospital starts a doctor down a slippery slope. To better understand medical practice outside of the mainstream, I spoke with Luke Steinbach, the lawyer who represented Dr. Owens and Dr. Orusa in their medical board disciplinary proceedings. Steinbach has made a niche practice out of representing doctors and nurses facing board discipline, and he is the only person I've met who makes a regular practice out of checking the disciplinary history of his and his kids' doctors in the state database.[24]

Steinbach told me that losing hospital privileges or being removed from an insurance panel makes a provider less attractive to partners. So does another collateral consequence, at least in Tennessee, of a probated license: the inability to supervise mid-levels.[25] Mid-levels like physician assistants and nurse practitioners are often referred to as "extenders" because they multiply the number of patients a given physician can bring through a practice. To a practice group, a physician that can't take private insurance, supervise mid-levels, or share in the hospital work is dead weight. Steinbach told me that discipline can get you kicked out of your group and can make joining one almost impossible.[26]

At this particular point on the slippery slope, where private, prestigious employers are off the table, a professional that's been disciplined still has a few options. Public institutional employers can be an option for a professional with some disciplinary history. Many public providers of professional services have some combination of features that make attracting top-notch professionals difficult: remote geography, high-risk populations, and publicly funded wages that fall short of those in the private sector. But they have something special to offer a troubled provider. Because these institutions can self-insure, they can offer employment to providers whose disciplinary history makes it hard for them to get private malpractice insurance.[27] These employers may feel that having some tolerance for board discipline is the only way to keep their hospitals staffed or to provide constitutionally required criminal representation.

In the medical context, federal insurance programs like Medicaid and Medicare tend to have a lower threshold than private insurance for accepting providers with serious discipline. (Professor Hyman's study found that the Illinois hospitals with the highest percentage of disciplined doctors also had high numbers of Medicaid patients.)[28] Medicaid's already low standard can be troublingly flexible. For example, an investigation in 2018 by the *Milwaukee Journal Sentinel* revealed that more than two hundred doctors remained on Medicaid rolls despite licensure history that should disqualify them according to federal rules. In 2015 alone, these doctors billed taxpayers $25.8 million.[29]

Likewise, the US Department of Veterans Affairs has faced a similar scandal for violating its own policy of not hiring physicians with a revoked license in any state. *USA Today* reported in 2017 that the Iowa City VA hired John Henry Schneider, a neurosurgeon with a long history of malpractice and wrongful death suits involving misplaced screws and devices, undiagnosed infections, and repeated surgeries to correct prior surgical mistakes. The Wisconsin medical board took action when, on top of the mounting evidence of surgical incompetence, Dr. Schneider killed a patient by prescribing him fentanyl, oxycodone, Valium, and Demerol. Wisconsin revoked his license, but his license in Montana remained intact, allowing for a fresh start at the Iowa City VA, where he went on to perform more botched surgeries before resigning when the illegality of his hiring came to light.[30]

There are other employers who might offer a disciplined provider a second chance. For example, jails and prisons are especially likely to hire a provider with a checkered past. One in five doctors employed by Georgia's public prisons has serious discipline in his licensing history, making a prison doctor eight times more likely to have been disciplined than the average Georgia physician.[31] American Indian reservations, too, seem to attract providers with disciplinary histories. In 2019, the *Wall Street Journal* ran a story about medical malpractice at Indian Health Service facilities. Many of the doctors involved in questionable care had previous board discipline; their offenses ranged from sexual abuse to unlawful prescribing. Some were hired despite IHS policy requiring unrestricted licenses.[32] When I asked Steinbach where his clients go to work after the conclusion of their disciplinary case, American Indian reservations were high on the list.[33]

Other professions have their own version of the institutional employer with high tolerance for board discipline. In law, criminal courts responsible for appointing defense attorneys to represent indigent clients may be more open-minded about an attorney's licensure file than, say, a white-shoe law firm. The court-appointment process stems in part from a 1963 Supreme Court opinion called *Gideon v. Wainwright*,[34] which recognized a constitutional right to a defense attorney for all criminal defendants—even those who could not afford one. Most states responded by creating or expanding public defender offices in their major cities, the best of which view indigent defense as a fully professionalized calling. They train, supervise, and hold their attorneys to account. But these public defenders' offices cannot handle all criminal cases with indigent defendants because of conflicts of interest, resource constraints, and geography. A lot of indigent criminal defense, especially in rural areas, falls on court-appointed lawyers paid out of state coffers. The pay rate varies among states, ranging from below-market to abysmally below-market.[35]

Systematic studies of disciplinary rates among court-appointed defense attorneys are rare, but the example of Maine suggests that appointed lawyers may be more likely than others to have checkered pasts. Maine is the only state that does not have any public defender offices—all indigent defense is provided through what amounts to an appointment system. ProPublica reported that appointed lawyers account for just 15 percent of the attorneys in the state but represent more than a quarter of the state's attorneys who have faced major discipline in the last ten years.[36]

ProPublica's investigation revealed breaches of professional conduct that ran the gamut from helping clients commit crimes to indecent exposure. One appointed defense lawyer convicted of possessing child pornography was denied access to the jails because of his criminal history, a problem that he addressed by representing only clients out on bond while "simply hoping" none of them got rearrested. Law professor Bob Cummins said of the system in Maine: "We're allocating the indigent criminal work to individuals who are already in that class of lawyers who too often get in trouble."[37]

Studies of death row inmates and their lawyers also paint a dark picture of indigent defense at the bottom of the barrel. Journalists found that nearly one in five Pennsylvania defendants sentenced to death in the last ten years were represented by an attorney who had been disciplined for professional misconduct at some point in his or her career. In 58 percent of the cases, the discipline had preceded the capital representation, and in 45 percent of the cases the attorney had been disciplined more than once.[38]

Indigent criminal defendants can make attractive victims for predatory lawyers, not only because they have no choice in who represents them but also because they are often in dire straits when the attorney-client relationship begins. For example, two of the victims of Gerald Moothart, the attorney from Chapter 6 who kept his license after sexually abusing several clients, were women he was appointed to represent because they could not afford an attorney. One said she acquiesced to his request for oral sex because she feared the consequences of saying no. "I was in a pretty tough situation," she said. "[I was] going to lose my kids."[39]

## The Employer of Last Resort

Sometimes discipline is so serious that even institutional employment is out of reach. This was the trap Dr. Lapaglia's lawyer referred to at his board hearing, the place where "no employer will touch him." Here, a professional with a valid but tainted license has to turn to the employer of last resort: himself.

Recent empirical evidence of how discipline affects employment reveals that indeed discipline tends to shunt providers toward solo practice. A recent study of the labor market for attorneys finds that public discipline makes it harder for an attorney to stay at a firm, and makes it more likely they will turn to solo practice. The study finds that 12 percent of solo practice lawyers with a disciplinary record moved into solo practice *after* discipline, where they are most likely to serve the underserved, such as immigrants, personal injury victims and, of course, indigent defendants.[40]

Perhaps it's not a coincidence, then, that solo practitioners make up a significantly higher percentage of lawyers and doctors who have been disciplined.[41] Although there are alternate explanations for this phenomenon, including board bias against rural and solo practice, one likely explanation is that there actually are more troubled lawyers and doctors in solo practice than in group settings.[42] A disciplinary focus on solo and small practice professionals may make sense if it's where the disciplinary system itself puts professionals more likely to break the rules.

Cash-based solo practice, in medicine and law, is unaccountable to almost anyone but the state licensing board. There is no health insurance auditor to come inspect your clinic. There is no hospital peer review panel to weigh in on a case gone wrong. There is no senior partner to supervise your legal strategy for defending a capital murder case. And cash-based solo practitioners—whether the country doctor serving the uninsured or the lawyer eking a living out of court-appointment fees—tend to serve a clientele that is disproportionately poor, unsophisticated, and, especially in the case of incarcerated defendants, uniquely vulnerable. It is not, to say the least, a good place to park providers with a troubling history of professional discipline. To make matters worse, whatever temptations the fallen professional had to cut corners *before* her fall are even more intense at the bottom of the market. Non-elite solo practitioners make money by handling high volumes of cases or patients. The lower the pay, the higher the volume required to make ends meet.

Understanding the economics of solo practice requires distinguishing between professionals paid by the hour and those paid a flat fee for a service. Hourly pay, while prevalent in many professions, has a big drawback: it creates the temptation to work slowly and inefficiently to run up a client's bill. In some contexts, therefore, professions have settled on a model of fee-for-service; medicine has especially embraced this solution. A medical board member told me his wife liked to kid him, "you're a well-respected garment worker; you're paid by the piece!"[43] She's right; doctors at all tiers of practice are commonly paid by the procedure whether as a reimbursement from an insurance provider or directly by the patient. Pay-per-service fee structures solve the problem of slow-walking service and running up hourly bills, but they introduce the opposite problem of rushed professional work. In medicine, the pressure that pay-per-service has put on doctors to spend less time with their patients is well-documented.[44]

Dr. Anna Lembke, in her book *Drug Dealer, MD,* says the "Toyotaization of Healthcare"—the strive for healthcare efficiency as measured by patients seen per day—bears some of the blame for the opioid crisis. In a world where doctors are paid by the appointment, it is faster and cheaper to write a prescription than to explore other modalities of pain management or, what may be even more time-consuming, to confront or resist a drug-seeking patient. "Treat 'em and street 'em" is the best way to maximize reimbursements, a mentality that pushed the prescription pad to the fore of medical practice, to the ultimate detriment of public health.[45]

Though the problem pervades all strata of medical practice, it's particularly acute in capacity-constrained settings where reimbursement rates are low and the demand for prescriptions is high. That perfectly describes a solo practitioner serving the underserved. When a country doctor takes it a little too far, we call it a pill mill.

The phenomenon of the professional mill is not unique to medicine. Some lawyers, especially outside of the large firms, are also paid by the piece—$1,000 for a DUI defense; $450 for an uncontested divorce. Here, the incentives tempt lawyers to move volume through their practice by taking shortcuts. Similar incentives are found among court-appointed lawyers in criminal cases. Although states ostensibly pay these lawyers an hourly wage, many have caps on how much a lawyer can claim for each case in total. These caps have the effect of turning an hourly system into a pay-by-the-case arrangement.[46] Thus the appointed lawyers' tendency to "meet 'em and plead 'em," which has led many an innocent defendant to take a conviction based on weak proof.[47]

The incentive to rush—to turn quickly to a prescription pad or a plea deal—becomes even stronger as you descend the totem pole of professional service and the pay rates get lower. A doctor taking only Medicaid patients has to somehow find a way to support a practice on $50 a visit. And a defense lawyer to the indigent has to find a way to defend a murder charge—which can take years of investigation and litigation when done properly—for a single $3,000 fee from the state.[48] For professionals serving the poor, cutting corners isn't just a temptation. It's virtually required by the system.

### The Country Doctor

As I was watching the boards, a disciplinary case was plodding along against a doctor in the small city of Cookeville, located in a rural part of Tennessee about halfway between Nashville and the mountains to the east. The doctor's sign, hanging over the main street in Cookeville, says simply "Dr. Russell Stevenson, Internal Medicine" with a local phone number. He takes insurance, but also cash from his uninsured patients. His online reviews paint him as a caring, available doctor who gives out his personal email and cell phone number, makes himself available after hours and on weekends, and explains without talking down to his patients. The state record of his controlled substance prescribing is seven hundred pages long.[49]

I interviewed one of his patients, Dave Harlan, and he told me about another side of medical practice outside the hospitals and clinics where

I receive care in downtown Nashville. Dave grew up in the 1960s and 1970s in Wilder, Tennessee, an unincorporated community in Fentress County, in the foothills of the Appalachian Mountains. His father was a coal miner and a moonshiner on the side; it was as a child that Dave had his first taste of alcohol. He got married in 1989 and had a son in 1993. His drinking hit bottom in 2001. After eight DUI arrests and a divorce, Dave turned to AA and spent the next decade sober and connecting with the son whose early childhood he had missed. It was the first time, but not the last, that he would escape the clutches of addiction.[50]

Like his father and his grandfather, Dave worked in the mines. Long days fourteen feet underground took a toll on his knee, which had been injured in a work accident. When his family practitioner refused to give him more than very low-dose opioids (citing his history of addiction), Dave asked his coworkers at the zinc mine where he might find something stronger. They said, "you want pain pills, go see Dr. Stevenson, he'll fix you right up."

Dave found a willing prescriber in Dr. Stevenson. The doctor didn't raise the issue of Dave's past struggles with addiction, but rather seemed keen to keep Dave coming back. Dave told me he used to sell a little marijuana on the side, and he recognized Dr. Stevenson's "keep the customer satisfied" approach to prescribing. He told me it was like Dr. Stevenson was saying, "hey, you know, I'll move you from 120 Percocets to 180, and down the road I'll give you some Xanax, too, to help you along. And if these 180 Percocets aren't enough then we can go up a milligram or two." Dave told me that Dr. Stevenson never turned him down, and never asked him about his increasingly disheveled appearance or desperate state of mind. When he had insurance from his mining job, he paid a co-pay; when he didn't, he paid $55 cash.

Things just got worse for Dave as Dr. Stevenson doubled, then redoubled the opioids, added Xanax (a benzodiazepine that increases opioid overdose risk), and then upped that, too. Dave would fill Dr. Stevenson's prescriptions but, feeling like it wasn't enough, he'd take more than had been prescribed. When he ran out before the end of the month, he'd buy more off the street, then come back to Dr. Stevenson for another prescription. Dave bounced between overdoses of Percocet and then

Xanax, using one as an upper and the other as a downer. He took so many pills he would vomit them up. He hit bottom when his son walked in on him snorting his medication.

When I interviewed Dave in 2019, he was two years sober and working part time. He was also living with chronic pain—six years of pain pills gave him no long-term relief. But he was happy to be on the other side of his ordeal and reconnecting with his son. When he told me that, I said, "six years is a long time to lose." He corrected me: "Six years is a long time to live."

Dave's was not the only chart presented at Dr. Stevenson's trial before the medical board. In fact, board prosecutors presented so much evidence of dangerous prescribing that the hearing took eight trial days, and because the board so rarely meets to hear disciplinary cases, the trial lasted eighteen months. Prosecutors showed that the doctor regularly prescribed patients almost twenty times the threshold dose that the CDC says presents a significant overdose risk. He routinely combined his opioid prescribing with benzodiazepines, he didn't check the state-controlled substance database, and he did no pill counts. Dr. Stevenson's lawyer argued, however, that revocation would "depriv[e] 3,500 people in the underserved upper Cumberland region of Tennessee" of a physician.[51] Evidently, the board agreed. It placed his license on probation, but otherwise kept Dr. Stevenson in practice and preserved his authority to prescribe.[52] He still works under that sign in Cookeville, and he is still taking new patients.

## The Professional Caste System

Many would argue that, however unfortunate, the fact that the poor and vulnerable get inferior professional providers is inevitable in a market-based system. Poor clients and patients can't afford to pay for long appointments, hours of investigation and advocacy or, in the case of pain treatment, fancy alternative modalities. So they get what they pay for (or don't): a quick plea deal or an opioid prescription. Until we have fully public systems for the provision of professional services, we have to accept that people who can't pay will get less.

Whatever wisdom there is in our system of using markets to allocate professional services (and whether there is any wisdom to it is beyond the scope of this book), professional licensing is supposed to protect the public from the worst providers that might haunt the lowest tranche of an unregulated market. Not only is the disciplinary system failing to weed out the bad seeds, but by slapping wrists without taking licenses, it's pushing the most problematic providers toward the most needy populations. Licensing boards' light disciplinary touch creates a self-reinforcing caste system of professional service. Whether board members understand this phenomenon isn't entirely clear.

Most board members seemed unaware of the effect their light disciplinary touch had on at-risk patients and clients. It seemed inconceivable to board members—whose high-achieving professional career depended on things like hospital privileges, insurance credentials, and a rock-solid reputation—that there is a professional substratum where a different kind of provider can survive.

Although board members didn't directly acknowledge their role in the professional caste system, I did observe some troubling indifference to the problem. After the hearing where the medical board relicensed Dr. Owens, a public member of the board (who had voted along with most of the doctors in favor of relicensure) remarked: "I wouldn't send my daughter to see him." A physician member reassured her that the Memphis OBGYN "only sees TennCare patients." That fit with an argument in favor of relicensure that a different board member had offered at the hearing: that his victims were not "your friends and neighbors." That board member told me later what she meant—that the patients were prostitutes.[53]

Whether board members are clueless or indifferent about the caste system they perpetuate, it is wrapped up in something they do talk a lot about, if only in disciplinary cases: prioritizing access to care. Provider shortages are rarely addressed by boards working the ratchet or defending turf but make for a compelling consideration when boards take a light disciplinary touch. Many board members I interviewed about discipline cited this as a good reason for second chances. In protecting the people of the state, they told me, you have to consider the patients of an accused provider who would have to go without.

There is a certain logic to this argument. But together with the reality that the problem doctors tend to drift toward the neediest patients and clients, it endorses a double standard in professional competence and ethics—one for those who serve the privileged, and one for those who serve the poor. As a former executive director of the Mississippi medical board told me, boards in disciplinary cases seem to think "[any] physician is better than no physician," even one with major ethical or competency problems.[54] And board members seemed blind to the hypocrisy at the heart of their own regulation. Boards limit the supply of providers with entry and ethics rules, all in the name of minimum competency, and then fail to hold the line against unethical and incompetent providers, allowing market forces to shunt these providers toward the patients and clients most harmed by the very scarcity they created in the first place.

I saw a lot of providers accused of misconduct use their at-risk patients and clients to advocate for a lighter disciplinary touch, and it usually worked. Dr. Owens was a good example. Steinbach pointedly mentioned at his hearing that the doctor saw mainly at-risk, inner-city Black mothers. After his hearing, when I asked Dr. Owens why he thought he got his license back, he told me: "OBGYNs don't grow on trees."[55]

In states with large, underserved rural populations, the argument is particularly persuasive to licensing boards.[56] When reporters for the *Atlanta Journal Constitution* confronted the executive director of the Georgia medical board about their findings—that most sexually abusive doctors in the state return to practice—he cited access to care as a reason for putting them back in practice. He pointed out that many patients in the state are desperate for care. "You do not think so? Then leave Atlanta and go down to a little Georgia town and get sick," he said. "See how far they have to go to find a doctor."[57]

In my own state, I saw the small-town argument work, too. One example was Dr. Carl Samuelson, whom I saw appear in front of the medical board for the third time for over-prescribing opioids. Despite the board's lingering concerns about his prescribing habits, it reinstated his ability to prescribe, in part because he said his clinic provided care to the underserved. "Fifty percent of our patients are unemployed and below poverty," he told the board. Full restoration of his prescribing ability was essential to the success of his clinic, he explained, because his only partner was also under board discipline for over-prescribing and had lost his DEA number.[58]

This line of argument was troubling enough when accused providers used it to invoke access-to-care issues. But sometimes it seemed to have an even darker purpose: to reassure the board that the troubled provider would stay out of the upper echelons of professional practice, where they might encounter the "friends and neighbors" of the board who are the proper focus of licensing's protection. For example, when I saw particularly troubled physicians appear before the medical board—such as a psychiatrist who failed her licensing and specialty board exams three times each, or the sex addict who dismissed a patient in order to pursue an affair with her—bewildered board members would ask where the physician planned to work if they took mercy. When the doctors responded with an answer outside of the mainstream (the Department of Corrections and the VA, respectively), the board acquiesced.[59]

At least one board takes a more deliberate approach to matching troubled providers with at-risk populations. The Louisiana medical board sometimes imposes discipline that restricts a physician's practice to an "institutional setting," a restriction justified by the board's executive director as ensuring oversight.[60] He told the *Times-Picayune:* "In the right setting, with the right level of supervision, [disciplined doctors] have the skills, and their medical judgment may be quite good. Even if they're not doing so well in other aspects of their life, and they're providing a needed service."[61]

But the way that the Louisiana medical board defines an "institutional setting" is based less on the availability of supervision and mentorship, and more on the kinds of populations found in that institution. Marier told the *Times-Picayune* that the designation precludes employment at a teaching hospital, but allows practice in prisons, mental health facilities, and homes for developmentally disabled children. In fact, the *Times-Picayune* reported that the medical board employs a headhunter who has helped disciplined doctors land jobs in the state's prisons.[62]

Thus, it isn't an accident—nor merely the work of the invisible hand of the market—that the rate of disciplinary action among Louisiana's prison doctors is even higher than in most other states. In 2021, BuzzFeed

News ran a story revealing that 80 percent of the state's prison doctors had had their license restricted or suspended at some point. (Their offenses ranged from dealing drugs to sexual misconduct.) Louisiana also happens to have the highest per capita rate of incarceration in the United States, and the highest rate of prisoner deaths from 2003 to 2011. A man who had been released recently from Angola State Prison—where *all* staff physicians had a history of professional discipline—told BuzzFeed: "The doctors they hired there are there serving a sentence of their own."[63]

### Arsonist and Fireman

To the list of patients and consumers who get the lowest caste of professionals—people serving prison sentences, indigent defendants, and patients without insurance—we can add the three million Americans living with opioid use disorder. Physicians with the authority to prescribe Suboxone, the state-of-the-art treatment for opioid addiction, are far more likely to have a history of discipline than other physicians. For example, in Louisiana and Ohio, Suboxone doctors are ten times as likely to have been disciplined than their counterparts in other areas of medicine. The numbers of disciplined providers are especially high for doctors authorized to see the maximum number of Suboxone patients.[64]

Although Suboxone is covered by some insurance programs (and in Tennessee it is generously covered by TennCare), it is also a cash business. Because addiction treatment is stigmatized in the medical and nursing professions, the field suffers from a shortage of providers. On top of that, until recently, federal law limited how many patients those few Suboxone providers could see. With so many addicted Americans seeking this safe and lifesaving treatment, demand far exceeds the supply of providers who are willing to bother with the treatment specifications (like talk therapy and drug screens) and safety protocols (like not co-prescribing Suboxone with Adderall and benzos) imposed by health insurance companies. So, prescribers can make a lot of money with a cash-based addiction practice.[65] And where there is a cash clinic, there will be providers who have been disciplined.

Often, Suboxone prescribers' disciplinary history involves overprescribing opioids. Samson Orusa received his certification to prescribe Suboxone in 2016, the year he ranked fourth in controlled substance prescribing among Tennessee's family practitioners (he would go on to climb to first place before being federally indicted, and years before facing any consequence to his medical license). Anand Rajan, the physician from Chapter 6 who was disciplined three times by the medical board for inadequate record keeping, then sexually touching a patient, and finally for improper prescribing through his pain clinic, started prescribing Suboxone in the same year. The *New York Times* investigated the disciplinary histories of thousands of Suboxone providers around the country and concluded that "an unmet demand for treatment has created a commercial opportunity for prescribers, attracting some with histories of overprescribing the very pain pills that made their patients into addicts."[66]

For a provider whose revenue streams have been impaired by board discipline, prescribing Suboxone for cash is an attractive option.[67] During a break at his July 2019 disciplinary hearing, Dr. LaPaglia told me about EHC's business model: $400 a visit, serving 8,000 patients a month.[68] Shortly before the owner of the clinic was indicted on federal drug trafficking charges, he sold EHC to Revelstoke, a private equity firm run by Harvard Business School grads, for $18 million.[69] Under Revelstoke's ownership, the clinic still operated in that strip mall in East Tennessee with drawn blinds and what appeared to be a bouncer sitting outside. When I observed the clinic in 2020, I saw patients come and go at a rate of about twenty an hour.

Prescribing Suboxone in bulk for profit is neither as dangerous nor as unethical as running an opioid pill mill. And until we reduce the stigma of addiction medicine, we will have to settle for a cash market for something that should be affordable (or free). In other words, turning Suboxone into a cash cow is better than not prescribing it at all. But the bottom line is, if you suffer from opioid use disorder in Tennessee and seek treatment, you are seven times more likely to receive care from a doctor that has been disciplined than if you were another kind of patient. There is something tragic about forcing addicts—the victims of unethical opioid prescribers and the licensing boards who didn't stop them—back into the care of the providers who got them hooked in the first place.

That irony was driven home to me when I went to Clarksville in 2020 to take a photograph of Samson Orusa's clinic, where a few years before patients were called like cattle to receive their opioid prescriptions. The clinic had been torn down, and where it once stood was an empty field with a bright yellow sign that read "Addicted? We can help!!" and below that, the phone number for a new Suboxone clinic in town.

## Pushing Back against the Caste System

Many of our country's most vulnerable—like the inmates at Angola State Prison—have no choice when it comes to medical services. That's also true about legal services, and it's something that Dawn Deaner, former Public Defender for Nashville, wants to change. But she's getting a lot of heat from her own licensing board over the project.[70]

*Gideon* gave everyone the right to be represented by a lawyer in their criminal case—even people who couldn't afford one. But what does that mean? For many indigent defendants, not much. Lawyers who show up drunk to court or fall asleep during trial have been held to meet the minimum standard of professionalism demanded by the Constitution.[71]

When Dawn was the head of the public defender's office, she had the ability to hire, fire, and train the defense lawyers on her team according to her high sense of professionalism that put client communication and advocacy first. But the thousands of clients her office had to turn away every year—mostly because of conflicts of interest—were fed into the grinder of our state's court-appointment system, where representation is, at best, a mixed bag. Dawn says some court-appointed lawyers are great, but they tend to move on (the state sets low caps on how much they can earn per case). The ones who stick around learn they can only "make a living by handling a high volume of cases and billing quickly," says Dawn. Often that involves no time for client communication or advocacy. She says one of the highest-earning appointed defense lawyers in town blocks all calls from the jail on his phone.

What she saw happen to the clients she turned away led her to start a nonprofit after stepping down as public defender. She started the Choosing Justice Initiative to connect indigent defendants unhappy with their appointed lawyer with her roster of competent lawyers willing to take on criminal cases pro bono. The idea was that indigent defendants—no less than wealthy ones—should have the right to fire an incompetent or unresponsive lawyer and obtain adequate counsel. But introducing choice into the process threatened to disrupt the long-established professional norms that have kept lawyers-to-the-poor from having to worry about things paid lawyers do: client satisfaction and effectiveness in advocacy.

The way the system is currently set up, Dawn told me, appointed lawyers compete only "to kiss the judge's ass." Often this involves not bothering judges with motions to reduce bonds or cluttering up their dockets with suppression hearings.[72] She thought, "if we got the power centered in [the clients]" rather than the judges, then their lawyers would have to work to deliver value.

For that, the attorney licensing board threatened her with disciplinary action. The Tennessee Board of Professional Responsibility claimed that when Dawn communicated with clients who were at the time represented by someone else—however ineffectually—she violated a rule of professional ethics. The argument made no sense (it was a patent misreading of the ethics rule) but the board persisted for more than a year. She believed that was because she angered judges, a professional no-no. Even worse, her business model violated an unspoken but strong norm in my profession: never publicly speak ill of a fellow lawyer. Eventually, the board dropped its investigation, but not without having an impact on her mission of bringing choice to indigent defendants. She's also under a judge's gag order to not speak to any represented clients in that court without their lawyer's permission.

If not a licensing board, then what will take a bad provider out of the market, once and for all? Next, we'll learn about how the criminal system has stepped in to regulate where boards won't, and whether it's a good thing.

# 9

# Crime and Punishment

*Criminal law has stepped into the regulatory void left by lax professional discipline. Can locking up dangerous professionals keep us safe?*

When Dr. LaPaglia got his license back in July 2019, he entered the job market with a probated medical license, two rounds of serious board discipline, a federal conviction for using his license to deal drugs, and no DEA number. He had yet to be sentenced for his federal crimes, so he was living—and working—with the sword of Damocles hanging over his head in the form of a possible prison sentence. As Dr. LaPaglia's lawyer told me at his 2019 medical board hearing, "once the feds get involved, you're screwed." Dr. LaPaglia hoped that information he shared with prosecutors about other prescribers would be enough to convince them to advocate for a "downward departure" in his federal sentence. But in the end, his freedom depended on more than what usually matters in informant cases. For Dr. LaPaglia, it also came down to the way he practiced medicine.

When Dr. LaPaglia got his license back in July 2019, his professional options were limited. Like many providers whose professional discipline put mainstream practice out of reach, his only real option was to hang a shingle. Working under the name Elite Healthcare, he operated as a sort of travelling doctor-of-all-trades, offering house calls for cash.[1] One set of patients were the residents of Volunteers for Recovery, a chain of "sober living facilities" where criminal defendants and recently released inmates lived by court order.[2] The owner of the recovery house, who demanded total abstinence from all drugs including addiction medications like Suboxone, testified at one of LaPaglia's criminal hearings that 99 percent of her clients didn't have health insurance but were in desperate need of medical care, especially for psychiatric issues. She described Dr. LaPaglia's help writing maintenance psychiatric prescriptions and treating infections as an "absolute blessing." Her residents paid him in cash, having nowhere else to go but to the local emergency room, the de facto primary care provider to the uninsured.[3]

When, in early 2021, the judge presiding over Dr. LaPaglia's criminal case learned that he was treating COVID patients without a mask and that he forged his own positive COVID test result to avoid a court-ordered drug screen, she modified the terms of his pre-sentencing release to preclude solo medical practice.[4] The owner of Volunteers for Recovery testified that since then, her residents were back to using the Knoxville ERs for primary care or going without it altogether.[5]

In modifying the terms of his release, the federal judge wanted some kind of assurance that if Dr. LaPaglia practiced medicine he would do so safely and responsibly. The medical board clearly could not be counted on in that area, nor could the federal supervised release office which had no medical expertise. Grasping at straws, she turned to an equally unlikely regulator: the Tennessee Medical Foundation (TMF), the state's health program for physicians. "The conditions [of the TMF] will become the conditions of his release," she said at the hearing in February 2021.[6] Her order placed the authority of the federal criminal system—essentially the power to lock up Dr. LaPaglia—in the hands of a private entity dedicated to physician welfare, run by one individual.[7] TMF works confidentially; we don't know what limits were placed on Dr. LaPaglia's practice in the spring of 2021.

### When More Is Less

Some professional misconduct is so bad it's literally criminal. When professional practice meets the elements of a crime—fraud, rape, drug dealing, or assault—two regulators are potentially in play. Licensing boards, of course, have the authority to restrict or revoke a license for conduct that violates a profession's code of ethics, which certainly describes criminal professional practice. (A closer question that I will address later is whether boards should take disciplinary action for crimes conducted outside of someone's professional life.)

The other "regulator"—though we are not perhaps used to using that term in this context—is the criminal justice system. Most people think of the primary purpose of the criminal system as punishment for major social transgressions, but it is (at least secondarily) *regulatory* in the sense that it shapes human behavior. By threatening to punish people for crimes, it creates incentives that influence how people act. And after someone is caught up in the system, its power to control people gets even stronger because the government can set conditions for bail, probation, and parole. Finally, the criminal justice system can "regulate" someone's behavior—essentially stop it—through the ultimate coercive act: incarceration.

Having two regulators that might shape professional practice for the better sounds like a good thing. We might expect that one can fill in the gaps left by the other, or double the chances of a bad actor getting caught. The reality, though, is that having these two authorities regulate professional practice may be worse than having just one.

## Nature Abhors a Vacuum

On April 16, 2019, federal prosecutors for the Appalachian Region Prescription Opioids (ARPO) Strike Force held a press conference in Ohio, alongside Attorney General William P. Barr and Health and Human Services Secretary Alex Azar (who, one year later, would implore states to rollback medical licensing rules as COVID ravaged New York City). Standing in front of a sea of cameras, in front of royal blue drapes and next to an oversized American flag, the feds announced the arrest and indictment of fifty-three medical professionals involved in the unlawful distribution of prescription opioids. Most of them held medical or nursing licenses in Tennessee.[8]

Although there were some familiar names on the list—like Charles Brooks (Dr. LaPaglia's partner), and Darrel Rinehart, the doctor from Chapter 6 whose prescribing allegedly led to at least five overdose deaths—many of these nurses and doctors had clean licenses. According to the state database, twenty-one of them had no history of medical board discipline at the time of the sweep. Of the prescribers who had been disciplined, the measures taken against them were clearly inadequate, given the facts known by the board and described in their disciplinary orders. In the absence of meaningful, commonsense regulation by a licensing board, another government actor had stepped in. With a very different set of priorities, to say the least.

One of these indicted prescribers who had been lightly disciplined was Jeff Young, a nurse practitioner who was known to his patients in Jackson as a work-hard, play-hard bad boy with a pilot for his own reality show he called "The Rock Doc."[9] Over prosecutors' objections, a federal judge granted him pretrial release the day after his arrest on April 16, 2019. The prosecutors appealed that decision, arguing that his freedom—and license to practice and prescribe—was a threat to society.[10]

When his lawyer countered that the nursing board didn't see it that way, the government called the board investigator who had been following the nurse practitioner for years to the stand and, for a day and a half, put the Tennessee Board of Nursing on trial. It was a rare glimpse into the timeline of a licensing board investigation, the details of which were usually kept private. The testimony offered at this second detention hearing described long-term board inaction in the face of damning evidence against Jeff Young—a portrait of a regulatory vacuum. Prosecutors argued that someone had to stop the Rock Doc, and it wouldn't be the nursing board.[11]

At the detention hearing, the board investigator told the federal judge that she started looking into Jeff Young in 2014, in response to a series of complaints that he was prescribing controlled substances, including high doses of opioids, Adderall, and benzodiazepines without seeing the patient at all. She learned that he was intoxicated—on one occasion unconscious—when patients arrived for care. She viewed his social media pages where he could be seen disparaging rival medical providers in Jackson and identifying his patients—a HIPAA violation that patients said they found threatening. At this stage, the board responded to these findings by sending Nurse Young a private letter admonishing him to refrain from keeping alcohol at his clinic to avoid the "appearance of impropriety."[12]

The letter did not have its desired effect and the Rock Doc's improprieties multiplied. The investigator learned that he was serving alcohol to patients and treating them while they were intoxicated. She found that he engaged in billing fraud, prescribed controlled substances to known drug dealers, and falsified charts. He prescribed enough opioids and other drugs with street value to raise a red flag with the state system that tracks prescribing (a Tennessee Bureau of Investigations officer testified that he prescribed 800,000 doses of opioids and 600,000 of benzos). He gave high-school boys testosterone.[13]

Years passed as his practice spun out of control. Still the nursing board did nothing. One woman to whom he prescribed opioids while she was pregnant died of an overdose. More patients came forward saying they were threatened by him. He posted a picture of a patient on social media with the caption "THIS CUNT TALKS ABOUT HOW I WON'T PRESCRIBE HER NARCOTICS." Other evidence suggested that Nurse Young might have been trading sex for scripts. The situation was becoming untenable for the investigator herself, whose findings continued to be ignored by the board. She testified that she grew so afraid of Nurse Young that she started carrying a gun.[14] The board responded with another private letter asking the nurse to stop posting about patients on social media, observing that it "reflects poorly on the profession of nursing."[15]

Finally, in November 2018, the nursing board took public action against Nurse Young for the first time with an order that placed his license on probation, asked him to attend continuing education courses, and removed some of his prescribing authority, but otherwise kept him in practice.[16] One panel member recused himself from approving the order because he had heard too many things through the professional grapevine to be objective about Young's case. "I'd have been braiding the rope," he told me later.[17]

The 2018 discipline may have circumscribed the drugs he could pre-scribe, but it did little to change the character of his practice. In the six months after the nursing board order, he prescribed 15,000 doses of controlled substances with street value like Klonopin, Ambien, and phentermine.[18] Additionally, more stories of sexual predation began to surface. In early 2019, the board investigated a patient's allegation of rape and concluded that Nurse Young had been having sex with pa-tients for some time. The nursing board's response was to send an-other private letter asking him to stop.[19]

In arguing their case against pretrial release in his federal criminal case, the prosecutors made clear how much deference the judge should give the board's decision to keep Young in practice: none. The board could not say, as I have heard several members claim generally about board inaction against severe misconduct, that they were unaware of any wrongdoing until the criminal system got involved. Virtually all of the evidence presented by the government was available to the licensing board when it gave Nurse Young his third and fourth chances, with one notable exception. At the detention hearing, the government produced a cellphone video of Nurse Young having sex with a woman who ap-peared to be unconscious. This time the judge didn't hesitate. He re-voked Young's pretrial release and ordered him to remain in custody until his trial.[20]

## Foot Dragging and Free Riding

Two-thirds of the Tennessee providers indicted in April 2019 had even less professional discipline than Nurse Young—namely, none. Criminal charges (even ones not directly related to practice) can trigger discipline, yet none of the indicted doctors were on the agenda the next time the medical board met. And so it was with the meeting after that, and the one after that. One year later, half of the Tennessee providers under fed-eral indictment still had no reported discipline on their licenses.

One explanation for this was legal. It was difficult to proceed with a disciplinary case against providers with pending criminal charges because anything admitted to by the provider in the disciplinary proceeding could be used against him in the criminal case. Defendants couldn't be compelled to make incriminating statements, something very likely to happen in a disciplinary case about the same facts in a criminal indictment. If the board pushed it, the provider could ask a state court to stay the licensing proceeding pending resolution of the criminal case, which is what Samson Orusa did successfully when the medical board finally pursued discipline after his federal indictment.[21]

On the one hand, this was a likely explanation for board inaction and illustrated an important way in which the criminal and board systems do not work well together. A lot of time can pass while the board waits for the criminal system to do its thing; fifteen months after the indictments, only two of the twenty-eight providers' criminal cases had been resolved. Observers have noted the same problem in other states.[22]

On the other hand, the self-incrimination problem didn't explain why the boards didn't use their power to suspend a license on a temporary, emergency basis. In Tennessee, as in most states, a disciplinary panel can be convened on short notice to decide that the public welfare is immediately in danger based on proof offered by a Department of Health attorney.[23] The proceeding is not adversarial; the accused is not present nor able—let alone compelled—to make a potentially incriminating statement. Of course, the provider is given due process eventually; emergency suspensions are temporary. This seemed to me a reasonable way to deal with indicted providers who had clean medical licenses and, unlike Nurse Young, were out and about awaiting trial (as most of them were). But this power is rarely invoked, and indeed in Tennessee the boards pursued emergency suspensions against only two indicted doctors in 2019: Brooks and LaPaglia.[24]

Board members I talked to didn't agree with me that summary suspension was a good way to handle providers under indictment. Several told me that an indictment was just an accusation—it didn't prove anything.[25] Another told me they disfavored summary suspension because it stopped the provider "dead in the water." He said, "How are they going to feed their family?"[26] In these conversations, another explanation for board inaction emerged: free riding. It might take a long time, but something was going to happen with these criminal cases one way or the other. Why should a board expend limited resources on pursuing discipline when, in the end, there would be a set of facts produced by another regulator that could form a basis for discipline? In an inversion of the typical argument about letting professionals regulate other professionals, the board members seemed to be saying, about the criminal system, "better to sit back and let the experts handle it."

In the end, I viewed free riding as the most powerful explanation for the silence after the April sweep, and probably also for other instances of board foot-dragging when disciplining indicted providers. Free riding in this context is problematic. First, it pushes the regulatory void left by the boards indefinitely into the future. In the case of pill mill prescribers, that void raises the possibility that alleged drug dealers would be out practicing medicine and prescribing controlled substances while awaiting trial. Second, as I would learn by observing how boards disciplined (or didn't) convicted providers on the other end, justice deferred is often justice denied.

There was no mention of the doctors indicted in the April sweep at the next medical board meeting, but there was a new face sitting near me in the audience. He was big, tall, square, and dressed in a detective suit. He wore a DEA pin and carried a folder with a federal crest on it. When he spoke, his voice was loud and had a strong Maine accent. The typical vibe of the Tennessee medical board meeting is Southern genteel. To put it mildly, he did not fit in.

Despite the pin and the folder, he was not a DEA agent. He had retired from that job after decades of service, during which (as he told me later during a three-hour interview in which he swore like a sailor) he cooked meth undercover, busted dirty cops for internal affairs, and— most importantly for his current position—investigated prescription drug distribution rings throughout the United States. As the board meeting commenced, he was introduced as David Mercier, the new head of investigations for the health licensing boards.[27]

The head of investigations serves at the pleasure of our governor, not the licensing boards for which they investigate disciplinary cases. The governor's selection of Mercier was a shot across the bow to both the boards and the pill mill prescribers in my state. Indeed, Mercier had a decidedly more law-and-order attitude toward overprescribers than your average board member. He asked me, rhetorically, what the difference was between a crack dealer on the street and a doctor handing over prescriptions for cash. I gave the stock answer: a lab coat. "Well," Mercier told me, "I don't give a shit."[28]

He said Tennessee was just like all the other licensing boards he'd seen in other states, and that what they did would shock the average citizen. He was prone to exaggeration, but he explained board discipline this way: "You're guilty of a federal felony for a million-dollar fraud, you've got alcohol and drug abuse problems, and you're on supervised release, but hey, you're a great doctor!"

He was hired to shake things up at the department, and in particular to facilitate information-sharing between the boards, other state agencies, and the federal authorities. But he had already gotten criticism for being from out of state, and he suspected that while he had the support of the governor, he was making too many waves with the boards and the Department of Health. By the time of the next medical board meeting a month after our interview, he had already quit.

My conversation with Mercier and two other interviews with federal law enforcement agents convinced me that the April indictments could be viewed, at least in part, as a vote of no confidence in the board's regulation. One agent told me (with more oratorical restraint than Mercier), that there "seems to be a disconnect" between how boards and the feds saw these prescribers.[29] As I followed some of these cases from indictment through trial, I learned that the feds' priority wasn't just getting the conviction, but also controlling the defendant's ability to practice medicine. In other words, they had stepped into the regulatory void.

## A Nontraditional Approach

Mercier's attitude toward drug-dealing doctors was not unique. At the press conferences announcing ARPO's sixty indictments in April 2019, a federal agent gave law enforcement's party line on pill mill doctors: "the only difference between a doctor and a drug dealer is a white coat." But even he wasn't entirely convinced, because a moment later he acknowledged that using criminal law to rein in overprescribers feeding the opioid crisis in Appalachia was a "nontraditional" approach.[30]

Locking up doctors for bad professional behavior is certainly non-traditional. It's also relatively ineffective as a way to stop unethical prescribing. More generally, using the criminal law to regulate professional practice is far less efficient than using a functional administrative process (not the one we have). Using criminal prosecutions to control the professions is like trying to use lightning to trim trees. So few professionals will ever face criminal sanctions for their professional misconduct that it cannot serve as a meaningful deterrent, and when it happens it's imprecise, arbitrary, and draconian.

Criminal cases against professional misconduct are rare in part because they are so hard to win. First, law enforcement must investigate the case thoroughly, which in the professional context usually requires viewing charts and other professional work product. Licensing boards have the authority to access patient charts and client files through a subpoena process.[31] The police, in contrast, must get a judge to sign a warrant saying that the search is likely to turn up evidence of a crime.

Then, supposing the police are able to correctly interpret patient charts and professional records, and supposing there is evidence of bad practice, they can only bring a case if it also meets the elements of a crime. Not all conduct worthy of professional discipline is also a crime, in part because professional regulation and criminal justice ask two different questions. Professional regulation is supposed to protect the public by asking whether a provider has the minimum level of competence and judgment to practice safely. The criminal justice system asks whether the accused's conduct is so antisocial as to justify incarceration. It's often not possible to characterize even very dangerous and unethical professional practice as drug dealing, assault, rape, or murder.

Finally, the criminal system can only bring a professional to heel if it can convince a jury *beyond a reasonable doubt* that his practice is literally criminal. Licensing boards, at least theoretically, use a lighter standard of proof—usually either a preponderance of evidence or clear and convincing evidence.[32] (I say "theoretically" because in practice, as we have seen, providers are almost always given the benefit of the doubt.) Proving something beyond a reasonable doubt requires the government not only to produce a lot of evidence, but also to put it together in a clear, simple story for a lay jury. Cases about professional practice, definition-ally uncommon knowledge, can be particularly confusing to a jury.

On top of that, professionals, as some of the most trusted and esteemed members of society, get tremendous deference in their criminal cases. It's hard to convince a jury that doctors and lawyers are criminals. Even judges, too, tend to give professionals the benefit of the doubt. I observed this myself when watching doctors' criminal cases, and Mercier told me about a judge staying late on a Friday to let an arrested doctor out on bail so he wouldn't have to spend the weekend in jail, a courtesy Mercier had never seen extended to any other kind of defendant.[33]

The cases against professionals that go forward tend to be factually simple and well-documented. It's no accident that most prosecutions against pill mill prescribers allege over-billing insurance or forging documents, because fraud tends to leave a paper trail. But so much egregious professional misconduct—especially sexual—involves proof much messier than a forgery. That leaves a lot of unsafe or unethical practice out of the reach of the criminal law.

Unless, of course, we're talking about Dr. Christopher Duntsch.

## "A Surgeon So Bad It Was Criminal"

In the summer of 2012, Dallas-based neurosurgeon Dr. Robert Henderson was asked to perform a repair surgery on a patient who had come into his hospital two days before for a spinal fusion. As neurosurgery goes, spinal fusions are routine, yet this one had gone very badly. The patient was in horrible pain and barely able to move her legs. Dr. Henderson looked at the CT scan in disbelief. The hardware that was supposed to hold the vertebrae together was sunk in muscle, inches away from her spine.[34]

As Dr. Henderson later told the *Dallas Observer,* what he saw when he performed the repair surgery on Mary Efurd made him believe the hospital had an imposter in its midst. The previous surgeon had inexplicably amputated a nerve root and left multiple screw holes "everywhere but where he had needed to be." It was inconceivable to the doctor that an actual neurosurgeon had performed this surgery. Dr. Henderson found a picture of the new guy—Dr. Christopher Duntsch—and faxed it over to the University of Tennessee, where Duntsch claimed he had done his residency. The school confirmed his identity.[35]

The more Dr. Henderson learned, the worse it got. As Dr. Duntsch was operating on Ms. Efurd, another of Duntsch's spinal-fusion patients lay dying in her recovery bed. Floella Brown's surgery had gone even worse—Dr. Duntsch nicked an artery during the operation that bled so much it soaked the drapes and dripped onto the floor. When Duntsch arrived at work the next day he was advised that Ms. Brown was in critical condition. Yet he went ahead with Ms. Efurd's surgery, and by the end of the day Ms. Brown was brain dead.[36]

Dr. Henderson started by calling around to area medical societies, but in the end he decided to call the Texas Medical Board. The person who answered the phone told him to file a complaint and that it would be read in about a month. If there was something there, they would investigate. He recalled the conversation when interviewed for "Dr. Death," a six-part podcast about Christopher Duntsch's short and bloody career as a neurosurgeon in Dallas. "You don't seem to understand," he said. "This guy already killed somebody [and] made a partial paraplegic out of my patient. He needs to be stopped." His words had no effect.[37]

Dr. Henderson's was not the only complaint the board received that summer. A different surgeon who had cleaned up after another of Duntsch's botched surgeries also complained, as did a member of the medical board who had heard the rumors: since Dr. Duntsch began performing spinal surgeries just six months earlier, he had maimed four and killed two patients. With at least three credible complaints filed with the board, the creaky wheels of board discipline began to turn.[38]

In the meantime, Dr. Duntsch remained busy in the operating room. At the time of the complaints to the medical board, he was only one third of the way through the thirty-seven spinal surgeries he would perform, thirty-three of which left the patients maimed or dead. All the while, area hospitals played a game of hot potato with the surgeon. As they learned about his performance, they asked him to resign quietly. No hospitals outright fired him, knowing that doing so would trigger a report to the National Practitioner Data Bank. That, in turn, could expose the hospital to a suit from Dr. Duntsch claiming the Data Bank hit impaired his professional prospects.[39]

When, a full year after his initial complaint, Dr. Henderson received an email from University General Hospital inviting him to a "Meet Our Specialist Dinner" featuring their newly hired neurosurgeon Dr. Christopher Duntsch, he knew it would take more than a medical board to stop the doctor. (University General serves a low-income population in South Dallas; it was the third hospital to take on the surgeon in less than two years.) Dr. Henderson reached out to the District Attorney's office and, against the odds, found a prosecutor interested in making a criminal case against the surgeon.[40]

The theory of the case was unconventional. I interviewed Michelle Shughart, the lead prosecutor in case, who said as far as she knew, she was the first prosecutor to argue that bad surgery was a crime. Although thirty-three patients had been injured or killed on Dr. Duntsch's table, the prosecution went forward with only their strongest case—Mary Efurd's. The indictment accused Dr. Death of "assault with a deadly weapon" (the scalpel), which required the prosecution to prove that he "knowingly injured" Efurd during surgery.[41]

Yet the prosecution had little evidence of what Dr. Duntsch "knew" about his surgical performance. He maintained a bravado about his own practice—he said every case was complicated and the bad outcomes were not his fault—that was either a sign of egotism or mental illness, but not necessarily criminality. The closest thing the prosecution had to direct evidence of his bad intent was a long, rambling email Dr. Duntsch sent to a girlfriend in which he said, "I am ready to leave the love and kindness and goodness and patience that I mix with everything else that I am and become a cold-blooded killer."[42]

The indictment was a gamble. Without other similar cases to use as a template, Shughart said "we felt like we were starting from scratch." The prosecution's success got a boost when the judge allowed evidence of other surgeries that had gone wrong as a way of proving Dr. Duntsch knew he was injuring patients (the law typically bars evidence of uncharged prior bad acts).[43] After hearing testimony from Mary Efurd, four other maimed patients, and the husband of a patient killed by Dr. Duntsch, the jury convicted and sentenced him to life in prison.[44]

It takes a lot to put a professional away for being bad at his job. In fact, only two out of the three judges that considered Dr. Duntsch's appeal felt the prosecution had produced adequate proof of his intent. If anything had been different in his case—if he hadn't written that email about being a killer, if the judge hadn't let the prior bad acts in as evidence, if his conduct had been just slightly less egregious, prosecutors probably could not have gone forward with the case. Dr. Duntsch would have been left in the regulatory void, and his patients left to the mercy of hospitals watching their bottom line.

## The Sledgehammer and the Fly

Although the Christopher Duntsch case was groundbreaking and unconventional, it's hard to see it as prosecutorial overreach given the extent of suffering he left in his wake. Yet it's easy to imagine that when a punitive system that has only blunt tools—incarceration and intimidation—comes after a professional loaded for bear, there is a significant risk of it going too far.

That is, at least arguably, what happened in federal prosecutions against pill mill prescribers in the wake of the opioid crisis. Not all of the prescribers swept up in the 2019 ARPO indictments overprescribed with the flair of the Rock Doc or with the body count of Rinehart. I interviewed Caleb Thompson, the defense attorney for one of those "small fry" prescribers. His client, Timothy Abbott, was a podiatrist accused of prescribing hydrocodone (Vicodin) without adequate records on six occasions over a span of four years. Given that I had seen much worse prescribers successfully claim—at least in licensing board proceedings—that cutting a few corners was hardly malpractice, Abbott's criminal case seemed to me to strongly favor the defense.

Caleb said that might have been true twenty years ago. The statute that made trafficking narcotics a federal crime created a carveout for medical professionals prescribing controlled substances for "a legitimate medical purpose" and "within the usual course of professional practice."[45] Legitimacy, of course, is in the eye of the beholder, and defense attorneys tried to argue that even if it was bad medicine by any objective standard, prescriptions written in good faith were for "legitimate" medicine.

But as the opioid crisis raged on, and licensing boards continued to let dangerous prescribers slip through the regulatory cracks, that put additional political pressure on federal prosecutors to secure convictions. That, in turn, put pressure on the courts to lighten the government's burden in opioid cases. Thus, in 2018, the Sixth Circuit (whose cases control federal law in Appalachian states such as Tennessee, Ohio, and Kentucky) effectively did away with the "good faith" defense in overprescribing cases in *United States v. Godofsky*.[46]

Caleb said that winning a case under the *Godofsky* standard meant arguing that your client strictly followed professional norms. "You're proving your innocence," he said, and for that you need good medical records. As an older doctor nearing retirement, Dr. Abbott wasn't a great documentarian. "How do you win in that scenario?" Caleb asked. Sending Abbott to prison, at his age and with COVID raging, felt like a death sentence. So he pled guilty to felony drug trafficking, in exchange for no prison time. He also agreed to permanently give up his medical license.[47]

Caleb wasn't the only one who saw *Godofsky* as an overreach. In 2022, the US Supreme Court decided *Ruan v. United States*,[48] which overturned *Godofsky* and reinstated the possibility of a "good faith" defense. This U-turn in federal precedent solved some problems but introduced others; Samson Orusa, who, quite unlike Dr. Abbott, prescribed millions of pills out of his Clarksville clinic for a number of years, turned a blind eye to overdoses in his waiting room, and allegedly sent away cash to overseas accounts, was able to take advantage of the new precedent. Although a jury found him guilty after a two-week trial of thirty-six counts, including trafficking in narcotics and running his clinic as a drug house, he petitioned to have those convictions vacated in the wake of *Ruan*.[49] After two years of litigation, the judge ruled in his favor for all but the healthcare fraud convictions, vacating most of his 2021 convictions. Although the government could have retried the doctor under the *Ruan* standard, it opted instead to drop Orusa's overprescribing charges altogether.[50]

It's hard to tell how many opioid prosecutions are overreaches, but based on the ever-shifting legal standard and the enthusiasm with which the government is looking for someone to hold accountable for the opioid crisis (both of which are partially a product of board inaction) the percentage could be nontrivial. It's just another reason to doubt that criminal law can pick up the slack left by the licensing board disciplinary system.

Incarceration, the threat in every prosecution, is the most direct way of regulating a professional's practice. But there are less obvious ways in which the criminal system steps into the regulatory void, such as by setting terms of release that limit practice in certain ways, or extending plea offers conditional on a professional surrendering his license, as in the Abbott case. When the criminal law gets involved at this level of detail in a defendant's professional life, it raises the question: is the criminal system suited to deciding the how and whether of professional practice?

After the ARPO indictments, I started following the criminal cases of the providers who had clean licenses. All of them were granted pretrial release; only the Rock Doc and another doctor who had attempted to flee to the Marshall Islands lost the privilege.[51] Perhaps unsurprisingly, in most of the cases the judge set limits on what they could do professionally (typically no controlled substance prescribing).

This is sensible, of course, but consider it as an alternative to licensing board regulation. Setting practice limits as a matter of criminal law puts a federal criminal judge, with no expertise in medicine, in the position of overriding a medical or nursing board's judgment about fitness to practice. Defense attorneys have been quick to point out this incongruity and ask the judge to defer to the board's judgment. For example, the attorney for the Rock Doc argued for deference to the board of nursing's decision to keep him in practice, saying that the board "would not have placed him back out into the community, would not have allowed him to continue practicing . . . if, in fact, he was found by them to be a threat to his community. They are the experts in this field."[52] Although this argument is not persuasive in the context of someone like the Rock Doc, for providers accused of slightly less egregious conduct it might hold water, especially with judges who don't know the truth about professional discipline.

## Debts Paid and Time Served

There are plenty of reasons, if not all good ones, for a licensing board to sit back while the criminal system proceeds against a practitioner. But what happens when the criminal case is concluded? One might expect that once a professional is found guilty of using his license to commit a crime, the board will free ride on those factual findings to revoke his license.

But boards take a different perspective. In many cases, the fact of conviction seems to militate *against* board discipline rather than for it. A professional appearing before a board after the conclusion of his criminal case has already suffered severe consequences for his behavior, professionally and personally. Some have even done prison time. With the proverbial (and sometimes literal) "debt to society" paid, boards are not eager to pile on the consequences. Here, the idea of second chances and redemption are yet again in play, as might be the assurance that comes with knowing that the provider's days of mainstream practice are over, no matter what the board does.

Thus, many convicted felons return to practice—and even after crimes directly relating to their professional practice. The Tennessee medical board put back into practice Dr. Carl Lindblad, who had taken a federal felony for his participation in a pain cream scam that defrauded the military out of $65 million. At the time of the scheme, he was on his second round of discipline with the licensing board.[53] In a similar case involving a federal conviction for a multi-million-dollar fraud scheme, one a board member remarked, "I don't see what a federal charge and conviction over a billing matter has to do with us giving him a license to return to practice."[54]

Ironically, some boards may be tougher on crimes committed *outside* of professional practice. This is especially true in law. Professor Deborah Rhode writes, in her book *The Trouble with Lawyers*, "[w]hatever its inadequacies in responding to misconduct that occurs within a lawyer-client relationship, the bar has often been highly vigilant in its response to criminal offenses occurring outside it." Professor Rhode attributes this double standard, at least in part, to maintaining appearances.[55] A lawyer convicted of domestic violence or a DUI makes the profession look bad, or, in the words of a court affirming professional discipline for a lawyer convicted of owning child pornography, effect a "stain upon the legal profession."[56] At the same time, if the victim is a client, boards seem less willing to pile professional consequences on top of criminal.

## Not above the Law

By May 27, 2021, Dr. LaPaglia's medical career had, at least for the moment, run out of road. That was the date when the federal judge would finally announce his sentence for his guilty plea from more than two years before. Dr. LaPaglia sat in a cavernous, oaky courtroom with a freshly vacuumed royal blue carpet depicting symbols of federal power: an eagle, a flag. With the latest pre-sentence report, the prosecutors had dropped a bomb. Not only would they not be arguing for a "downward departure" in his prison sentence, but the government would argue for an *upward* departure from the recommended six to twelve months of prison time. As the prosecutor put it, with his forged COVID test he had "ruined" his credibility and would no longer be a useful witness in the government's other cases.[57]

In fact, Dr. LaPaglia's medical practice since the licensing board gave him back his license in 2019 was worse than the feds apparently knew. I interviewed one of his patients who saw him in 2020 after learning that the doctor was offering house calls giving "second opinion" COVID tests to people who had turned up positive PCR results at a clinic. These tests were a scam: LaPaglia used antibody tests, which weren't appropriate to diagnose COVID because it could take the body up to two weeks to produce antibodies after infection was detectable by PCR. The patient I interviewed said she had plans to visit her elderly parents and although she had symptoms, she was shocked by the positive PCR test. Dr. La-Paglia came to her home, did a pick-prick test, and gave her the news she wanted to hear. She told me, "He looked me in the eye and said, 'You've got something, but it's not COVID.'"[58] He charged $50 for the visit. Even without the benefit of these additional details about his medical practice, the federal judge could see that Dr. LaPaglia was undeserving of yet another chance. She took testimony from friends and acquaintances of Dr. LaPaglia who spoke to his compassion and professionalism, but in the end, she read from a pre-written order.

Through L&B, Dr. LaPaglia had used his position of trust as a physician to "take advantage of his patients who were suffering from addiction," it said. Moreover, the doctor was remorseless. "Dr. LaPaglia has consistently showed that he believes himself to be above the law." After reading her statement, she pronounced Dr. LaPaglia's sentence: eighteen months in prison, six months more than the recommended maximum sentence for his offense.[59]

Two months after his sentencing and just before reporting to prison, one more order concerning Dr. Michael LaPaglia was presented to the Tennessee Board of Medical Examiners: a consent order that would represent LaPaglia's fourth round of discipline from the board. Department of Health investigators had evidently learned about the antibody testing scam and the falsified positive COVID test he presented to the pretrial release office, and the board had opened new charges against his license. As presented to the board in July 2021, the doctor would voluntarily revoke his license, and agree not to seek relicensure for three years.

It also, however, described a route back to licensure for the doctor, involving compliance with the TMF, practice monitoring, and a practice plan that must include a description of "what patient population Respondent intends to serve."[60] As the board voted to approve it, one member praised the order because it described "a pathway that, should he want to return to practice, could be possible."[61]

Can anything be done to fix our broken system of professional licensing? Next, we will imagine a world with less professional licensing and, for the professions that need it, a regulatory system without licensing boards.

# Conclusion

## Fixing Professional Licensing

*The licensing system fails America's workers, patients, and clients. It's time to find a better way to regulate the professions.*

Solutions to a one-hundred-and-fifty-year-old problem won't come easily, especially because the licensing system works perfectly well for everyone with the power to change it. The professions like it because it maximizes their autonomy. State governments like it because it allows them to avoid the effort and expense it would take to truly balance the interests at stake in regulating the professions. Meaningful reform will involve building the political will to confront the reality that the system doesn't work for everyone else. Meaningful reform will also have to confront the heart of the problem—self-regulatory state licensing boards.

### A Stalled-Out Reform Movement

Before developing a promising agenda for reform, it is important to understand what has been tried already and why it hasn't brought about widespread change. Lawsuits asserting a right to be free from onerous professional regulation, as discussed in Chapter 3, play an important role in holding the line against too much licensing, but they are a limited tool for the full-scale reform that's necessary. These cases are hard to win and only target extreme overreach; they cannot address the problem of licensing regulation that doesn't go far enough. The direct effect of these suits can therefore be characterized as trimming the edges of a problem that's bigger and deeper than the reach of constitutional law.

There has, however, been an indirect effect of these suits that is perhaps more important than their win / loss record in the courtroom. Libertarian lawfare has brought attention to bad licensing policy, placing pressure on the entities with the real power to change licensing for good: state legislatures. The Institute for Justice, for example, augments its legal work with lobbying and research projects that have moved the needle toward more reasonable licensing regulation in several states. It was the same tactic Braden Boucek of Tennessee's Beacon Center used to eliminate the high-school degree requirement for barbers in 2020, by bringing a bill to the legislature and filing suit in the same year.

Indeed, pressure on legislatures to roll back licensing laws is coming from all directions. In 2017, the US Department of Labor gave a $7.5 million grant to the National Conference of State Legislatures (NCSL) and the Council of State Governments (CSG) to organize a consortium of states to study their licensing laws and pursue reform.[1] In those states—and in just about every other one, too—each new legislative session carries a spate of bills looking to cut some of licensing's red tape. Some of them even pass, despite the best lobbying efforts of the professions and the licensing boards they control. I heard several references to this movement in board meetings, such as when the executive director of the architecture and engineering board from Chapter 2 invoked the "temperature of things" at the legislature in an effort to pull the board back from reigniting a turf war.

It is worth celebrating the successes of these efforts. One area of strength for the legislative-reform movement has been improving interstate mobility. It's hard to justify separate licenses for every state—the needs of consumers and clients in Texas wouldn't seem to be that different from those in Tennessee. As an advocate for interstate mobility for teachers observed at a NCSL conference about licensing reform, "if you crossed a state line, you haven't stopped being the person that you were."[2] This intuition has proved powerful in lobbying state legislatures, who have recently experimented with various ways to boost professional mobility. Arizona has even gone so far as to create "universal recognition," which purports to make any professional license from any state good in Arizona.[3] Less drastic measures, like streamlined reciprocity for military spouses and interstate compacts—where states join forces to create a kind of umbrella license that works in all member states—have been even more widespread.[4]

Many states have also implemented a "sunset" review process that automatically terminates a licensure law and abolishes the board unless the legislature affirmatively renews it every few years.[5] However, this review almost never actually results in the demise of a professional board and its licensing regime.[6] (There are some exceptions to this, like when my state eliminated licensing for beauty pageant operators and locksmiths in 2018.)[7] But sunset review does require boards to publicly account for their regulation and face sometimes heated questioning from the legislatures that oversee them, contributing to regulatory transparency. Indeed, a significant amount of the research for this book was based on board documents and testimony prepared for sunset hearings.

Finally, some states have attempted to slow the growth of newly licensed professions by implementing "sunrise" review, a structured legislative process that places the burden on the licensed profession to show that licensure will lead to better, safer practice in a way that justifies the associated higher prices and scarcity. The Institute for Justice has studied sunrise review and found that states that implemented it have been able to significantly cut down on new licensure regimes. They also found that it works best in combination with sunset review.[8]

As important as these legislative efforts are, they are not enough. In a report on the success of the federal grant that funded licensing reform in a consortium of states, NCSL noted that member states have used the grant to *slow* the growth of new professional licenses, but they have not stopped it. In fact, in states funded by the grant, bills creating a new professional license still outnumber bills delicensing a profession by more than four to one.[9]

Legislative reform has been particularly slow going in the professions with the highest stakes for consumers. Nearly every state licensing reform statute I have come across exempts the state's medical board. More generally, aside from a few victories for nurse practitioners seeking a broader scope of practice, virtually no health care professions have seen a meaningful rollback of licensing requirements. Here, the legislative wins have been to mobility, where nursing and medical compacts have slightly increased the flow of labor.[10]

If the legislative reform movement has been lackluster when it comes to cutting back on licensing, it has been DOA when it comes to the other set of problems identified in this book. The idea that boards are insufficiently protective of the public in their disciplinary decisions was not one I heard discussed at any of the national meetings I attended about licensing and reform. Besides Tennessee's legislative attempt to set mandatory minimum discipline for opioid overprescribers, I did not run across any major legislative effort to curb board leniency. A few bills have been introduced (and even fewer passed) to increase the transparency of the disciplinary process, but I have not heard of one that actually changes its basic structure or outcomes.

Legislative reform has, so far, been a limited tool for change because of the political economy of licensing reform. As we learned in Chapters 1 and 5, organized professions are good at convincing legislatures that licensing is a win-win for the profession and the public. The more prestigious the profession, the more convincing its lobbyists. The result has been a legislative reform movement focused on what one state senator I interviewed called "the low-hanging fruit of professional licensing"—the restrictions that are the hardest to justify on the basis of consumer protection and the least likely to be successfully blocked by organized professional groups.[11]

The low-hanging fruit of licensing reform includes small professions without a strong lobbying presence; not a single industry representative showed up at the hearing where Tennessee's licensing law for beauty pageants faced the chopping block.[12] Mobility is also a relatively easy legislative fix because it benefits professionals as much as it does consumers, and so professions tend not to fight it. These are low-risk, low-reward strategies. As we experienced so acutely during COVID, there is only so much interstate mobility can do—it cannot actually expand the number of overall providers. The abolition of the beauty pageant license may have been sensible, but it hardly opened up any major professional opportunities for the citizens of my state.

Most problematically, the low-hanging fruit of licensing tends to include lower-income professions, like cosmetology and barbering. That puts the burden of reform on workers who are already on the edge and gives a free pass to the high earners, whose licensing rules have a greater potential to harm the public. That's not an argument against rolling back licensing in the low-income professions, but the unfairness of focusing *only* on those professions is another reason to be disappointed in the reform movement so far.

## The Case That Shall Not Be Named

There is another, more fundamental reason why neither libertarian lawfare nor the legislative reform movement haven't done more for consumers and patients: both ignore the role of boards. Libertarian lawyers mounting constitutional challenges accept the existence of, and processes used by, professionally dominated boards as legitimate—they attack only the substance. Legislatures pass reform laws imagining that their edicts will become policy through the same administrative process applied to their other laws—for example, through the state's department of education or environment. But, when it comes to licensing, the work of the legislature is operationalized by a board that is often indifferent—or hostile—to state policy.

A regulatory system is only as strong as its weakest link. This was driven home for me at a conference where a speaker was touting Arizona's "universal recognition law," which purported to allow anyone with a license in any state to automatically practice in Arizona.[13] After the presentation, a member of Arizona's psychology board told me that her board had interpreted the new law to preclude reciprocity for anyone whose qualifications weren't identical to those required in Arizona.[14]

For a moment in the recent history of licensing reform, it looked like boards might get their due. On February 25, 2015, the US Supreme Court handed down their first case about professional regulation in more than a decade. Unlike other cases decided that year—same-sex marriage, lethal injection, and Obamacare were on the docket—virtually no one was waiting on the edge of their seat for the outcome of *Federal Trade Commission v. North Carolina Board of Dental Examiners*.[15] No one, that is, except me.

I had spent the previous few years researching the legal issue in the case, writing articles about it, and authoring an amicus brief (a kind of advisory document often filed by experts and academics) for the Court to consider. When the opinion came down, it adopted my argument into law: professional licensing boards are cartels. When they go too far in their regulation at the expense of consumers, board members can be sued—individually, and for money damages—for antitrust violations.

But if I or any of the justices thought this would mean real change for how the professions are regulated, we were wrong. There were some qualifications in the opinion that made it less powerful than it might have been—most importantly that boards "actively supervised" by state government were exempt from antitrust suits. However, the Court was not very clear about what counts as "supervision," and in the years since *North Carolina Dental*, boards have been able to exploit that uncertainty to avoid antitrust liability.[16]

Ultimately, the Supreme Court's opinion in *North Carolina Dental*, despite focusing on boards as the crux of what's wrong with professional licensing, was thus reduced to the same status as the other avenues for reform: tinkering around the edges. Since 2015, several lawsuits have been allowed to proceed, perhaps giving boards pause before defending their turf in ways that are obviously bad for competition.[17] The Federation of Associations of Regulatory Boards calls it "the case that shall not be named," and several times I heard board staff in Tennessee use the case to try pull back board members from their protectionist instincts.[18]

Real reform will have to take on the state licensing board system more directly. That requires some clear thinking about what licensing is good for in the first place, and whether licensing boards—as we know them—are good for anything at all.

# A Theory of Professional Licensing

Recall that I define professional licensing as a government-granted privilege to work that's given after a significant investment in human capital measured in months or years, without which professional practice is illegal. Recall that this kind of regulation almost certainly adds a hefty tax to services, has an unproven effect on service quality, erects high barriers to entry and mobility restrictions for workers, and can result in tragic scarcity of services for those who need them most. It's time to recognize that it should be a regulatory intervention of last resort, not a way to regulate three hundred professions and one-fifth of the American workforce, as we do now.

We can use a process of elimination to arrive at a theory for when to use licensing to regulate the market for professional services. First, we may ask whether governmental intervention is necessary at all. We learned in Chapter 3 that market forces can protect consumers where there is good information about provider quality, and the effects of bad practice are not particularly widespread. When someone raises the problem of bad professional service, we might first ask whether the market cannot be expected to protect the public because of information asymmetries and externalities.

If so, we would next ask questions about other regulatory interventions—ones that already exist, or ones that might serve as alternatives to professional licensing. Licensing is clumsy because it asks professionals to engage in months or years of education on topics they may never need to know about when they specialize. For example, a criminal attorney must demonstrate proficiency in contracts and property to get a license, and cosmetologists must learn perming and coloring even if they only plan to cut hair.

Other governmental regulation is narrower. For example, in Tennessee, day care centers are regulated not by professional licensing for providers but by premises licenses that demand short, targeted trainings for workers (on CPR, for example) and adherence to straightforward rules of practice. Regulations created by the Department of Human Services require, for instance, that babies sleep on their backs and that toddlers eat while secured in highchairs.[19] Note that the choice to use something other than licensing doesn't mean that childcare is less important or less dangerous than other work; indeed, it is hard to think of a job with higher stakes.

Premises licenses, backed up by inspections, govern establishments where sanitation and safe handling of chemicals is important, such as restaurants and dry cleaners. For the hair professions, we may think that a combination of market forces (for the bad haircuts)[20] and codified rules about sanitation (for the possibility of infection) are more reasonable means of protecting the public than a year of education and two examinations.

Where the risks to the public are harder for a regulator to observe during an inspection—such as fraud or theft—there are still other regulatory interventions that are more targeted and therefore more efficient than full-blown professional licensing. If an auctioneer absconds with a client's funds or misrepresents an item at auction, the criminal and civil systems may respond. To mitigate the risk that an auctioneer may slip through the cracks in these systems, states that don't require licensure for auctioneers do require them to post a bond and carry insurance to compensate aggrieved consumers.[21]

Rules that specify what is and isn't allowed (rather than vague ethical standards that require interpretation) and bonding or insurance requirements are simpler to enforce, cost consumers less, and create a much lower barrier to entry for workers than full-blown professional licensing. Perhaps most importantly, these forms of regulation do not need professional expertise to be administered, obviating the need for self-regulation.

The clearest illustration I have found of the difference between professional licensing and codified regulation comes from the death industry. In Tennessee, both a funeral director and someone operating a cemetery may handle dead bodies (neither can embalm—that's a separate license) and both deal with vulnerable consumers who are unlikely to be repeat customers. Both professionals are trusted to honor long-term promises, as when a funeral director makes a "pre-need" sale to a living person, or a cemetery commits to the upkeep of the burial grounds for future mourners. These similarities would suggest that the risks to the public posed by each of these professions are similar.

Their regulatory frameworks, however, are not. Funeral directors are regulated through professional licensure by a board dominated by funeral directors.[22] In contrast, cemeterians are regulated by the Burial Services Section program which is led by an assistant commissioner of the Department of Commerce and Insurance who's a full-time state employee and combines this work with other administrative and regulatory duties.[23]

Regulatory structures have dictated regulatory outcomes. Both regimes impose special reporting and financial requirements on pre-need sales, but only the funeral board enforces a year-long education requirement and a high-school degree on its licensees.[24] The regulatory focus of the funeral board is on disciplining unlicensed practice, where they take action in more than 90 percent of complaints (while only acting on about half of consumer complaints about service quality).[25] The assistant commissioner, in contrast, focuses his enforcement of the cemetery permit on compliance with the statutory financial and reporting requirements.[26]

If we removed from the current set of licensed professions those that could be well-regulated by the market, or through a codified set of rules administered by bureaucrats, what would be left? Another way of asking the question is this—for what kind of work is it impossible to reduce good practice to a finite set of straightforward rules of dos and don'ts?

Professional licensing is only appropriate for work that requires what I will call "professional judgment." This is the process of applying a complex system of knowledge to an individual case. The complexity of the abstract knowledge on the one hand, and the variety of possible individual needs of a client or patient on the other, create a nearly infinite matrix of appropriate professional choices. It's not possible, let alone desirable, for the government to try to tell these professionals how to handle their work at each step of the way. Relatedly, work that's appropriate for professional licensing will often be done independently, where professionals are given the autonomy to be their own boss and to decide for themselves how to handle their cases and clients. The more structured the work environment, the less appropriate the profession is for full-blown licensure.

Although it is possible to assess professional judgment after the fact (that is, or at least should be, the role of professional discipline), beforehand we can only enforce it indirectly. The best we can do is to ask the provider to go to school, pass an exam, and adhere to necessarily vague ethical rules of practice. We believe that someone who does these things is likely to have the necessary professional judgment to be a safe and effective provider. But notice how inefficient that regulation is. It requires extensive investment (often years!) before society can have confidence in that provider, and even then, we cannot really know if they will do a good job. We are just guessing based on their background and experience. That's another reason why, as a regulatory intervention, professional licensing should be somewhat of a last resort.

If we limit professional licensing to work that applies complicated knowledge on a case-by-case basis, then it will naturally include some high-status, high-prestige professions like medicine and law. But not all professions that are important or dangerous are ripe for professional licensing, as the childcare example makes clear. We need to decouple the idea of the seriousness or the social value of a profession from the idea of licensing. Of course, the ingrained sociological meaning of professional licensure will make this difficult, but we should nevertheless try to resist arguments for licensure based in social status and parity with other professions.

## Culling Professional Licensing

This theory of licensing would suggest that many professional licenses should be eliminated and others should be significantly streamlined. This legislative work can be achieved with bolder and more widespread use of sunset and sunrise review, which should be implemented in every state and for every profession.

Sunrise review, properly designed, can reframe the political debate about new or expanded licensure away from the "win-win" outcome sometimes perceived by legislatures who don't look hard at the costs of licensing. At the moment, sunset review frames the question in deregulatory terms—asking whether the government or the market best protects consumers. But states should be asking a less binary question— whether the profession in question poses a risk to the public *that cannot be mitigated through codified practice rules.* Sunset review should be designed to force legislatures to ask a similar set of questions of an existing licensed profession—whether licensing is necessary for this profession at all, and if so, whether the current rules can be justified in light of other regulatory possibilities.[27] Many currently licensed professions could not answer these questions satisfactorily.[28] In eliminating licensing through sunrise and sunset review, legislatures should be careful not to opt only for low-hanging fruit—the professions that lack the political clout to fight deregulation. Fairness and equality demand that all professions failing the test for licensure should face the chopping block.

By providing a middle path where the government regulates not though onerous educational or testing requirements but directly through codes and inspections, legislative review that applies my theory of licensing has a better chance of halting the spread of professional licensing than an all-or-nothing deregulatory approach, even if it does not stop governmental intervention when consumer protection calls for it.

## Fixing Boards

For work that poses a significant risk of harm to the public, and where good practice requires professional judgement, regulation requires an effective administrative system. The board system we have now works against public protection by increasing costs and the scarcity of professional services while also exposing the public to unacceptable risks from dangerous providers. Professional licensing, if done right, may be good for some professions (though fewer than we use it for today), but professional licensing boards, as currently conceived, aren't good for much at all. Boards have three main weaknesses: they are hopelessly underresourced, they are controlled by members of the profession they are supposed to regulate, and they use casual, collegial procedures for making decisions. Reform must take on all three problems.

First, boards need to be given the money, staff, data, and expertise to do their work. They need a budget that adequately covers timely investigations and allows for proactive measures, like periodic background checks, that would turn up criminal charges against a licensed professional. Boards should also have the funds to more extensively use databases like the National Practitioner Data Bank and state-controlled substance-monitoring programs that would reveal a pattern of dangerous or unethical practice. More information would lead to more cases, so resources must also be allocated to hiring more staff to follow up on investigations and prosecute cases. Less obviously, boards need more resources to pursue reasonable rulemaking; without access to systematic data and expert reports about how a rule might affect practice and the availability of providers, boards are left guessing and revert to learned patterns of protectionism.

These solutions to well-documented problems are obvious, and they have been proposed many times. Why, then, are boards still not given what they need to do their work? The simple answer is that it's expensive for states. But as the saying goes, you get what you pay for. States have had to pay millions to settle suits over state-employed doctors whose misdeeds were enabled by a licensing board.[29] Tennessee alone has spent billions of dollars to combat an opioid crisis enabled by nonexistent discipline for prescribers.[30] Add to that the financial burdens states and the federal government have had to take on because of an overwhelmed healthcare system whose pathologies include licensing turf wars and ever-higher professional barriers to entry. It's time for states to recognize that underfunding boards is penny wise and pound foolish.

Second, board membership needs to reflect the true set of stakeholders in professional practice, not just the profession itself. When I attended licensing board meetings, the word "stakeholder" was always used to refer to members of the profession. But the true stakeholders in a profession's regulation go well beyond its practitioners. In other areas of state administration, the boards reflect a range of perspectives. For example, Tennessee's Air Pollution Control Board comprises a physician, an engineer, a professor, a farmer, a member of the auto industry, three people in manufacturing, a conservationist, an environmentalist, two people from city government, and two administrators from state government.[31] The board's work has analogies to professional licensing; it makes rules, issues permits (like licenses), and decides individual controversies about violations and variances (like disciplinary action).

A licensing board could reflect this structure. In the course of my research, I had many occasions to meet people with important perspectives on professional regulation, from advocates for patients' rights fighting for safer medical boards to professors studying the lack of legal services for the poor. For example, I got to know Monti Herring, who works for Prevention Partnership, a Nashville-based nonprofit organization that provides Narcan and training on how to use it to homeless shelters and first responders. (Narcan is an overdose-reversing drug that saves lives that would otherwise be lost to the opioid crisis.) As someone in recovery himself, Monti has deep professional experience in how the practice of medicine has contributed to the crisis of addiction in our state. I asked him if he would be willing to sit on a hypothetical medical licensing advisory board, and he said "absolutely." He speculated that he "would ask totally different questions" from the physician members.[32]

In setting the statutory membership rules for licensing boards, legislatures should give a voice to advocates for consumer and patient rights— experts on licensing's effects on public health, employment, equality, and access to services. The few public members who currently serve on professional licensing boards are inadequate to represent these interests because they don't have expertise to offer beyond the common sense they've acquired as an occasional consumer of professional services. Professional members should comprise a minority on the board, there to provide professional expertise as one of several inputs into the decision-making process.

Members should be selected based on merit, not political patronage, through an open, competitive process and according to pre-identified, relevant qualifications. When necessary to attract qualified candidates, board members should be compensated for their time at a rate commensurate with their expertise. This would ensure not only expert, engaged decision-makers, but it would also allow them to devote enough time to their regulatory work.

Third, board procedure needs to be overhauled to be less like a collegial, private meeting and more like the government regulation it purports to be. Boards should not be allowed to go into executive session except for deliberations in disciplinary cases, where having to hash out a disciplinary order in front of the accused cuts against public protection. Meetings should be live-streamed and recordings made available on easily-found state websites. Boards should post public records like budgets and minutes as a matter of course.

Professional discipline, especially, needs a procedural overhaul, from the complaint process to the resolution of cases. All states should use an online complaint system that does not bully patients and clients into keeping mum. Complainants, including employers such as hospitals, should receive immunity from lawsuits for complaints filed in good faith.[33] States should publish anonymized complaint data about providers and hold all complaints for context in the event of future complaints, even after the statute of limitations (which, in most cases, should be lengthened) has run.

Next, investigations should be swift, thorough, and as independent from professional bias as possible (the Tennessee system of giving a physician the authority to secretly decide whether a case warrants investigation and, again, whether an investigation merits charges, is unacceptable). Investigations and charging decisions should be guided by clear, detailed, and public guidance. Charging documents should be public, as they are in the criminal and civil legal systems, and plea deals should not be allowed. Any professional whose misconduct is serious enough to merit the filing of charges should be subject to a public airing of the facts, not a curated "consent order" with sanitized information about the wrongdoing.

Contested cases should be more adversarial, structured, and guided by clear criteria. Cases should apply a "preponderance of the evidence" standard, not something more generous to the accused professional, as some states do.[34] They should be bifurcated into a fact-finding phase and a sanction phase, where during the latter the rules of evidence are relaxed to give the tribunal a fuller picture of the professional's life and career before the alleged misconduct. And the decision-makers should be guided by rules and policies—created by the board through notice-and-comment rulemaking—about everything from the theory of professional discipline to the minutiae of board orders like when to use practice monitoring. States should create advisory sanction ranges for given offenses to promote uniformity and counter the tendency to cut slack in individual cases. Failure to adhere to guidelines or advisory ranges should increase the risk that a court will throw out the disciplinary decision as "arbitrary and capricious."

Finally, cases should be heard by panels that have training and expertise in professional regulation, where no more than one member is from the profession of the accused. Panels should include at least one lawyer to provide some expertise in the adversarial system (this may be an administrative law judge, the kind that rules on procedural issues in Tennessee). To the extent more expertise is necessary to understand the conduct in question, the parties could call expert witnesses. That's how medical malpractice trials use experts. The idea that a doctor is entitled to a malpractice jury made up of mostly other doctors would offend notions of due process in civil trials, as it should in professional administrative hearings.

## Finding Models for Board Reform

Some elements from the three categories of reform—increasing boards' resources, diversifying their membership, and changing their procedures—have precedent in at least one state. (As we'll see later, most of the suggestions found above are used in concert, and to notable success, in the United Kingdom.)

None of the fifty states dedicate enough funds to regulate the professions that need it, but some seem to do more with less. A few states "continuous query" the National Practitioner Data Bank for instant information on changes to their licensees' criminal status, hospital discipline, and malpractice history. In Colorado, an umbrella agency provides the necessary staffing, data, and analysis that its boards need to understand the impact of their licensing decisions. That state's Department of Regulatory

Agencies (DORA) comprises six hundred regulatory staff who, among other regulatory tasks, review new and existing professional licenses to "ensure that they are necessary, fair, effective, and efficient."[35]

Diversifying board membership has been a slow process since the reform was first suggested decades ago, but in a few states and for a few professions, nonprofessional board members have achieved parity or even dominance over professional members. California seems to be the leader here, with professionals dominating less than half of its licensing boards. But even there, boards governing the healthcare professions— where the stakes of regulation are perhaps the highest—tend to be dominated by practitioners.

Likewise, examples of better board decision-making procedures can be found around the country. Tennessee records and posts board meetings and does not allow boards to discuss matters privately. Some states have more robust board member training systems than the brief intro Dr. Loyd was given when he joined Tennessee's medical board. Delaware provides explicit, public guidance for boards in disciplinary cases, even if a close reading reveals that many of the recommended sanction ranges are too wide to meaningfully constrain boards' decision-making.[36] In a minority of states, an administrative law judge tries disciplinary cases, not a panel dominated by professionals. This is an improvement on the typical disciplinary system where professionals truly face a jury of their peers. But even in this handful of states, the judge's opinion is merely advisory; a board dominated by professionals must give it the green light.

To see what all these reforms might look like in the aggregate, we have to go abroad. The United Kingdom, for example, uses two different regulatory bodies to oversee the profession of medicine, both of which improve upon the American model.[37] The members of the General Medical Council (GMC), the body responsible for setting the terms of professional entry and practice, are merit-selected, trained in their regulatory role, and paid a competitive wage for their part-time work. Only half the seats go to physicians. The GMC investigates disciplinary cases, but hands off adjudications to the Medical Professional Tribunal Service (MPTS).[38]

The MPTS follows a decision-making protocol far more guided, transparent, and adversarial than that used by the typical American licensing board. Plea bargaining doesn't exist; all cases are tried to a panel of three drawn from a pool of people who are also merit-selected, trained, and paid.[39] A disciplinary panel must comprise one lawyer, one doctor, and one lay member; in most cases, this has the effect of limiting the number of doctors to one-out-of-three members.[40] Panelists are constrained by more than forty official documents guiding their decisions about facts, fitness to practice, and sanction.[41] Decisions are internally reviewed for appropriateness and consistency, and may also be appealed by an arm of the National Health Service as well as by the physician.[42]

Any comparison between systems so different—an American state licensing board and a national regulator of healthcare providers in a country with socialized medicine—should be taken with a grain of salt. Yet the empirical evidence we have suggests that the British disciplinary system works better. British patients complain less frequently about their doctors and, based on recent data I collected with a colleague in the UK, the British system imposes a serious sanction more frequently in almost any category of offense. For example, fraud was punished more harshly in the UK (serious sanctions in 89 percent of cases with a finding of fraud versus 63 percent in Tennessee). And the UK suspended or revoked a license in 95 percent of cases where the board found that the doctor had engaged in sexual misconduct. In Tennessee, that number is just 33 percent.[43]

Importing the British system of professional licensure to the United States is not, of course, a straightforward task. One of the biggest differences between the two jurisdictions is that the UK enjoys the economies of scale lost in a state-by-state system. But even if recreating the British system for every state and every profession would be prohibitively expensive, efficiencies could be found by combining professions within a state. For example, New York uses an agency housed in the Department of Education to hear disciplinary cases for most professions.[44] Cases are heard by three-person panels drawn from a large and diverse set of professionals and lay people. In practice, quorum rules—that a panel must comprise two members of the "relevant" board—recreate the professional bias so problematic in American professional discipline, but the example suggests that combining professions under one state regulatory authority may be a way to keep down the costs of adequate regulation.[45]

A more dramatic way to achieve economies of scale would be to create federal professional licenses that preempt state regulation altogether. If we were writing on a clean slate, this may be a plausible design. Not only would national licenses for each profession be efficient in terms of regulatory resources, but they would ease interstate mobility. One serious downside to a national license, however, is that to achieve political viability, the license may have to approximate the requirements from the most onerous state so as not to be seen as *reducing* public safety anywhere. The effect, of course, would be to increase licensure burdens for just about everyone, in the name of bureaucratic efficiency and interstate mobility. Indeed, something like this ratchet effect is in play in interstate compacts—agreements among participating states to honor a single license—where requirements tend to be especially burdensome.

To be clear, we are not writing on a clean slate. Hundreds of years of state regulation of the professions has created strong political winds against federal preemption in this area and the professions themselves can be expected to cling to the status quo. They will raise arguments about tradition, states' rights, and perhaps even the constitutionality of federal professional licensing.[46] Until the crisis of professional regulation becomes so acute that Congress decides to take the drastic step of preempting state licensure and risk being batted down by the Supreme Court, reform will have to be state by state.

## . . . Or Eliminating the Board System as We Know It

Will these changes to licensing boards' resources, membership, and procedures be enough? There is only one way to find out. But if not, there is another approach, one suggested by the fact that the state professional licensing board is a regulatory anomaly. States could scrap the board system altogether and use what they do for virtually every other kind of regulation: a governmental agency, vested with the authority to make decisions in its own right, that uses input from industry as one of several sources of information.

As I watched licensing boards at work, I often felt like the people in the room who knew the most about the practice acts being interpreted and applied, and who seemed best positioned to decide in the public interest, were the state employees who had no vote—the executive directors, attorneys, full-time consultants, and administrative law judges. In many other areas of regulation, civil servants do the deciding while industry does the lobbying. Professional licensure could be like that, too.

For some professions, legislatures could replace the decision-making body with a single bureaucrat, like the assistant commissioner who runs the Burial Services Sector program in Tennessee. Administrative law requires certain processes for rulemaking and disciplinary decisions; each of these provides an opportunity for input from the regulated entities. If the head of a licensing program needed professional expertise beyond what's provided at these hearings, he or she could hire a consultant or convene a taskforce. The crucial difference between a commissioner-run program and a licensing board is that experts from within industry would be providing information, not making the decision in the final instance.

For complex professions, legislatures may recognize that expertise will be needed in a more sustained way. One way of harnessing expertise, and one with precedent in state government, is to use an advisory board. My personal favorite in this category is Tennessee's Elevator and Amusement Device Safety Board, which advises the Department of Labor and Workforce Development on "everything that goes up and down and round and round."[47] The board comprises representatives from the industry (when I attended a board meeting, the COO of Dollywood was a member), public representatives, and someone from the insurance industry.[48] Final decision-making power, however, is vested in the Department of Labor.

At least one state uses advisory licensing boards. Vermont, which holds itself out as a state with less-than-average professional red tape, vests final decision-making authority over professional licensing decisions in a state official. In implementation, however, the system falls short of the fully accountable, bureaucratized system I have in mind. The Vermont boards—which are, of course, dominated by professionals—do not merely advise, they perform all the rulemaking and disciplinary work in the first instance, subject to a final sign-off from the commissioner.[49] The commissioner does sometimes veto board decisions, and the threat of her disapproval undoubtedly pushes regulation at least slightly more toward public protection, but it is easy to imagine that the sign-off often acts as a rubber stamp. If states are to wrest regulation away from the professionals themselves, they may have to do so in a more robust way.

We should, of course, be aware of the downsides of bureaucratizing professional licensing. Regulating the professions through the political process may address the problems identified in this book, but also creates new ones. Issues that once seemed like ethical or scientific debates internal to the professions have become explicitly politicized. There are many examples in medicine, from COVID-vaccine safety, to the ethicality of abortion, or gender-affirming care. Law, too, has seen its share of political controversy over bar rules about nondiscrimination in client selection and mandated antiracism trainings for new lawyers. Likewise, psychologists have clashed with state governments over whether the profession can ban gay conversion therapy as a matter of professional ethics. Giving the licensing system a more direct line of accountability to the legislature risks taking these questions out of the professions' hands and putting them in the hands of the electorate.

Whether you think this is a good or a bad thing in the individual case probably depends on which professional rule we're talking about and what state you live in. But the current state of professional licensing is bad enough that some tradeoffs would seem appropriate. It is also not clear that the system we have isn't already subject to political influence of the kind we might worry about in a more bureaucratized system. In 2021, as licensed physicians were pushing a social media campaign spreading misinformation about the safety of the COVID vaccine (that it would "magnetize" your body, for example), the Tennessee Medical Board posted to its website a policy that such misinformation was grounds for professional discipline. After my state legislature pressured them to take it down (under threat of "dissolving" the medical board), they did so.[50]

It is also not clear that the risks of politicization are as high for other professions as they are for law and medicine, nor that they couldn't be mitigated through proper regulatory design. For example, licensing agencies could be designed as "independent" agencies—not subject to removal and reappointment with every change in leadership, or financially independent from the legislature. In any case, reform that makes professional licensing more politically accountable should account for unintended consequences.

Old problems die hard. For more than a century, we have put the professions on a pedestal, defined their identity as one of exclusion, and then given them legal authority to decide who is in and who is out of their club. We defined the value of a profession by whether it has a state licensing board, and as a result their number and the percentage of workers organized under them has exploded. We gave these ostensible state agencies power without accountability, with higher costs to the public than most people realize.

There is no silver bullet for a problem this complex and longstanding. Easy solutions will help a little, but real change will take hard work. The first step is to realize that our experiment of giving the professions unfettered autonomy over their regulation has been a failure. The next is to see that we need to use licensing as a regulatory last resort and to administer it in the public interest. Convincing the people in power that these things are true will be difficult, but not impossible. Indeed, if we want a system that does more than protect the public in name only, then it is essential.

# Notes

## INTRODUCTION

1.    April 9, 2018, meeting of Tennessee Board of Cosmetology and Barber Examiners.

2.    Keith M. Macdonald, *The Sociology of the Professions* (London: Sage, 1995), 1.

3.    Sociologists have long debated what constitutes a "profession." For example, see Rudy Volti, *An Introduction to the Sociology of Work and Occupations,* 2nd ed. (Los Angeles: Sage, 2012), 153–156. My definition is not sociological but legal: if you have a personally held license that you earned through a significant investment in human capital, you are a licensed professional.

4.    Because this book concerns professional licensing (requiring a significant investment in human capital), I was not able to rely directly on existing estimates of the rate of *occupational* licensure, which includes some licenses requiring more minor qualification, like attending a training or posting a bond. To learn how much of the American workforce was covered by professional licensing as I have defined it, I requested public records from a sample of American states (California, Illinois, and Tennessee) asking for the number of licenses issued by their professional boards. After excluding licenses issued to out-of-state workers, I extrapolated the number of licenses issued by each of those three states to the rest of the country according to population, arriving at approximately thirty million licensed workers. This estimate is, of course, approximate, and it is predictably lower than existing estimates of *occupational* licensing which range from 22 percent to 32 percent of American workers. US Bureau of Labor Statistics, "Labor Force Statistics from the Current Population Survey," 2023, https://www.bls.gov/cps/cpsaat49.htm; Morris M. Kleiner and Evgeny Vorotnikov, "Analyzing Occupational Licensing among the States," *Journal of Regulatory Economics* 52, no. 1 (June 2017): 134; Beth Redbird, "The New Closed Shop? The Economic and Structural Effects of Occupational Licensure," *American Sociological Review* 82, no. 3 (June 2017): 600.

5.    The sum of workers that make the federal minimum wage or are illegally paid less than it constitutes less than 2 percent of all hourly workers. US Bureau of Labor Statistics, *Report No. 1085, Characteristics of Minimum Wage Workers, 2019* (2020), 1, https://www.bls.gov/opub/reports/minimum-wage/2019/pdf/home.pdf.

6.    US Bureau of Labor Statistics, *Union Members—2023* (2024), https://www.bls.gov/news.release/pdf/union2.pdf.

7.    Estimates of the premium licensing adds to the price of professional services vary from 5 percent to 33 percent, but most find a price effect of around or in excess of 10 percent. Morris M. Kleiner, *Guild-Ridden Labor Markets: The Curious Case of Occupational Licensing* (Kalamazoo: W. E. Upjohn Institute, 2015), 35.

8.    Researchers found the wage premium for unionization was 11 percent in 2020. David A. MacPherson and Barry T. Hirsch, "Five Decades of Union Wages, Nonunion Wages, and Union Wage Gaps at Unionstats.Com" (IZA Discussion Paper 14398, Institute of Labor Economics, Bonn, Germany, May 2021), 7.

9.    Department of the Treasury Office of Economic Policy, Council of Economic Advisers, and Department of Labor, *Occupational Licensing: A Framework for Policymakers* (2015), https://obamawhitehouse.archives.gov/sites/default/files/docs/licensing_report_final_nonembargo.pdf; Brink Lindsey and Steven Teles, *The Captured Economy* (New York, Oxford University Press, 2017).

10.    For but one example from a large volume of work on the subject, see Kleiner, *Guild-Ridden Labor Markets,* 30.

11.    Aaron S. Edlin and Rebecca Haw, "Cartels by Another Name: Should Licensed Occupations Face Antitrust Scrutiny?," *University of Pennsylvania Law Review* 162, no. 5 (April 2014): 1093–1161; Rebecca Haw Allensworth, "The New Antitrust Federalism," *Virginia Law Review* 102, no. 6 (October 2016): 1387–1445; Rebecca Haw Allensworth, "Foxes at the Henhouse: Occupational Licensing Boards Up Close," *California Law Review* 105, no. 6 (December 2017): 1567–1609; North Carolina State Board of Dental Examiners v. FTC, 574 U.S. 494, 500 (2015) (citing Edlin and Haw, "Cartels,"); Department of the Treasury Office of Economic Policy, Council of Economic Advisers, and Department of Labor, *Occupational Licensing: A Framework for Policymakers* (2015) (citing Edlin and Haw, "Cartels,"); *Barriers to Opportunity: Do Occupational Licensing Laws Unfairly Limit Entrepreneurship and Jobs: Hearing before H. Comm. on Small Business,* 113th Cong., 2d. Sess. (2014) (congressional testimony, statement by Rebecca Haw) https://www.govinfo.gov/content/pkg/CHRG-113hhrg87281/html/CHRG-113hhrg87281.

htm; *Occupational Licensing: Regulation and Competition: Hearing before H. Comm. on Judiciary,* 115th Congress, 1st Sess. (2017), https://www.govinfo.gov /content/pkg/CHRG-115hhrg29777/html/CHRG-115hhrg29777.htm (congressional testimony, statement by Rebecca H. Allensworth).

12.  *Dent v. West Virginia,* 129 U.S. 114 (1889), conferred upon the states the right to license professions in the name of public health, welfare, or safety, allowing licensing to proliferate in the ensuing decades. That regulation crowded out federal involvement when the Court expanded federal regulatory authority to its modern-day extent in *Wickard v. Filburn,* 317 U.S. 111 (1942).

13.  S. David Young, *The Rule of Experts: Occupational Licensing in America* (Washington, DC: Cato Institute, 1987), 81.

14.  Kara Schmitt, *Demystifying Occupational and Professional Regulation* (Orlando: Professional Testing, 2015), 41; Stanley J. Gross, *Of Foxes and Hen Houses: Licensing and the Health Professions* (Westport, CT: Quorum Books, 1984), 97–98.

15.  Allensworth, "Foxes at the Henhouse," 1570.

16.  Benjamin H. Barton, "Do Judges Systematically Favor the Interests of the Legal Profession?," *Alabama Law Review* 59, no. 2 (2008): 455.

17.  Benjamin Shimberg, *Occupational Licensing: A Public Perspective* (Princeton, NJ: Educational Testing Service, 1980), 22–25.

18.  Gross, *Foxes and Hen Houses,* 102.

19.  For an excellent account of the unpaid drudgery of board work (among many other contributions made by this remarkable book—one of the few academic books about licensing boards), see Ruth Horowitz, *In the Public Interest: Medical Licensing and the Disciplinary Process* (New Brunswick, NJ: Rutgers University Press, 2013).

20.  Allensworth, "Foxes at the Henhouse," 1570.

21.  Some states even require that governors only appoint board members from a list provided by the state association. "Occupational Licensing: A Framework for Policymakers," *Occupational Licensing: Benefits, Costs, and Issues,* ed. Margie Castro (New York: Nova, 2016), 51.

22.  Eliot Freidson, *Profession of Medicine: A Study of the Sociology of Applied Knowledge* (New York: Harper & Row, 1970), 185, 368.

23.  The facts about this physician's 2017 discipline are from his contested case hearing (Docket No. 17.18-183745A, 47–48, 68–69 [Tennessee Board of Medical Examiners, March 8, 2017]) and board order (Case No. 17.18–183745A [Tennessee Department of Health, September 26, 2017]).

24. March 20, 2018, meeting of the Tennessee Board of Medical Examiners.

25. Morris M. Kleiner and Evgeny Vorotnikov, "Analyzing Occupational Licensing among the States," *Journal of Regulatory Economics* 52, no. 1 (June 2017): 132–158; Carrie Teegardin and Saurabh Datar, "How Well Does Your State Protect Patients?," *Atlanta Journal-Constitution,* https://doctors.ajc.com/states/.

26. Wilbert E. Moore and Gerald W. Rosenblum, *The Professions: Roles and Rules* (New York: Russell Sage Foundation, 1970).

27. Richard Susskind and Daniel Susskind, *The Future of the Professions: How Technology Will Transform the Work of Human Experts* (New York: Oxford University Press, 2015), 21–23.

28. Susskind and Susskind, *Future of the Professions,* 22.

## 1. THE RATCHET

1. All biographic details about Fatou Diouf are from interviews with the author in May 2018 and November 2020.

2. Tenn. Code Ann. § 62-4-110(e)(2) (2023).

3. Valerie Bayham, *A Dream Deferred: Legal Barriers to African Hairbraiding Nationwide* (Arlington, VA: Institute for Justice, December 2005), https://ij.org /report/a-dream-deferred/.

4. Ayana Byrd and Lori L. Tharps, *Hair Story: Untangling the Roots of Black Hair in America* (New York: St. Martin's Griffin, 2014); Princess Gabbara, "The History of the Afro," *Ebony,* March 2, 2017, https://www.ebony.com/the-history-of-the-afro/.

5. Mark Flatten, "Protection Racket: Occupational Licensing Laws and the Right to Earn a Living," *Regulatory Reform / Taxes* (blog), Goldwater Institute, December 6, 2016, https://www.goldwaterinstitute.org/protection-racket-occupational -licensing-laws-and/.

6. Evan Carter, "Salon Owner Gets Tangled in Licensing Laws," *Detroit News,* August 1, 2017, https://www.detroitnews.com/story/opinion/2017/08/01/licensing -hair-braiding/104210462/; Eric Stern, "The Legal Tangle over Braids," *St. Louis Post-Dispatch,* March 11, 2001, https://www.proquest.com/newspapers/legal -tangle-over-braids/docview/404086334/se-2; William Mellor and Dick M. Carpenter II, *Bottleneckers: Gaming the Government for Power and Private Profit* (New York: Encounter Books, 2016).

7. Tenn. Code Ann. § 62-4-102(3) (2019).

8. Tenn. Code Ann. § 62-4-110(e)(2) (2023).

9. EMTs must complete about 180 hours of training total. Tennessee Department of Health, Initial License Requirements for Emergency Medical Technician (EMT), https://www.tn.gov/content/dam/tn/health/events/Initial%20License%20for%20Emergency%20Medical%20Technician.pdf.

10. Director of graduate counseling program, Trevecca Nazarene University, in discussion with the author, May 2020.

11. National Conference of State Legislatures, "Occupational Licensing: Assessing State Policy and Practice" (Washington, DC: NCSL, 2019); S. David Young, *The Rule of Experts: Occupational Licensing in America* (Washington, DC: Cato Institute: 1987).

12. April 5, 2019, Tennessee Board of Alcohol and Drug Abuse Counselors.

13. December 19, 2019, Tennessee Senate Committee on Government Relations meeting (at 1:32:30).

14. Patrick A. McLaughlin, Matthew D. Mitchell, and Anne Philpot, *The Effects of Occupational Licensure on Competition, Consumers, and the Workforce* (Fairfax, VA: Mercatus Center, George Mason University, November 3, 2017), https://www.mercatus.org/publications/corporate-welfare/effects-occupational-licensure-competition-consumers-and-workforce; Aaron S. Edlin and Rebecca Haw, "Cartels by Another Name: Should Licensed Occupations Face Antitrust Scrutiny?," *University of Pennsylvania Law Review* 162, no. 5 (April 2014): 1093–1161.

15. American Medical Association, *Report of the Council on Medical Service: Cover of and Payment for Telemedicine,* June 2014, https://www.jonesday.com/en/insights/2014/06/american-medical-association-offers-new-telemedicine-recommendations. At the January 14, 2015, Tennessee Board of Medical Examiners meeting, members expressed concerns that telemedicine could "open [. . .] the door for fraud and abuse."

16. Wilbert E. Moore and Gerald W. Rosenblum, *The Professions: Roles and Rules* (New York: New Russell Foundation, 1970).

17. Richard Posner writes about the "professional mystique" that accompanies a profession's claim of elite or learned status, noting that the shakier a profession's knowledge claims, the most urgent the need for this mystique. Richard A. Posner, "Professionalisms," *Arizona Law Review* 40, no. 1 (1998): 1–15. Licensure can provide the required mystique.

18. National Association of Alcohol and Drug Abuse Counselors, *How-To Series: Licensing of Addiction Professionals in States* (March 2011), https://www.naadac.org/assets/2416/naadac_model_state_licensure_bill.pdf.

19.  November 8–9, 2018, Council for Interior Design Qualification Conference, Nashville, TN.

20.  Student, Austin Beauty College, attending April 9, 2018, meeting of the Tennessee Board of Cosmetology and Barber Examiners.

21.  Richard Susskind and Daniel Susskind, *The Future of the Professions: How Technology Will Transform the Work of Human Experts* (New York: Oxford University Press, 2015); Keith McDonald, *The Sociology of the Professions* (London: Sage, 1995).

22.  Dental hygienist and advocate, in discussion with the author, May 2018. This point is echoed in the sociological literature on licensing. *See* Eliot L. Freidson, *Profession of Medicine: A Study of the Sociology of Applied Knowledge* (New York: Dodd, Mead, 1970), 368 ("autonomy is the prize sought by virtually all occupational groups").

23.  National Traffic and Motor Vehicle Safety Act of 1966, Pub. L. No. 89-563, 80 Stat. 718 (1966); Banking Act of 1933 (Glass-Steagall Act), Pub. L. No. 73-66, 48 Stat. 162, 162 (1933).

24.  S. David Young, *The Rule of Experts: Occupational Licensing in America* (Washington, DC: Cato Institute, 1987).

25.  Morris M. Kleiner, *Guild-Ridden Labor Markets: The Curious Case of Occupational Licensing* (Kalamazoo: W. E. Upjohn Institute, 2015), 30; Charles Wheelan, "Occupational Licensure: The Elephant in the Labor Market," *University of St. Thomas Journal of Law & Public Policy* 5, no. 2 (January 2011): 16–28.

26.  Julie Fellmeth (professor and staff attorney, Center for Public Interest Law at University of California, San Diego), in discussion with the author, June 2018.

27.  November 8–9, 2018, Council for Interior Design Qualification Conference, Nashville, TN.

28.  Academics writing about the political economy of licensing have long made this observation. Morris M. Kleiner, *Licensing Occupations: Ensuring Quality or Restricting Competition?* (Kalamazoo: Upjohn Press, 2006); Mellor and Carpenter, *Bottleneckers,* XI; Donald L. Martin, "Will the Sun Set on Occupational Licensing?," in *Occupational Licensure and Regulation,* ed. Simon Rottenberg (Washington, DC: American Enterprise for Public Policy Research, 1980), 148. Their accounts fit with what I heard during my interviews with Tennessee legislators.

29.  National Conference of State Legislatures, "Full- and Part-Time Legislatures," July 28, 2021, https://www.ncsl.org/research/about-state-legislatures/full-and-part-time-legislatures.aspx.

30. This was a common justification I heard for new professional licenses—that insurance companies would only cover a service if it was licensed by the state. While licensure that facilitates third-party payment is clearly good for professionals, its effect on the rest of the public is unclear. For insured patients wanting to use that service, licensure that comes with third-party payment may increase access because they can now obtain the service more cheaply, perhaps with a mere copay. However, because licensure increases prices, the license is also likely to increase the *actual* cost of the service to the insurance company. That cost is likely to be passed on to all insured patients in the form of higher premiums. How this nets out is an empirical question that should be answered before we accept the idea of third-party payment as a public-regarding justification for licensure. Even more fundamentally, we should ask why insurance companies would insist on licensure—effectively raising their own costs—for reimbursement. I suspect that the answer is to assure quality. Insurance companies believe they cannot cost-effectively monitor providers' safety and competence, and so they outsource this regulation to state boards. If this is the reason for the insistence on licensure, however, the lessons of Part II teach us that insurance companies' reliance on quality control from boards may be misplaced.

31. Joe Pitts (member, Tennessee House of Representatives) in discussion with the author, July 2018.

32. Tenn. Code Ann. § 63-11-401 (2022).

33. North Carolina State Board of Dental Examiners v. FTC, 574 U.S. 494 (2015).

34. As an administrative law judge told me during a break from a contested disciplinary case over which he was presiding, the professionals who get selected as board members are those who are "at the top of their profession who know everything and the governor, too." Steve Darnell (administrative law judge), in discussion with the author, May 2019.

35. Former member of the Tennessee Board of Chiropractic Examiners, in discussion with the author, June 2018.

36. For two examples, see July 30–31, 2019, Tennessee Board of Medical Examiners; December 7, 2017, Tennessee Board of Architectural and Engineering Examiners.

37. April 9, 2018, Tennessee Board of Cosmetology and Barber Examiners.

38. July 2018, Tennessee Taskforce of the Board of Physical Therapy (statement of the chair).

39. S.B. 2473, 110th Gen. Assemb., Reg. Sess. (Tenn. 2018).

40. Former member of the Tennessee Board of Chiropractic Examiners, in discussion with the author, June 2018.

41. Former member, Tennessee Board of Massage Licensure, in conversation with the author, June 2021 ("elevate"); member, Tennessee Board of Veterinary Medical Examiners, in conversation with the author, April 2018 ("advocate for"); cosmetologist attending January 23, 2020, Federation of Associations of Regulatory Boards, Colorado Springs, CO ("keep us regulated").

42. June 21, 2022, National Conference of State Legislatures, "The National Occupational Licensing Meeting," Las Vegas, NV.

43. Member, Tennessee Board of Medical Examiners, in discussion with the author, July 2019.

44. July 30–31, 2019, Tennessee Board of Medical Examiners.

45. June 14, 2018, Tennessee Board of Architectural and Engineering Examiners; April 20, 2018, Tennessee Board Alcohol and Drug Abuse Counselors; May 18, 2018, Tennessee Board of Physical Therapy; March 20, 2018, Tennessee Board of Medical Examiners.

46. April 26, 2018, Tennessee Board of Dentistry.

47. Interview not for attribution, in discussion with the author, June 2018.

48. Advanced practice registered nurse and member of the Tennessee Board of Nursing and Opioid Minimum Discipline Taskforce, in discussion with the author, April 2019.

49. Tennessee Comptroller of the Treasury, *Performance Audit Report: Regulatory Boards in the Department of Commerce and Insurance* (2017), 22–23.

50. November 17, 2015, Tennessee Board for Licensing Contractors. In addition to this one-time payment, the board also pays 50 percent of its surplus to Go Build Tennessee on an ongoing basis. For a similar arrangement where a board's surplus goes to the professional association, see Stanley J. Gross, *Of Foxes and Hen Houses: Licensing and the Health Professions* (Westport, CT: Quorum Books, 1984), 100.

51. January 23, 2020, Federation of Associations of Regulatory Boards, Colorado Springs, CO.

52. Interview not for attribution, in discussion with the author, June 2018.

53. Benjamin Powell and Evgeny Vorotnikov, "Real Estate Continuing Education: Rent Seeking or Improvement in Service Quality?," *Eastern Economic Journal* 38, no. 1 (2012): 71.

54. "US Continuing Medical Education Market—Industry Outlook & Forecast 2023–2028," Arizton, July 2023, https://www.arizton.com/market-reports/us-continuing-medical-education-market. ("The US continuing medical education market size was valued at USD 2.91 billion in 2022 and is expected to reach USD 4.23 billion by 2028, growing at a CAGR of 6.43% during the forecast period.")

55. April 11, 2019, Tennessee Board of Dentistry; May 3, 2018, Tennessee State Board of Accountancy; August 29, 2018, Tennessee Opioid Minimum Discipline Taskforce.

56. Licensed professional counselor and professor at Middle Tennessee State University, in discussion with the author, May 2020.

57. May 18, 2018, Tennessee Board of Physical Therapy.

58. May 18, 2018, Tennessee Board of Physical Therapy; June 1, 2018, Tennessee Board for Licensed Professional Counselors, Licensed Marital and Family Therapists and Licensed Clinical Pastoral Therapists.

59. "Application and Instructions for Licensure as a Dietitian / Nutritionist," Tennessee Department of Health, https://www.tn.gov/content/dam/tn/health/health profboards/nursing/DN_Online_Application.pdf; "CDR's Roles and Governance," Commission on Dietetic Registration, February 2, 2023, https://www.cdrnet.org /cdrs-roles.

60. Licensed professional counselor and professor at Middle Tennessee State University, in discussion with the author, May 2020.

61. "Taking the United States Medical Licensing Examination," National Board of Medical Examiners, accessed February 3, 2024, https://www.nbme.org /examinees/united-states-medical-licensing-exam-usmle#exam-fees; "Step 3 Application Fees," Federation of State Medical Boards, accessed February 3, 2024, https://www.fsmb.org/step-3/step-3-application-fees/.

62. "2024 Graduate Degree Requirement—Registration Eligibility," Commission on Dietetic Registration, accessed February 3, 2023, https://www.cdrnet.org/ graduatedegree.

63. Stephen Elliott, "Supreme Court Rules Argentine Can Take Tennessee Bar," *Nashville Post*, August 4, 2017, https://www.nashvillepost.com/business /legal/article/20971591/supreme-court-rules-argentine-can-take-tennessee-bar. The total cost of attendance for Vanderbilt Law School's one-year LLM program in 2022–2023 was $95,928. "LL.M. Cost & Financial Aid," Vanderbilt Law School, updated 2023, https://law.vanderbilt.edu/prospective-students/llm-program-/llm budget.php.

64. "Federation of Associations of Regulatory Boards," FARB, updated 2023, https://farb.org/home; "Federation of State Medical Boards," FSMB, updated 2018, https://www.fsmb.org/.

65. Humayun Chaudhry (president and CEO, Federation of State Medical Boards) in discussion with the author, May 2018.

66. The National Auctioneer License Law Officials Association (NALLOA) holds an annual seminar in conjunction with the National Auctioneer Association (NAA) Conference. "About Us," NALLOA, https://nalloa.org/about-us/.

67. *Sunset Laws: Hearing on S.B. 1555 before the S. Gov't Operations Comm.,* 2018 Leg., 110th Sess. (Tenn. 2018).

68. Director of graduate counseling program, Trevecca Nazarene University, in discussion with the author, May 2020.

69. As one board member told me, about attending board meetings with her educator colleague, "most of the time we're there. If [the board has] an issue, they'll just stop the meeting and ask us." Licensed professional counselor and professor at Middle Tennessee State University, in discussion with the author, May 2020.

70. May 18, 2018, Tennessee Board of Physical Therapy.

71. April 9, 2018, Tennessee Board of Cosmetology and Barber Examiners.

72. Harold L. Wilensky explained that professional associations and university professional programs grow together in "The Professionalization of Everyone?," *American Journal of Sociology* 70, no. 2 (September 1964): 137–158.

73. "Alcohol and Drug Abuse Counselors: Applications," Tennessee Department of Health, https://www.tn.gov/health/health-program-areas/health-professional -boards/ad-board/ad-board/applications.html.

74. April 20, 2018, Tennessee Board of Alcohol and Drug Abuse Counselors.

75. July 13, 2018, Tennessee Board of Alcohol and Drug Abuse Counselors.

76. April 20, 2018, Tennessee Board of Alcohol and Drug Abuse Counselors.

77. Board member, Tennessee Board of Alcohol and Drug Abuse Counselors, in conversation with the author, April 2019.

78. April 5, 2019, Tennessee Board of Alcohol and Drug Abuse Counselors.

## 2. FENCES AND TURF

1. In 2018, Tennessee had only 156 natural hair licensees in total. Tenn. Gen. Assemb. Fiscal Rev. Comm., Fiscal Note, HB 1809—SB 2233 (February 18, 2018).

2.    Fatou Diouf (owner of a hair-braiding salon), in discussion with the author, November 2020.

3.    April 9, 2018, Tennessee Board of Cosmetology and Barber Examiners.

4.    Transcript of Oral Argument at 41, North Carolina State Board of Dental Examiners v. FTC, 574 U.S. 494 (2015) (No. 13–534).

5.    President of the Tennessee Trial Lawyers Association, in discussion with the author, May 2018.

6.    Elliot A. Krause, *Death of the Guilds: Professions, States, and the Advance of Capitalism, 1930 to the Present* (New Haven: Yale University Press, 1996), 9–14; Morris M. Kleiner, *Licensing Occupations: Ensuring Quality or Restricting Competition?* (Kalamazoo: W. E. Upjohn Institute, 2006), 19.

7.    Carl F. Ameringer, *State Medical Boards and the Politics of Public Protection* (Baltimore: Johns Hopkins University Press, 1999), 15–19.

8.    For a discussion of the role of medical societies as a stepping stone to licensing boards, see David A. Johnson and Humayun J. Chaudhry, *Medical Licensing and Discipline in America* (Plymouth, UK: Lexington Books, 2012), 5.

9.    May 20, 2018, Tennessee Auctioneer Commission.

10.    April 11, 2019, Tennessee Alarm Systems Contractors Board.

11.    Attorney for the Tennessee Real Estate Commission, in discussion with the author, June 2018.

12.    April 11, 2019, Tennessee Alarm Systems Contractors Board.

13.    Obamacare augmented this effect by seeming to mandate parity in reimbursement rates for medical services, regardless of what kind of provider did them. Patient Protection and Affordable Care Act, 42 U.S.C.A. § 300gg-5 (2010). The language of the statute, however, was far from crystal clear on this point, and some nurse practitioners have recently observed that they are reimbursed at a different rate than physicians. Letter from the American Association of Nurse Practitioners et al. to Xavier Becerra, Secretary of the Department of Health and Human Services, Martin Walsh, Secretary of the Department of Labor, and Janet Yellen, Secretary of the Department of the Treasury (March 8, 2022) (on file with author).

14.    Morris M. Kleiner, Allison Marier, Kyoung Won Park, and Coady Wing, "Relaxing Occupational Licensing Requirements: Analyzing Wages and Prices for a Medical Service," *Journal of Law and Economics* 59, no. 2 (May 2016): 286; Coady Wing and Allison Marier, "Effects of Occupational Regulations on the Cost of

Dental Services: Evidence from Dental Insurance Claims," *Journal of Health Economics* 34, no. 1 (March 2014): 142.

15. Member of the Tennessee Board of Medical Examiners, in discussion with the author, May 2018.

16. Eliot Freidson, *Professionalism Reborn: Theory, Prophecy, and Policy* (Cambridge: Polity Press, 1994); Sarah N. Heiss, Kristen K. Smith, and Heather J. Carmack, "Waging a Professional Turf War: An Examination of Professionalization as a Strategic Communication Practice Used by Registered Dietitians," *Qualitative Research in Medicine & Healthcare* 2, no. 3 (2018): 122, 129.

17. Department of Justice, General Counsel Division, State of Oregon, opinion letter (May 19, 2017), https://www.doj.state.or.us/wp-content/uploads/2017/06 /op2017-2.pdf (dry needling); Elizabeth Aguilera, "Facing Doctor Shortage, Will California Give Nurse Practitioners More Authority to Treat Patients?," *Cal Matters*, February 13, 2020, https://calmatters.org/projects/doctor-shortage-nurse -practitioners-california/ (prescribing); Dr. Michael Mashni (dentist), in conversation with author, May 2018 (oral surgery); Lindsay Boyd Killen, "The Dirty Dozen: Animal Massage Therapist," *Beacon*, October 16, 2017, https://www.beacontn .org/the-dirty-dozen-animal-massage-therapist/ (animal massage); May 20, 2018, Tennessee Auctioneer Commission (car auctions).

18. US Department of Health and Human Services, "Reforming America's Healthcare System through Choice and Competition" (2018), https://www.hhs.gov /sites/default/files/Reforming-Americas-Healthcare-System-Through-Choice -and-Competition.pdf.

19. Morris M. Kleiner, *Licensing Occupations Ensuring Quality or Restricting Competition?* (Kalamazoo: W. E. Upjohn Institute, 2006), 59–63.

20. Milton Friedman noted that licensure is "the key to [the medical profession's] ability to restrict technological and organizational changes in the way medicine is conducted." *Capitalism and Freedom* (Chicago: University of Chicago Press, 1962), 154.

21. Harold L. Wilensky, "The Professionalization of Everyone?," *American Journal of Sociology* 70, no. 2 (September 1964): 145.

22. For example, in the 1970s, dental hygienists declared for themselves the authority to see patients "as the primary provider of initial services," prompting dentists to counter that hygienists are "auxiliaries who must work under the supervision of a dentist." The professions have been locked in a turf war ever since. Morris M. Kleiner and Kyoung Won Park, "Battles among Universally Li-

censed Occupations," *Stages of Occupational Regulation* (Kalamazoo: W. E. Up-john Institute, 2013), 176.

23. Member of the Tennessee Board of Veterinary Medical Examiners, in discussion with the author, April 2018; H.R. 2288, 110th Gen. Assemb., Reg. Sess. (Tenn. 2018); S. 2154, 110th Gen. Assemb., Reg. Sess. (Tenn. 2018). Similarly, the esthetician member of the cosmetology board asked the board, during a meeting, to back her in her profession's turf war with physicians over microdermabrasion. December 9, 2019, Tennessee Board of Cosmetology and Barber Examiners.

24. For example, I learned at a national conference about licensing that the Maryland physical therapy board sent cease-and-desist letters to acupuncturists doing dry needling. September 27–30, 2018, Federation of Associations of Regulatory Boards, Portland, OR.

25. January 23, 2020, Federation of Associations of Regulatory Boards, Colorado Springs, CO.

26. For a discussion of the value of term protection, see Eliot Freidson, *Professional Powers* (Chicago: University of Chicago Press, 1986), 67–68.

27. Tenn. Code Ann. § 62-2-102(a) (2022); Tenn. Code Ann. § 62-2-105(b)(1), (c) (2009).

28. June 14, 2018, Tennessee Board of Architectural and Engineering Examiners.

29. April 11, 2018, Tennessee Board of Veterinary Medical Examiners.

30. Adam Jackson (founder, Edge AI), in discussion with the author, October 2018.

31. June 22, 2017, Tennessee Alarm Systems Contractor Board.

32. Cemetery professional, in discussion with the author, July 2018.

33. Cemetery professional, in discussion with the author, April 2018.

34. Cemetery professional, in discussion with the author, July 2018.

35. Cemetery professional, in discussion with the author, April 2018.


## 3. THE WILD, WILD WEST

1. 1996 Tenn. Pub. Acts Ch. 897.

2. Fatou Diouf (owner of a hair-braiding salon), in discussion with the author, November 2020.

3.    Dale Atkinson (executive, Federation of Associations of Regulatory Boards), at the 2020 FARB Forum with the author in attendance, January 2020.

4.    For example, the Tennessee Board of Alarm Systems Contractors used the phrase in resisting the sunset of licensure for their profession. *See June 18, 2019, Hearing before the S. Gov't Operations Comm.*, 111th Gen. Assemb., Reg. Sess. (Tenn. 2019), https://tnga.granicus.com/player/clip/17810?view_id=420&redirect =true&h=e76664366ab62e36932751b54f8b919d.

5.    Shannon Lantzy and David Anderson, "Can Consumers Use Online Reviews to Avoid Unsuitable Doctors? Evidence from RateMDs.com and the Federation of State Medical Boards," *Decision Sciences* 51, no. 4 (August 2020): 975.

6.    George A. Akerlof, "The Market for 'Lemons': Quality Uncertainty and the Market Mechanism," *Quarterly Journal of Economics* 84, no. 3 (August 1970).

7.    Aaron Edlin and Rebecca Haw, "Cartels by Another Name: Should Licensed Occupations Face Antitrust Scrutiny?," *University of Pennsylvania Law Review* 162, no. 5 (April 2014): 1115–1116; Hayne E. Leland, "Quacks, Lemons, and Licensing: A Theory of Minimum Quality Standards," *Journal of Political Economy* 87, no. 6 (December 1979): 1329.

8.    For an example of a study unable to show that licensing increased service quality, see Morris M. Kleiner, "Regulating Occupations: Quality or Monopoly?," *Employment Research Newsletter* 13, no. 1 (Kalamazoo: W. E. Upjohn Institute, 2006): 2. Relatedly, economists have shown that giving more responsibility to professionals from a profession with lower barriers to entry did not negatively affect quality: J. Nellie Liang and Jonathan D. Ogur, *Restrictions on Dental Auxiliaries: An Economic Policy Analysis* (Washington, DC: Federal Trade Commission, 1987), 49–51, https://hdl.handle.net/2027/mdp.39015020801117; Morris M. Kleiner, Allison Marier, Kyoung Won Park, and Coady Wing, "Relaxing Occupational Licensing Requirements: Analyzing Wages and Prices for a Medical Service," *Journal of Law and Economics* 59, no. 2 (May 2016): 286. For a study that does find an increase in quality as a result of licensing restrictions, see D. Mark Anderson, Ryan Brown, Kerwin Kofi Charles, and Daniel I. Rees, "Occupational Licensing and Maternal Health: Evidence from Early Midwifery Laws," *Journal of Political Economy* 128, no. 11 (October 2020): 4340.

9.    For scholarship arguing that licensing may *decrease* health and safety outcomes, see Adriana D. Kugler and Robert M. Sauer, "Doctors without Borders? Relicensing Requirements and Negative Selection in the Market for Physicians," *Journal of Labor Economics* 23, no. 3 (July 2005): 440; Morris M. Kleiner and Robert T. Kudrle, "Does Regulation Affect Economic Outcomes? The Case of Dentistry," *Journal of Law & Economics* 43, no. 2 (October 2000): 570.

10.  For a recent collection of empirical studies designed to assess the quality effect of licensing, see Morris M. Kleiner and Maria Koumenta, *Grease or Grit? International Case Studies of Occupational Licensing and Its Effects on Efficiency and Quality* (Kalamazoo: W. E. Upjohn Institute, 2022).

11.  Dick M. Carpenter II, "Testing the Utility of Licensing: Evidence from a Field Experiment on Occupational Regulation," *Journal of Applied Business and Economics* 13, no. 2 (2012): 36 (florists); Edward J. Timmons and Anna Mills, "Bringing the Effects of Occupational Licensing into Focus: Optician Licensing in the United States," *Eastern Economic Journal* 44 (January 2018): 76–77, 80 (opticians).

12.  Peter Q. Blair and Bobby W. Chung, "How Much of Barrier to Entry Is Occupational Licensing?," *British Journal of Industrial Relations* 57, no. 4 (December 2019): 928, 930 (17–27 percent); Morris M. Kleiner and Evan J. Soltas, "A Welfare Analysis of Occupational Licensing in U.S. States" (working paper, August 2020, https://dx.doi.org/10.2139/ssrn.3140912) (29 percent); Maya N. Federman, David E. Harrington, and Kathy J. Krynski, "The Impact of State Licensing Regulations on Low-Skilled Immigrants: The Case of Vietnamese Manicurists," *American Economic Review* 96, no. 2 (May 2006): 238 (additional required training reduces the number of Vietnamese manicurists by 17.6 percent).

13.  Morris M. Kleiner, *Licensing Occupations: Ensuring Quality or Restricting Competition?* (Kalamazoo: W. E. Upjohn Press, 2006), 115 (2000 figure adjusted upward for inflation).

14.  For example, the Federal Trade Commission has observed that consumers may "'do without' certain health care services because of higher prices." Carolyn Cox and Susan Foster, *The Costs and Benefits of Occupational Regulation* (Washington, DC: Federal Trade Commission, 1990), 35–36, https://www.ftc.gov/system/files/documents/reports/costs-benefits-occupational-regulation/cox_foster_-_occupational_licensing.pdf.

15.  Gillian K. Hadfield, "The Cost of Law: Promoting Access to Justice through the (Un)corporate Practice of Law," 38 *International Review of Law and Economics* (June 2014): 43, 46, 61.

16.  See *Shaw v. Shand,* 460 N.J. Super. 592 (App. Div. 2019).

17.  Andrea Estes, "FBI Investigating State's Licensing of Massage Therapists with Fake Credentials," *Boston Globe,* February 26, 2020, https://www.bostonglobe.com/2020/02/26/metro/fbi-investigating-states-licensing-massage-therapists/.

18.  The Department of the Treasury Office of Economic Policy, the Council of Economic Advisers, and the Department of Labor, *Occupational Licensing: A*

*Framework for Policymakers* (2015), 3, https://obamawhitehouse.archives.gov/sites
/default/files/docs/licensing_report_final_nonembargo.pdf.

19.   North Carolina State Board of Dental Examiners v. FTC, 574 U.S. 494, 496 (2015).

20.   "About Us," Institute for Justice, accessed September 19, 2022, https://ij.org
/about-us/.

21.   "California Firefighter Fresh Start," Institute for Justice, accessed September 19, 2022, https://ij.org/case/california-firefighter-fresh-start/; "Breast-feeding Battle: IJ Defeats Georgia's License for Lactation Consultants," Institute for Justice, accessed September 19, 2022, https://ij.org/case/georgia-lactation
-consultants/.

22.   W. Coast Hotel Co. v. Parrish, 300 U.S. 379, 391 (1937).

23.   Aaron Edlin and Rebecca Haw, "Cartels by Another Name: Should Licensed Occupations Face Antitrust Scrutiny?," *University of Pennsylvania Law Review* 162, no. 5 (April 2014): 1127–1130.

24.   Recognizing the difficulty of winning rationality review cases, the IJ has turned to another constitutional provision that doesn't seem to raise the specter of *Lochner*—the right to free speech found in the First Amendment. For more about these suits and a criticism of their effect on free speech doctrine and professional regulation, see Rebecca Haw Allensworth, "The (Limited) Constitutional Right to Compete in an Occupation," *William & Mary Law Review* 60, no. 4 (March 2019).

25.   "IJ's Cases," Institute for Justice, accessed September 24, 2022, https://ij.org
/cases/?&status-filter=&topic-filter=10

26.   Rob Johnson (attorney, Institute for Justice), in conversation with the author, February 2018.

27.   Meadows v. Odom, 360 F.Supp.2d 811 (M.D. La. 2005).

## 4. STRESS TEST

1.   Jordan Allen et al., "Coronavirus in the US: Latest Map and Case Count," *New York Times,* updated March 23, 2023, https://www.nytimes.com/interactive/2023
/us/covid-personalized-tracker.html.

2.   Joseph Goldstein and Brian M. Rosenthal, "Coronavirus in NY: Will a Surge in Patients Overwhelm Hospitals?," *New York Times,* March 14, 2020, https://www
.nytimes.com/2020/03/14/nyregion/coronavirus-nyc-hospitals.html
?searchResultPosition=25; Jason Horowitz, "Italy's Health Care System Groans

under Coronavirus—a Warning to the World," *New York Times,* March 12, 2020, https://www.nytimes.com/2020/03/12/world/europe/12italy-coronavirus-health-care.html.

3.   Goldstein and Rosenthal, "Coronavirus in NY."

4.   Brian M. Rosenthal and Joseph Goldstein, "New York May Need 18,000 Ventilators Very Soon. It Is Far Short of That," *New York Times,* March 17, 2020, https://www.nytimes.com/2020/03/17/nyregion/ny-coronavirus-ventilators.html?searchResultPosition=14.

5.   Goldstein and Rosenthal, "Coronavirus in NY."

6.   Siobhan Roberts, "Flattening the Coronavirus Curve," *New York Times,* March 27, 2020, https://www.nytimes.com/article/flatten-curve-coronavirus.html.

7.   This observation was confirmed by several physicians I interviewed about the early days on the front lines of COVID. For example, Dr. Jon Bauman (director, St. John's Riverside Hospital), told me in June 2021 that "our biggest fear was ventilators" but that he ended up having an easier time getting those than staff. Another intensivist in New York said, "we never ran out of ventilators" but her hospital did run out of personnel. Interview not for attribution, in conversation with the author, July 2021. Other cities had the same experience during their surges. An intensivist in New Orleans told me that, during their peak case load, "I told people, if we ever run out of ventilators, we will have run out of nurses thirty ventilators ago." Dr. Dave Janz (director of Medical Critical Care Services at University Medical Center, New Orleans), in discussion with the author, June 2021.

8.   Jonathan Martin, "Trump to Governors on Ventilators: 'Try Getting It Yourselves,'" *New York Times,* March 16, 2020, https://www.nytimes.com/2020/03/16/us/politics/trump-coronavirus-respirators.html?searchResultPosition=9.

9.   Exec. Order No. 202, N.Y. Comp. Codes R. & Regs. tit. 9, § 8.202 (2020).

10.   Bobby Allyn, "Cuomo Makes Plea to Medical Workers Nationwide: 'Please Come Help Us in New York,'" National Public Radio, March 30, 2020, https://www.npr.org/sections/coronavirus-live-updates/2020/03/30/823970536/cuomo-makes-plea-to-medical-workers-nationwide-please-come-help-us-in-new-york.

11.   New York State Governor's Press Office, "Amid Ongoing Covid-19 Pandemic, Governor Cuomo Announces Completion of First 1,000-Bed Temporary Hospital at Jacob K. Javits Convention Center," press release, March 27, 2020, https://www.governor.ny.gov/news/amid-ongoing-covid-19-pandemic-governor-cuomo-announces-completion-first-1000-bed-temporary.

12.  Nicole Hong, "Volunteers Rushed to Help New York Hospitals. They Found a Bottleneck," *New York Times,* April 8, 2020, https://www.nytimes.com/2020/04 /08/nyregion/coronavirus-new-york-volunteers.html?searchResultPosition=9.

13.  Hong, "Volunteers."

14.  Olivia Goldhill, "'People Are Going to Die': Hospitals in Half the States Are Facing Massive Staffing Shortages as Covid-19 Surges," STAT, November 19, 2020, https://www.statnews.com/2020/11/19/covid19-hospitals-in-half-the-states-facing -massive-staffing-shortage/.

15.  Dhruv Khullar, "America Is Running Out of Nurses," *New Yorker,* December 15, 2020, https://www.newyorker.com/science/medical-dispatch/america -is-running-out-of-nurses.

16.  Brian M. Rosenthal, Joseph Goldstein, Sharon Otterman, and Sheri Fink, "Why Surviving the Virus Might Come Down to Which Hospital Admits You," *New York Times,* July 1, 2020, https://www.nytimes.com/2020/07/01/nyregion /Coronavirus-hospitals.html.

17.  Michael Schwirtz, "Nurses Die, Doctors Fall Sick and Panic Rises on Virus Front Lines," *New York Times,* March 30, 2020, https://www.nytimes.com/2020/03 /30/nyregion/ny-coronavirus-doctors-sick.html.

18.  Chief of anesthesiology, St. John's Riverside Hospital, in discussion with the author, June 2021.

19.  Khullar, "Running Out of Nurses."

20.  A CDC report on COVID in New York City spanning March through May 2020 estimated the fatality rate at 32.1 percent among hospitalized patients. Corinne N. Thompson et al., "COVID-19 Outbreak—New York City, February 29-June 1, 2020," *Morbidity and Mortality Weekly Report* 69 (2020): 1725, http://dx .doi.org/10.15585/mmwr.mm6946a2. The national rate during this period appears to have been much lower—between 10 percent and 20 percent. Lynn Finelli et al., "Mortality among US Patients Hospitalized with SARS-CoV-2 Infection in 2020," *JAMA Network Open* 7, no.4 (2020), doi:10.1001 / jamanetwork open.2021.6556.

21.  Erin Durkin, "NYC's Poorest Neighborhoods have Highest Death Rates from Coronavirus," *Politico,* May 18, 2020, https://www.politico.com/states/new-york /city-hall/story/2020/05/18/poorest-nyc-neighborhoods-have-highest-death -rates-from-coronavirus-1284519; Elisabeth Ryden Benjamin, *How Structural Inequalities in New York's Health Care System Exacerbate Health Disparities during*

the *COVID-19 Pandemic: A Call for Equitable Reform* (New York: Community Service Society, June 4, 2020), https://www.cssny.org/news/entry/structural -inequalities-in-new-yorks-health-care-system. Bronx County, for example, had the most severe physician deficit and the highest rate of COVID infections in April 2020. Rosenthal, Goldstein, Otterman, and Fink, "Which Hospital Admits You"; Larry Neumeister and Marina Villeneuve, "Call for Virus Volunteers Yields Army of Health Care Workers," Associated Press, April 1, 2020, https://apnews .com/article/7fca3117e7fa0f394bc7b2dba9e26316.

22. Thompson et al., "COVID-19 Outbreak," 1725.

23. IHS Markit Ltd for the Association of American Medical Colleges, *The Complexities of Physician Supply and Demand: Projections from 2017–2032* (April 2019), https://specialtydocs.org/wp-content/uploads/2019/06/2019_update_-_the _complexities_of_physician_supply_and_demand_-_projections_from_2017 -2032.pdf.

24. Xiaoming Zhang et al., "United States Registered Nurse Workforce Report Card and Shortage Forecast: A Revisit," *American Journal of Medical Quality* 33, no. 3 (November 2017): 229–236, https://doi.org/10.1177/1062860617738328. Burnout from the COVID-19 pandemic may expand these projections. Gretchen Berlin, Meredith Lapoint, Mhoire Murphy, and Joanna Wexler, *Assessing the Lingering Impact of COVID-19 on the Nursing Workforce* (New York: McKinsey and Company, May 11, 2022), https://www.mckinsey.com/industries/healthcare /our-insights/assessing-the-lingering-impact-of-covid-19-on-the-nursing-work force.

25. Peter Jaret, "Attracting the Next Generation of Physicians to Rural Medicine," Association of American Medical Colleges, February 3, 2020, https://www.aamc .org/news-insights/attracting-next-generation-physicians-rural-medicine; Jack Pitsor, *Improving Rural Health: State Policy Options for Increasing Access to Care* (Washington, DC: National Conference of State Legislatures, June 23, 2020), https://www.ncsl.org/research/health/improving-rural-health-state-policy-options -for-increasing-access-to-care.aspx#intro.

26. Kritee Gujral and Anirban Basu, "Impact of Rural and Urban Hospital Closures on Inpatient Mortality" (working paper 26182, National Bureau of Economic Research, Cambridge, MA, August 2019), http://www.nber.org/papers/w26182; Jaya Khushalani et al., "Impact of Rural Hospital Closures on Hospitalizations and Associated Outcomes for Ambulatory and Emergency Care Sensitive Conditions," *Journal of Rural Health* 39 no. 1 (May 2022): 79.

27.  Jaret, "Next Generation."

28.  "State and Federal Efforts to Enhance Access to Basic Health Care," Commonwealth Fund, https://www.commonwealthfund.org/publications/newsletter -article/state-and-federal-efforts-enhance-access-basic-health-care.

29.  "The Road to Becoming a Doctor," Association of American Medical Colleges, November 2020, https://students-residents.aamc.org/ (detailing the "journey of becoming an MD"); James Youngclaus and Julia A. Fresne, "Physician Education Debt and the Cost to Attend Medical School," Association of American Medical Colleges, October 2020, https://www.aamc.org/data-reports/students -residents/report/physician-education-debt-and-cost-attend-medical-school.

30.  Leah Pierson, "The AMA Can Help Fix the Health Care Shortages It Helped Create," *Bill of Health* (blog), Harvard Law School Petrie-Flom Center, March 15, 2022, https://blog.petrieflom.law.harvard.edu/2022/03/15/ama-scope-of-practice -lobbying/. The Medicare cap is especially bad for hospitals serving lower-resourced areas, which depend on Medicaid funding for most or all of their residency funding. Keren Landman, "Why Well-Qualified Medical School Graduates Can't Get Jobs—Despite Doctor Shortages," *Vox,* March 25, 2022, https://www .vox.com/22989930/residency-match-physician-doctor-shortage-pandemic -medical-school.

31.  Silva Mathema, *Immigrant Doctors Can Help Lower Physician Shortages in Rural America* (Washington, DC: Center for American Progress, July 29, 2019), https://www.americanprogress.org/article/immigrant-doctors-can-help-lower -physician-shortages-rural-america/; Emma Goldberg, "'I Am Worth It': Why Thousands of Doctors in America Can't Get a Job," *New York Times,* February 19, 2021, https://www.nytimes.com/2021/02/19/health/medical-school-residency -doctors.html.

32.  American Association of Nurse Practitioners, *The State of the Nurse Practitioner Profession 2020,* 2021, https://storage.aanp.org/www/documents/no -index/research/2020-NP-Sample-Survey-Report.pdf; E. Kathleen Adams and Sara Markowitz, *Improving Efficiency in the Health-Care System: Removing Anticompetitive Barriers for Advanced Practice Registered Nurses and Physician Assistants* (Washington, DC: Brookings Institution, June 2018), https://www.brookings .edu/research/improving-efficiency-in-the-health-care-system-removing-anti competitive-barriers-for-advanced-practice-registered-nurses-and-physician -assistants/.

33.  Nurse practitioners currently have full practice authority in twenty-four states, while thirteen require reduced practice, and the remaining thirteen require

restricted practice. "State Practice Environment," American Association of Nurse Practitioners, accessed January 25, 2023, https://www.aanp.org/advocacy/state /state-practice-environment. Physician assistants are even more restricted—in forty-four states and the District of Columbia they require physician supervision, while Alaska, Illinois, and Michigan allow collaborative practice agreements, and New Mexico, North Dakota, and Utah allow them to work independent of a physician. Edward Timmons and Conor Norris, "Potential Licensing Reforms in Light of COVID-19," *Health Policy Open* 3, 100062 (December 2022), https://www.ncbi .nlm.nih.gov/pmc/articles/PMC8654457/.

34. Brendan Martin and Kyrani Reneau, "How Collaborative Practice Agreements Impede the Administration of Vital Women's Health Services," *Journal of Midwifery and Women's Health* 65, no. 4 (July 2020): 487.

35. Nancy Rudner, "An Assessment of Physician Supervision of Nurse Practitioners," *Journal of Nursing Regulation* 7, no. 4 (January 2017), https://doi.org/10 .1016/S2155-8256(17)30017-0.

36. "Occupational Outlook Handbook: Physician Assistants," US Bureau of Labor Statistics, September 8, 2022, https://www.bls.gov/ooh/healthcare/physician -assistants.htm; "Nurse Practitioner Fact Sheet," American Association of Nurse Practitioners, April 2022, https://www.aanp.org/about/all-about-nps/np-fact -sheet.

37. Ruth M. Kleinpell et al., "Nurse Practitioners and Physician Assistants in Acute and Critical Care: A Concise Review of the Literature and Data 2008–2018," *Critical Care Medicine* 47, no. 10 (October 2019), https://journals.lww.com /ccmjournal/fulltext/2019/10000/Nurse_Practitioners_and_Physician _Assistants_in.21.aspx. Although most studies show mid-levels performing on par or even better than physicians, some do not. See, for example, a recent study showing that nurse practitioners use more resources and achieve poorer health outcomes in emergency departments than do physicians. David C. Chan and Yiqun Chen, "The Productivity of Professions: Evidence from the Emergency Department," National Bureau of Economic Research, revised June 2023, https://www .nber.org/system/files/working_papers/w30608/w30608.pdf.

38. According to the Health Resources and Services Administration, there were 256,220 full-time equivalent primary care physicians in the United States in 2018 (105,400 family physicians, 81,760 general internal physicians, 8,220 geriatric physicians, and 60,840 pediatric physicians). "Primary Care Workforce Projections," Health Resources & Services Administration, 2018, https://bhw.hrsa.gov/data -research/projecting-health-workforce-supply-demand/primary-health; Brian

Antono et al., *Primary Care in the United States: A Chartbook of Facts and Statistics* (Washington, DC: Robert Graham Center, February 2021), 12, https://www.graham-center.org/content/dam/rgc/documents/publications-reports/reports/PrimaryCareChartbook2021.pdf (about 136,000 mid-levels in primary care).

39. Kleinpell et al., "Nurse Practitioners."

40. Tony Y. Yang et al., "State Scope of Practice Laws, Nurse-Midwifery Workforce, and Childbirth Procedures and Outcomes," *Women's Health Issues* 26, no. 3 (2016): 262–267.

41. Jeffrey Traczynski and Victoria Udalova, "Nurse Practitioner Independence, Health Care Utilization, and Health Outcomes," *Journal of Health Economics* 58 (2018): 90–109.

42. Ying Xue et al., "Full Scope-of-Practice Regulation Is Associated with Higher Supply of Nurse Practitioners in Rural and Primary Care Health Professional Shortage Counties," *Journal of Nursing Regulation* 8, no. 4 (2018): 5–13.

43. About 82 percent of nurse practitioners and 83 percent of primary care physicians see Medicare patients. "NP Fact Sheet," American Association of Nurse Practitioners, accessed February 17, 2023, https://www.aanp.org/about/all-about-nps/np-fact-sheet; Nancy Ochieng et al., "Most Office-Based Physicians Accept New Patients, Including Medicare and Private Insurance," news release, Kaiser Family Foundation, May 12, 2022, https://www.kff.org/medicare/issue-brief/most-office-based-physicians-accept-new-patients-including-patients-with-medicare-and-private-insurance/#:~:text=Across%20most%20specialties%2C%20the%20majority,(96%25%20for%20both.

44. Adams and Markowitz, *Improving Efficiency;* E. Kathleen Adams and Sara Markowitz, *Reforming America's Healthcare System through Choice and Competition* (Washington, DC: US Department of Health and Human Services, 2018), https://www.hhs.gov/sites/default/files/Reforming-Americas-Healthcare-System-Through-Choice-and-Competition.pdf.

45. For a summary of the evidence in favor of this policy, see Edward Joseph Timmons, "The Effects of Expanded Nurse Practitioner and Physician Assistant Scope of Practice on the Cost of Medicaid Patient Care," *Health Policy* 121 no. 2 (February 2017): 195.

46. Letter from Alex M. Azar, secretary of Health and Human Services, to the United States' State Governors (March 24, 2020) (on file with the author).

47. "Coronavirus State Actions," National Governors Association, accessed February 3, 2023, https://www.nga.org/coronavirus-state-actions-all/; Interstate

Commission of Nurse Licensure Compact Administrators, *Nurse Licensure Compact Annual Report: Fiscal Year 2019*–20 (2020): 4–5, https://www.ncsbn.org/public-files/20-NLCAnnualReport.pdf.

48. Eight states waived or suspended PA supervision requirements entirely (Maine, Michigan, New Jersey, New York, Louisiana, South Dakota, Tennessee, and Virginia), and Massachusetts, New Jersey, and New York had executive orders in effect doing the same. "COVID-19 State Emergency Response," American Academy of Physician Associates, accessed January 23, 2023, https://www.aapa.org/cme-central/national-health-priorities/covid-19-resource-center/covid-19-state-emergency-response/. Thirteen more states waived all or part of PA supervision requirements via statute or regulation. Or. Admin. R. 847-035-0030 (Oregon 2023); Idaho Admin. Code R. 24.33.02.028.04 (Idaho 2023); Mont. Code Ann. § 37-20-410 (Montana 2023); N.D. Cent. Code Ann. § 43–17 (North Dakota 2022); Minn. Stat. § 147A.23 (Minnesota 2022); Iowa Code Ann. § 148C.4; 255 (Iowa 2019); Ill. Comp. Stat. Ann. § 95 / 7(b) (Illinois 2024); Ind. Code Ann. § 25–27.5-6-8 (Indiana 2022); 216 R.I. Code Reg. § 40-05–24.14 (Rhode Island 2021); Ala. Admin. Code r. 540-X-7-.25 (Alabama 2023); Tex. Occ. Code Ann. § 204.2045 (Texas 2022); HB 2477, 2022 Leg., Reg. Sess. (Kansas—expired January 20, 2023); Ariz. Rev. Stat. Ann. § 32.2535 (Arizona 2022).

49. Rachel Bluth, "California Resists Push to Lift Limits on Nurse Practitioners during Covid-19 Pandemic," STAT, April 17, 2020, https://www.statnews.com/2020/04/17/california-resists-push-to-lift-limits-on-nurse-practitioners-during-covid-19-pandemic/.

50. Assembly Bill 890, 2020 Reg. Sess. (Ca. 2019); Bluth, "California Resists."

51. "CMA Urges Additional Steps to Mitigate the Financial Impact of Pandemic on Physicians," California Medical Association, April 3, 2020, https://www.cmadocs.org/newsroom/news/view/ArticleID/48810/t/CMA-Urges-Additional-Steps-to-Mitigate-the-Financial-Impact-of-Pandemic-on-Physician-Practices.

52. "Assembly Bill 890—Status Update: FAQs," California Board of Registered Nursing, https://www.rn.ca.gov/practice/ab890.shtml#faqs; "Title 16, Division 14, Article 8, sections 1480, 1481, 1482.3, 1482.5, and 1487 Final Statement of Reasons: Categories and Scope of Nurse Practitioners," California Board of Registered Nursing, December 22, 2022, https://www.rn.ca.gov/pdfs/regulations/fsor-ab890.pdf.

53. "Urge Gov Newsom to Reject Bill that Would Create Two-Tiered Healthcare System," California Medical Association, September 1, 2020 https://www.cmadocs

.org/newsroom/news/view/ArticleID/49008/t/Urge-Gov-Newsom-to-reject-bill
-that-would-create-two-tiered-health-care-system.

54. Exec. Order N-39-20 (Ca. 2020); "Newsom Relaxes Workforce Rules While Protecting Physician Supervision Model," California Medical Association, March 31, 2020, https://www.cmadocs.org/newsroom/news/view/ArticleID/48796 /t/Gov-Newsom-temporarily-relaxes-scope-requirements-in-anticipation-of -COVID-19-surge.

55. Bluth, "California Resists."

56. Exec. Order 14 (Tenn. 2020).

57. Exec. Order 15 (Tenn. 2020).

58. March 25, 2020, Tennessee Board of Medical Examiners.

59. S.B. 0680, 109th Gen. Assemb., Reg. Sess. (Tenn. 2015).

60. 2016 Tenn. Pub. Ch. No. 1046.

61. Carole Myers, "Reflection on the Scope of Practice Task Force," *Tennessee Nurse* 80, no. 1 (2017): 3, 8, https://www.nursingald.com/articles/17844-reflection -on-the-scope-of-practice-task-force.

62. John W. Hale, Jr., "We Need More Collaboration in Healthcare, Not Less," *Nashville Medical News,* January 10, 2017, https://www.nashvillemedicalnews.com /we-need-more-collaboration-in-healthcare-not-less-cms-1534.

63. Myers, "Reflection" (noting that although the law creating the taskforce called for parity between nurses and physicians, two members ostensibly representing interests outside of the health professions—one a legislator and one a mayor—were in fact also physicians).

64. "Tennessee Senator Faces Unethical Medical Conduct Charges," Associated Press, July 18, 2019, https://apnews.com/article/15972b0e058841818f27473ad54 438d4; Joseph Hensley, MD, Case No. 2017014711, Tennessee Department of Health, November 9, 2020, https://apps.health.tn.gov/DisciplinaryExclusion/board order/display/1606_15978_110520.

65. "Tennessee Sen. Joey Hensley's Medical License on Probation for Ethics Violation: Board," *Fox17 News,* November 5, 2020, https://fox17.com/news/local /tennessee-republican-sen-joey-hensley-medical-license-on-probation-for -ethics-violation-board-hohenwald.

66. S.B. 523, 110th Gen. Assemb., Reg. Sess. (Tenn. 2017).

67. January 14, 2020, Tennessee Board of Medical Examiners.

68. January 14, 2020, Tennessee Board of Medical Examiners.

69. Alexi Nazem (co-founder and CEO of Nomad Health), in discussion with the author, May 19, 2021.

70. Director of the COVID Intensive Care Unit, Vanderbilt University Medical Center, in discussion with the author, May 18, 2021.

71. Melanie Evans and Jim Carlton, "Soaring Costs of Nurses during COVID-19 Pandemic Are at Center of Lawsuits," *Wall Street Journal,* April 8, 2021, https://www.wsj.com/articles/soaring-costs-of-nurses-during-covid-19-pandemic-are-at-center-of-lawsuits-11617914600.

72. Alexi Nazem, in discussion with the author, May 19, 2021.

73. New York's worst day in April 2020 saw 11,571 new cases. "New York: Cases," COVID Tracking Project, last visited January 21, 2022, https://covidtracking.com/data/state/new-york/cases. Texas's worst day of July 2020 reported 14,916 on July 17, 2020. "Texas: Cases," COVID Tracking Project, last visited January 21, 2022, https://covidtracking.com/data/state/texas/cases.

74. John Henderson (CEO, Texas Organization of Rural and Community Hospitals), in discussion with the author, May 5, 2021.

75. Khullar, "Running Out."

76. Khullar, "Running Out"; Olivia Goldhill, "'People Are Going to Die': Hospitals in Half the States Are Facing Massive Staffing Shortages as Covid-19 Surges," STAT, November 19, 2020, https://www.statnews.com/2020/11/19/covid19-hospitals-in-half-the-states-facing-massive-staffing-shortage/.

77. Director of the COVID Intensive Care Unit, Vanderbilt University Medical Center, in discussion with the author, May 18, 2021.

78. Alexi Nazem, in discussion with the author, May 19, 2021.

79. Director of the COVID Intensive Care Unit, Vanderbilt University Medical Center. in discussion with the author, May 18, 2021.

80. Sanjay Basu, MD (director of research, Harvard Medical School Center for Primary Care), in conversation with the author, May 20, 2021.

81. Nick Marquiss, "An Empirical Assessment of Occupational Licensing Reforms in the Healthcare Sector" (PhD dissertation, Vanderbilt University, May 14, 2021) (on file with author).

82. Sherill J. Smith and Sharon L. Farra, "The Impact of COVID-19 on the Regulation of the Nursing Practice and Education," *Teaching and Learning in Nursing* 17, no. 3 (July 2022): 302–305.

83. Director of medical critical care services at University Medical Center, New Orleans, in discussion with the author, June 2021.

84. Alexi Nazem, in discussion with the author, May 19, 2021.

85. Laurel Rosenhall, "Unmasked: Doctors' Association Execs Joined Newsom at Lobbyist's Birthday Bash," *CalMatters,* November 18, 2020, https://calmatters .org/politics/2020/11/newsom-dinner-california-medical-lobby-french-laundry -pandemic/.

86. Don Thompson, "Most Enlistees Not Eligible to Join California Health Corps," Associated Press, May 1, 2020, https://apnews.com/article/5be17e90563d-6b5d45f8a8d11a26fd87; Daisy Nguyen, "California Desperately Searches for More Doctors and Nurses," Associated Press, December 22, 2020, https://www.pbs .org/newshour/health/california-desperately-searches-for-more-nurses-and -doctors.

87. John Antczak and Amy Taxin, "California's Hospitals 'Crushed' as Virus Patients Flood ICU's," Associated Press, December 18, 2020, https://krcrtv.com/news /local/california-hospitals-crushed-as-virus-patients-flood-icus.

88. Alicia Victoria Lozano, "1 Person Dies Every 6 Minutes: How LA Became the Nation's Largest Coronavirus Hot Spot," *NBC News,* January 14, 2021, https://www .nbcnews.com/news/us-news/1-person-dies-every-6-minutes-how-l-became -nation-n1254003.

89. Nguyen, "California Desperately Searches."

90. Lozano, "1 Person Dies."

## 5. AMERICAN DREAMS

1. S.B. 2233, 110th Gen. Assemb., Reg. Sess. (Tenn. 2018), https://wapp.capitol .tn.gov/apps/BillInfo/Default.aspx?BillNumber=HB1809&GA=110.

2. Morris M. Kleiner and Alan B. Krueger, "Analyzing the Extent and Influence of Occupational Licensing on the Labor Market," *Journal of Labor Economics* 34, no. 2 (2013): S175 (18 percent); Morris M. Kleiner and Evgeny Vorotnikov, "Analyzing Occupational Licensing among the States," *Journal of Regulatory Economics* 52 (June 2017): 144 (11 percent); Ryan Nunn, *How Occupational Licensing Matters for Wages and Careers* (Washington, DC: Brookings Institution, March 2018), 2 (5 percent to 8 percent); Brandon Pizzola and Alexander Tabarrok, "Occupational Licensing Causes a Wage Premium: Evidence from a Natural Experiment in Col-

orado's Funeral Services Industry," *International Review of Law and Economics* 50 (June 2017): 59 (11 percent to 12 percent).

3.   Morris M. Kleiner and Alan B. Krueger, "The Prevalence and Effects of Occupational Licensing," *British Journal of Industrial Relations* 48, no. 4 (December 2010): 681–682, 685.

4.   Keith M. Macdonald, "Social Closure and Occupational Registration," *Sociology* 19, no. 4 (November 1985): 541.

5.   For a typical cosmetology course, costing $14,995 in tuition and covering 1,500 hours of instruction in forty-five weeks, see "Cosmetology Program," Tennessee School of Beauty, accessed October 9, 2022, https://tennesseeschoolofbeauty .edu/cosmetology-program/.

6.   Knoxville barber school owner, in discussion with the author, May 2020.

7.   "Vibe Barber College," College Scorecard, US Department of Education, accessed January 17, 2023, https://collegescorecard.ed.gov/school/?483744-Vibe -Barber-College.

8.   Association of International Certified Professional Accountants, *Uniform CPA Examination Blueprints,* October 2021, 2, https://www.aicpa.org/resources /download/learn-what-is-tested-on-the-cpa-exam.

9.   US Bureau of Labor Statistics, *Certification and Licensing Status of Employed Persons 16 Years and Over by Selected Characteristics, 2021 Annual Averages* (2022), 1, https://www.bls.gov/cps/cpsaat51.pdf (22.7 percent for white workers, 19.6 percent for Black workers, 18.7 percent for Asian workers, and 14.1 percent for Hispanic workers).

10.   US Bureau of Labor Statistics, *Occupational Outlook Handbook: Barbers, Hairstylists, and Cosmetologists,* accessed January 17, 2023, https://www.bls.gov /ooh/personal-care-and-service/barbers-hairstylists-and-cosmetologists .htm#tab-1.

11.   Braden Boucek (director of litigation, Beacon Center), email correspondence to author, April 2018.

12.   Plaintiff's Complaint at 5–9, *Zarate v. Tennessee Board of Cosmetology Examiners* (filed May 2018), http://www.beacontn.org/wp-content/uploads/2018/06 /Complaint.pdf.

13.   Tenn. Code Ann. § 62-3-110(b)(2) (2023) (imposing high school or GED for barbers); Tenn. Code Ann. § 62-4-110(b)(2) (2023) (imposing no such requirement on cosmetologists).

14.  David E. Bernstein, *Only One Place of Redress: African Americans, Labor Regulations, and the Courts from Reconstruction to the New Deal* (Durham: Duke University Press, 2001), 28–45; Timothy Sandefur, *The Right to Earn a Living: Economic Freedom and the Law* (Washington, DC: Cato Institute, 2010), 146–149.

15.  Marc T. Law and Mindy S. Marks, "Effects of Occupational Licensing Laws on Minorities: Evidence from the Progressive Era," *Journal of Law & Economics* 52, no. 2 (May 2009): 363–364. The study has its limitations; the authors acknowledge that for some professions during this time—such as medicine—Black worker participation was so low that they could not statistically analyze the effect of licensure.

16.  Mary Roth Walsh, *Doctors Wanted: No Women Need Apply: Sexual Barriers in the Medical Profession 1835–1975* (New Haven: Yale University Press, 1977), 14–15.

17.  Peter Blair and Bobby Chung, "Occupational Licensing Reduces Racial and Gender Wage Gaps: Evidence from the Survey of Income and Program Participation" (HCEO Working Paper Series 2017–050, University of Chicago, June 2017), 4–5, http://humcap.uchicago.edu/RePEc/hka/wpaper/Blair_Chung_2017 _licensing_gender_racial_wage_gaps_r1.pdf (finding a 4 percent wage premium for white men compared to 14 percent for Black men).

18.  Peter Q. Blair and Bobby W. Chung, "How Much of Barrier to Entry Is Occupational Licensing?," *British Journal of Industrial Relations* 57, no. 4 (December 2019): 930, 934–935.

19.  Cat Wise and Sam Weber, "Occupational Licensing Hurts Job Prospects for People with Criminal Records," *Newshour*, PBS, September 20, 2023, https://www .pbs.org/newshour/show/occupational-licensing-hurts-job-prospects-for -people-with-criminal-records#transcript.

20.  Ann Carson, *Prisoners in 2020—Statistical Tables*, US Department of Justice, Bureau of Justice Statistics (2021), 13, https://bjs.ojp.gov/content/pub/pdf/p20st .pdf.

21.  Chidi Umez and Rebecca Pirius, *Barriers to Work: Improving Employment in Licensed Occupations for Individuals with Criminal Records* (Washington, DC: National Conference of State Legislatures, 2018), 5–9, https://compacts.csg.org/wp -content/uploads/2022/06/criminalRecords_v06_web.pdf.

22.  Stephen Slivinski, *Turning Shackles into Bootstraps: Why Occupational Licensing Reform Is the Missing Piece of Criminal Justice Reform* (Tempe: Center for the Study of Economic Liberty at Arizona State University, November 2016), 2, https://csel.asu.edu/sites/default/files/2019-09/csel-policy-report-2016-01 -turning-shackles-into-bootstraps.pdf.

23.  Nick Sibilla, *Barred from Working: A Nationwide Study of Occupational Licensing Barriers for Ex-Offenders* (Arlington, VA: Institute for Justice, August 2020), https://ij.org/wp-content/uploads/2020/08/Barred-from-Working-August-2020-Update.pdf.

24.  Alec C. Ewald, "Barbers, Caregivers, and the Disciplinary Subject: Occupational Licensure for People with Criminal Justice Backgrounds in the United States," *Fordham Urban Law Journal* 46, no. 4 (June 2019): 745–748, 770, 782.

25.  April 26, 2018, Tennessee Board of Dentistry.

26.  Ewald, "Barbers, Caregivers," 801–803.

27.  Fresh Start Act, Tenn. Pub. Ch. No. 793, https://publications.tnsosfiles.com/acts/110/pub/pc0793.pdf.

28.  Tenn. Code Ann. § 62-76-104(b)(3) (2022).

29.  Sugarman v. Dougall, 413 U.S. 634 (1973). Although as a legal matter the issue is settled, old laws banning lawful permanent residents from professional licensure remain on the books in many states, likely having a deterrent effect. Jennesa Calvo-Friedman, "The Uncertain Terrain of State Occupational Licensing Laws for Noncitizens: A Preemption Analysis," *Georgetown Law Journal* 102, no. 5 (June 2014): 1607, 1638–1639.

30.  Silva Mathema, *Immigrant Doctors Can Help Lower Physician Shortages in Rural America* (Washington, DC: Center for American Progress, July 2019), 12, https://www.americanprogress.org/article/immigrant-doctors-can-help-lower-physician-shortages-rural-america.

31.  "Information regarding the Examination," BarberCosmo, California Board of Barbering and Cosmetology, accessed January 24, 2023, https://www.barbercosmo.ca.gov/applicants/national.shtml (licensing exams are "available in English, Korean, Spanish, and Vietnamese"); "Examination Information," under "Available Languages," Florida Department of Business and Professional Regulation, accessed January 24, 2023, https://www2.myfloridalicense.com/examination-information/#1507738607304-4af04802-cab9 ("Examinations . . . are available in English and Spanish at no additional cost.").

32.  Maya N. Federman, David E. Harrington, and Kathy J. Krynski, "The Impact of State Licensing Regulations on Low-Skilled Immigrants: The Case of Vietnamese Manicurists," *American Economic Review* 96, no. 2 (May 2006): 240.

33.  Morris M. Kleiner and Alan B. Krueger, "Analyzing the Extent and Influence of Occupational Licensing on the Labor Market," *Journal of Labor Eco-*

*nomics* 31, no. 2 (2013): S177 (note that his figure representing the percentage of that holds a license is higher than mine; that's because he uses a definition of "occupational licensing" that is broader than my definition of "professional licensing").

34. Maury Gittleman and Morris M. Kleiner, "Wage Effects of Unionization and Occupational Licensing Coverage in the United States," *Industrial and Labor Relations Review* 69, no. 1 (January 2016): 147.

35. Nunn, *How Occupational Licensing Matters,* 2; Gittleman and Kleiner, "Wage Effects," 170.

36. Sociologist Beth Redbird recently published an article arguing for the preservation or even expansion of licensing as a means of protecting workers. Her observation that a license provides special benefits to marginalized workers is supported by other research in the field and should be considered in tallying up the pros and cons of licensing rules. But her argument that licensing is a redistributive labor intervention in the spirit of unionization isn't supported by what we know about the two institutions. And her main empirical finding— that licensing did not affect prices or wages—is anomalous given that every other study finds at least some wage and price premium from licensure. Beth Redbird, "The New Closed Shop? The Economic and Structural Effects of Occupational Licensure," *American Sociological Review* 82, no. 3 (2017).

37. Knoxville barber school owner, in discussion with the author, May 2020.

38. *March 7, 2018 Hearing on H.B. 1809 before the Gov't Operations Comm.,* 110th Gen. Assemb., Reg. Sess. (Tenn. 2018), https://wapp.capitol.tn.gov/apps /BillInfo/Default.aspx?BillNumber=HB1809&GA=110. This phenomenon isn't unique to Tennessee. At a national conference about licensing reform, a representative from Utah said (of hair industry representatives at legislative hearings about deregulating hair), "They can bring a thousand people to fill the room." National Conference of State Legislatures, November 29, 2018, Clearwater, FL.

39. *February 14, 2018 Hearing on H.B. 1809 before the Bus. and Utils. Comm.,* 110th Gen. Assemb., Reg. Sess. (Tenn. 2018), https://wapp.capitol.tn.gov/apps /BillInfo/Default.aspx?BillNumber=HB1809&GA=110; Debra Cassens Weiss, "Tennessee has Imposed Nearly $100k in Fines for Unlicensed Hair Braiding since 2009," *American Bar Association Journal,* March 16, 2018, https://www.abajournal .com/news/article/tennessee_has_imposed_nearly_100k_in_fines_for_unlicensed _hair_braiding_sin.

40. *February 14, 2018 Hearing on H.B. 1809 before the Bus. and Utils. Comm.*, 110th Gen. Assemb., Reg. Sess. (Tenn. 2018), https://wapp.capitol.tn.gov/apps/BillInfo/Default.aspx?BillNumber=HB1809&GA=110.

41. *February 28, 2018 Hearing on H.B. 1809 before the Gov't Operations Comm.*, 110th Gen. Assemb., Reg. Sess. (Tenn. 2018), https://wapp.capitol.tn.gov/apps/BillInfo/Default.aspx?BillNumber=HB1809&GA=110.

42. *February 28, 2018 Hearing on H.B. 1809 before the Gov't Operations Comm.*, 110th Gen. Assemb., Reg. Sess. (Tenn. 2018), https://wapp.capitol.tn.gov/apps/BillInfo/Default.aspx?BillNumber=HB1809&GA=110.

43. H.B. 2059, 110th Gen. Assemb., Reg. Sess. (Tenn. 2018).

44. Ayana D. Byrd and Lori L. Tharps, *Hair Story: Untangling the Roots of Black Hair in America* (New York: St. Martin's Griffin, 2001), 25–41, 69–70, 73–83, 86–90.

45. Byrd and Tharps, *Hair Story.*

46. Former instructor at Tennessee Department of Correction Prison for Women Cosmetology School, in discussion with the author, June 2020.

47. *February 28, 2018 Hearing on H.B. 1809 before the Gov't Operations Comm.*, 110th Gen. Assemb., Reg. Sess. (Tenn. 2018), https://wapp.capitol.tn.gov/apps/BillInfo/Default.aspx?BillNumber=HB1809&GA=110.

48. Jeff Yarboro (Tennessee state senator), in discussion with the author, May 2018.

49. Plaintiff's Complaint at 20–21, Zarate v. Tennessee Board of Cosmetology Examiners (filed May 2018), http://www.beacontn.org/wp-content/uploads/2018/06/Complaint.pdf.

50. *March 20, 2018, Hearing on S.B. 2293, before the S. Com. and Lab. Comm.*, 110th Gen. Assemb., Reg. Sess. (Tenn. 2018), https://wapp.capitol.tn.gov/apps/BillInfo/Default.aspx?BillNumber=SB2293&GA=110.

51. Memorandum in Support of Defendant's Motion for Summary Judgment at 11, Zarate v. Tennessee Board of Cosmetology Examiners (unpublished, filed May 2018), http://www.beacontn.org/wp-content/uploads/2018/06/Memorandum-in-support-of-Plaintiffs-MSJ_Redacted.pdf.

52. Memorandum and Order, Zarate v. Tennessee Board of Cosmetology Examiners (August 2020), http://www.beacontn.org/wp-content/uploads/2018/06/18-0534-II-Final-Memorandum-and-Order-JMN-SIGNED.pdf.

53. Professions and Occupations—Cosmetology—Hair Braiding, 2019 TN Laws Pub. Ch. 207 (S.B. 1185); Tenn. Code Ann. § 62-4-135 (2019).

## 6. LICENSED TO ILL

1.   Michael LaPaglia, MD, Case Nos. 2013015321, 2013019391 (Tennessee Department of Health, March 19, 2014), https://apps.health.tn.gov/Disciplinary Exclusion/boardorder/display/1606_42617_031914.

2.   Michael LaPaglia, MD, Case No. 201802040 (Tennessee Department of Health, January 2, 2019), https://apps.health.tn.gov/DisciplinaryExclusion /boardorder/display/1606_42617_010219.

3.   United States v. LaPaglia, No. 3:18-CR-172 (E.D. Tenn. 2018).

4.   March 19–20, 2019, Tennessee Board of Medical Examiners.

5.   July 30–31, 2019, Tennessee Board of Medical Examiners.

6.   Michael LaPaglia, MD, Docket No. 17.18-157362A (Tennessee Department of Health, August 13, 2019), https://apps.health.tn.gov/DisciplinaryExclusion /boardorder/display/1606_42617_081319.

7.   Data on disciplinary rates come primarily from medicine and law, and even in those professions good data are lacking. One study of physicians in Indiana found that about 1.2 percent of their sample of physicians had a disciplinary history. Jing Liu and David A. Hyman, "Physician Licensing and Discipline: Lessons from Indiana," *Journal of Empirical Legal Studies* 18, no. 3 (September 2021): 629. In law, studies suggest a slightly higher number—that approximately 3 percent of lawyers face discipline in the course of a twenty- to thirty-year career. Leslie C. Levin, "The Folly of Expecting Evil: Reconsidering the Bar's Character and Fitness Requirement," *Brigham Young University Law Review* 2014 no. 4 (2014): 793 (2.4 percent); Kyle Rozema, "Does the Bar Exam Protect the Public?," *Journal of Empirical Legal Studies* 18 no. 4 (December 2021): 814; Nicole C. Brambila, "Disorder in the Court: Troubled Attorneys Often Take on Capital Cases," *Reading Eagle,* October 25, 2015, https://www.readingeagle.com/2015/10/25/disorder-in -the-court-troubled-attorneys-often-take-on-capital-cases/.

8.   Case No. 201603945 (Tennessee Department of Health, March 7, 2017), https://apps.health.tn.gov/DisciplinaryExclusion/boardorder/display/1606 _27271_030717.

9.   July 30–31, 2019, Tennessee Board of Medical Examiners.

10.   Case No. 2014007621 (Tennessee Department of Health, May 17, 2016), https://apps.health.tn.gov/DisciplinaryExclusion/boardorder/display/1606_8772 _051916. Case No. 2019056321 (Tennessee Department of Health, July 20, 2021), https://apps.health.tn.gov/DisciplinaryExclusion/boardorder/display/1606_8772 _072021 (order of compliance restoring his license to "unencumbered" status).

11. "State Report Card: Wyoming," *Atlanta Journal-Constitution,* accessed July 16, 2022, https://doctors.ajc.com/states/wyoming_sex_abuse/.

12. Out of seventy-nine cases where the board found facts amounting to "prescribing or otherwise distributing any controlled substance not in the course of professional practice," the board kept fifty-two doctors in practice by imposing merely a reprimand or probation; many retained their prescribing authority. Note that this language used by the board to justify these relatively light sanctions closely tracks the language of the federal code that makes such prescribing a felony. See 21 U.S.C. § 841.

13. Danny Robbins, "Repeat Offender Still Licensed to Treat Georgia Patients," *Atlanta Journal-Constitution,* accessed July 22, 2024, https://doctors.ajc.com /georgia_doctor_sex_abuse/.

14. Darren Grant and Kelly C. Alfred, "Sanctions and Recidivism: An Evaluation of Physician Discipline by State Medical Boards," *Journal of Health Politics, Policy, and Law* 32, no. 5 (October 2007): 877 (showing that "physicians receiving a medium or severe sanction in period A" were thirty times more likely to receive serious discipline in subsequent period B than their peers).

15. Public member, Tennessee Board of Medical Examiners, in discussion with the author, May 2019 (paraphrasing another colleague on the board who had said, of Dr. Robert Windsor, "he'll be back"); Physician member, Tennessee Board of Medical Examiners, overheard lamenting that Dr. Owens "won't make it two years" after the hearing where he was outvoted in the decision to relicense Dr. Owens, March 2018.

16. Rachel Weiner, "'Pill Mill' Doctor Who Lost License Three Times Is Sentenced to Seven Years in Prison," *Washington Post,* April 26, 2019, https://www .washingtonpost.com/local/public-safety/pill-mill-doctor-who-lost-license -three-times-sentenced-to-seven-years-in-prison/2019/04/26/dc525b5c-669a -11e9-a1b6-b29b90efa879_story.html/.

17. Blythe Bernhard, "Few Missouri Doctors Face Discipline from State Medical Board in Heat of Opioid Crisis," *St. Louis Post-Dispatch,* January 26, 2018, https://www.stltoday.com/news/local/metro/article_8d5652e0-4fa5-50e9-bd12 -c8a82b9c321b.html?mode=comments&fb_comment_id=1816385591737049 _1816456415063300.

18. John Fauber and Matt Wynn, "Doctors Who Surrender a Medical License in One State Can Practice in Another—and You Might Never Know," WYKC Studios, November 30, 2018, https://www.wkyc.com/article/news/nation-world /doctors-who-surrender-medical-license-in-one-state-still-practice-in-others /507-619081091.

19.  Member, Tennessee Board of Nursing, in discussion with the author, May 2019.

20.  April 6, 2018, Tennessee Board of Physician Assistants.

21.  Azza AbuDagga, Sidney M. Wolfe, Michael Carome, and Robert E. Oshel, "Crossing the Line: Sexual Misconduct by Nurses Reported to the National Practitioner Data Bank," *Public Health Nursing* 36, no. 2 (March-April 2019): 113.

22.  Brett Kelman, "This Pain Clinic Nurse Gave a Patient 51 Pills a Day. And She Kept Her License," *Tennessean,* October 11, 2018, https://www.tennessean.com /story/news/2018/10/11/opioid-epidemic-tennessee-pill-mills-christina-collins /1488026002/.

23.  Christina Collins, RN, Case No. 17.19-138846A (Tennessee Board of Nursing, March 1, 2018) (no longer available on state website; copy on file with the author); Christina Collins, RN, Case No. 17.19-138846A (Tennessee Board of Nursing, February 28, 2022), https://apps.health.tn.gov/DisciplinaryExclusion/boardorder /display/1702_12828_022822; Kelman, "51 Pills a Day."

24.  Clark Kauffman, "Chiropractor Accused of Sexual Impropriety Keeps His License," *Iowa Capital Dispatch,* April 16, 2021, https://iowacapitaldispatch.com /2021/04/16/chiropractor-accused-of-sexual-impropriety-keeps-his-license /#:~:text=By%3A%20Clark%20Kauffman%20%2D%20April%2016%2C%20 2021%203%3A48%20pm&text=An%20Iowa%20chiropractor%20who%20 has,a%20state%20board%20has%20ruled.

25.  Arthur Kane, "Painful Mistakes: Dental Board's Lax Oversight Fails Patients," *Las Vegas Review-Journal,* Oct 28, 2019, https://www.reviewjournal.com /investigations/painful-mistakes-dental-boards-lax-oversight-fails-patients -1872676/.

26.  Executive director of the state of Nevada's Funeral and Cemetery Services, at the 2020 FARB Forum, with the author in attendance, January 2020.

27.  Leslie C. Levin, "The Case for Less Secrecy in Lawyer Discipline," *Georgetown Journal of Legal Ethics* 20, no. 1 (Winter 2007).

28.  Leslie C. Levin, "The Folly of Expecting Evil: Reconsidering the Bar's Character and Fitness Requirement," *Brigham Young University Law Review* 2014, no. 4 (2015): 793; Kyle Rozema, "Does the Bar Exam Protect the Public?," *Journal of Empirical Legal Studies* 18, no. 4 (December 2021): 814.

29.  BPR no. 029981 (Tenn. Bd. of Pro. Resp. August 26, 2020), https://www.tbpr .org/attorneys/029981.

30.  Leslie C. Levin, "The Case for Less Secrecy in Lawyer Discipline," *Georgetown Journal of Legal Ethics* 20, no. 1 (Winter 2007): 3.

31. BPR no. 014186 (Tenn. Bd. of Pro. Resp., Apr. 26, 2012); https://www.tbpr.org/attorneys/014186.

32. One researcher asserts that half of disbarred attorneys go on to be reinstated. Deborah L. Rhode, *In the Interests of Justice: Reforming the Legal Profession* (Oxford: Oxford University Press, 2000), 161. Another suggests the number is very small. Kyle Rozema, "Professional Discipline and the Labor Market: Evidence from Lawyers," *Journal of Law and Economics* (forthcoming) (manuscript at 19). For a study of outcomes among those who seek reinstatement, see Terry Carter, "Bounced from the Bar: Lawyers Who Lose Their Licenses for Fraud or Other Misconduct Can Win Reinstatement, if They Practice in the Right State," *ABA Journal* 89, no. 10 (2003): 56, 60.

33. Iowa Supreme Court Attorney Disciplinary Bd. v. Moothart, 860 N.W.2d 598, 602, 615–618 (Iowa 2015).

34. Docket No. 2014-2341-2-WM (Tenn. Bd. of Pro. Resp. January 15, 2015): 12. On appeal, the Tennessee Supreme Court increased the length of suspension, and Warner died before he was reinstated. No. M2015-00350-SC-BAR-BP, 482 S.W.3d 520, 544 (Tenn. 2016).

35. A former judge has noted that disciplinary decisions in cases involving abusive attorneys tend to sanitize descriptions of the violence, especially when they are decided by male-dominated panels. Mary Pat Gunderson, "Gender and the Language of Judicial Opinion Writing," *Georgetown Journal of Gender and Law* 21, no. 1 (2019).

36. Disciplinary Counsel v. Sarver, 119 N.E.3d 405, 409 (Ohio 2018).

37. Gillian R. Chadwick, "Time's up for Attorney-Client Sexual Violence," *University of Maryland Law Journal of Race, Religion, Gender and Class* 22, no. 1 (2022): 76, 85–90.

38. Georgia Department of Audits and Accounting, *Georgia Composite Medical Board—Physician Oversight* (2020), https://www.audits.ga.gov/PAO/19-14_GCMB.html.

39. Sidney Wolfe and Robert E. Oshel, *Ranking of the Rate of State Medical Boards' Serious Disciplinary Actions, 2017–2019* (Washington, DC: Public Citizen's Health Research Group, March 2021), 9, https://www.citizen.org/wp-content/uploads/2574.pdf. It should be noted, however, that comparing states, especially when only one is from the heart of the region most affected by the opioid crisis, compares apples to oranges. Still, the discrepancies are so large, they would seem difficult to explain by geography or other reasons for disparate base rates of misconduct.

40. Wolfe and Oshel, *Serious Disciplinary Actions.*

41.  American Bar Association, *Survey on Lawyer Discipline Systems (S.O.L.D.) 2021,* November 2023, https://www.americanbar.org/groups/professional_respon sibility/resources/surveyonlawyerdisciplinesystems/.

42.  David B. Wilkins, "Who Should Regulate Lawyers?," *Harvard Law Review* 105, no. 4 (February 1992): 822.

43.  Seth Oldmixon, *The Great Medical Malpractice Hoax: NPDB Data Continues to Show Medical Liability System Produces Rational Outcomes* (Washington, DC: Public Citizen, 2007), https://www.citizen.org/wp-content/uploads/npdb_report _final.pdf.

44.  David Hyman, Mohammad Rahmati, and Bernard Black, "Medical Mal-practice and Physician Discipline: The Good, the Bad, and the Ugly," *Journal of Empirical Legal Studies* 18, no. 1 (March 2021): 142.

45.  Alan Levine, Robert Oshel, and Sidney Wolfe, *State Medical Boards Fail to Dis-cipline Doctors with Hospital Actions against Them* (Washington, DC: Public Cit-izen, 2011), https://www.citizen.org/article/state-medical-boards-fail-to-discipline -doctors-with-hospital-actions-against-them/.

46.  Notice of Charges, In re: Samson Orusa, MD (Tennessee Department of Health, February 1, 2018).

47.  "Crash Data," Tennessee Department of Safety and Homeland Security, last visited February 28, 2023, https://www.tn.gov/safety/stats/crashdata.html (995 traffic fatalities in 2013, 1,015 in 2012).

48.  Notice of Charges, In re: Samson Orusa, MD (Tennessee Department of Health, February 1, 2018).

49.  Lenny Bernstein, "US Life Expectancy Declines Again, a Dismal Trend Not Seen since World War I," *Washington Post,* November 29, 2018, https://www .washingtonpost.com/national/health-science/us-life-expectancy-declines-again -a-dismal-trend-not-seen-since-world-war-i/2018/11/28/ae58bc8c-f28c-11e8 -bc79-68604ed88993_story.html.

50.  Notice of Charges, In re: Samson Orusa, MD (Tennessee Department of Health, February 1, 2018).

51.  Brett Kelman, "Tennessee Pain Clinic Handed Out Opioids at 'Cattle Calls,' Says Undercover Federal Agent," *Tennessean,* February 14, 2019, https://www .tennessean.com/story/news/health/2019/02/14/tennessee-pain-clinic-samons -orusa-opioids-undercover-investigation/2863256002/.

52.  Brett Kelman, "Tennessee Doctor, Accused of Drug Dealing, Ordered to Stop Seeing Patients," *Tennessean,* May 20, 2019, https://www.tennessean.com/story

/news/health/2019/05/20/tennessee-doctor-samson-orusa-drug-dealing
-ordered-stop-practicing-medicine/3693840002/.

53. "Samson K. Orusa, MD; Decision and Order," Drug Enf't Admin., 87 F.R. 2986, January 19, 2022, https://www.federalregister.gov/documents/2022/01/19 /2022-00952/samson-k-orusa-md-decision-and-order; US Attorney's Office for the Middle District of Tennessee, "Jury Convicts Clarksville Doctor of 36 Counts Related to Pill Mill Operation," press release, April 27, 2021, https://www.justice .gov/usao-mdtn/pr/jury-convicts-clarksville-doctor-36-counts-related-pill-mill -operation.

54. Government's trial brief, United States v. Samson Orusa, Case No. 3:18-cr-00342 (C.D. Tenn. 2021).

55. Brett Kelman, "Testimony: Drug-dealing Doctor Paid Himself Millions at Rundown Pain Clinic," *Tennessean*, September 23, 2021, https://www.tennessean .com/story/news/health/2021/09/23/clarksville-doctor-convicted-dealing-drugs -paid-himself-millions/8311028002/.

56. US Attorney's Office for the Middle District of Tennessee, "45-Count Indict-ment Charges Clarksville, Tennessee Physician with Massive Opioid Distribution and Healthcare Fraud Scheme," press release, December 14, 2018, https://www .justice.gov/usao-mdtn/pr/45-count-indictment-charges-clarksville-tennessee -physician-massive-opioid-distribution.

57. Nadia N. Sawicki, "Character, Competence, and the Principles of Medical Discipline," *Journal of Health Care Law & Policy* 13, no. 2 (2010): 302–303.

58. Terry Spencer, "Florida 'Pill Mills' Were 'Gas on the Fire' of Opioid Crisis," Associated Press, July 20, 2019, https://apnews.com/article/0ced46b203864d8fa6 b8fda6bd97b60e.

59. Federation of State Medical Boards, "Physician Sexual Misconduct: Report and Recommendations of the FSMB Workgroup on Physician Sexual Misconduct," *Journal of Medical Regulation* 106, no. 2 (May 2020): 26.

60. Reporting by the *Los Angeles Times* sparked the lawsuits against University of Southern California and "the largest sex crimes inquiry involving a single sus-pect in Los Angeles Police Department History." Dr. Tyndall was indicted in 2019 and died in 2023 awaiting trial. Richard Hinton and Harriet Ryan, "Former USC Gynecologist George Tyndall Charged with 29 Felonies in Sex Abuse Case," *Los Angeles Times*, June 26, 2019, https://www.latimes.com/local/lanow/la-me-george -tyndall-arrest-usc-sexual-abuse-20190626-story.html; Matt Hamilton, Harriet Ryan, and Paul Pringle, "George Tyndall, ex-USC Gynecologist Accused of Sexual

Abuse, Found Dead at Home," *Los Angeles Times,* October 5, 2023, https://www
.latimes.com/california/story/2023-10-05/george-tyndall-ex-usc-gynecologist
-accused-of-sexual-abuse-found-dead-at-home.

61.   Meredith Deliso, "Breaking Down University of Southern California's $1.1
Billion in Sex Abuse Settlements," *ABC News,* March 27, 2021, https://abcnews.go
.com/US/breaking-university-southern-californias-11-billion-sex-abuse/story
?id=76713012.

62.   For a general overview of how disciplinary procedure works at American
medical boards, for example, see US Department of Health and Human Services,
*State Discipline of Physicians: Assessing State Medical Boards through Case Studies*
(2006), https://aspe.hhs.gov/sites/default/files/migrated_legacy_files//41966/std
iscp.pdf; "Guide to Medical Regulation in the United States—Introduction,"
Federation of State Medical Boards, https://www.fsmb.org/u.s.-medical-regulatory
-trends-and-actions/guide-to-medical-regulation-in-the-united-states/intro
duction/. For a description of the procedure at the health-related boards in
Tennessee, see "Tennessee Board of Medical Examiners—About," Tennessee Department of Health, https://www.tn.gov/health/health-program-areas/health-pro
fessional-boards/me-board/me-board/about.html.

63.   For a description of how various medical boards use investigators, see Federation of State Medical Boards, *Legal Counsel and Board Investigators* (2021),
https://www.fsmb.org/siteassets/advocacy/regulatory/board-structure/legal
-counsel-and-board-investigators.pdf.

64.   The Tennessee rules about subpoenas can be found here: Tenn. Code Ann.
§ 63-1-117 (2019).

65.   The Tennessee rules about consultants can be found here: Tenn. Comp. R. &
Regs. R. 0880-02(4) (2017).

66.   For examples from medicine, see Federation of State Medical Boards, *US
Medical Regulatory Trends and Actions* (2018), 65, https://www.fsmb.org
/SysSiteAssets/advocacy/publications/us-medical-regulatory-trends-actions.pdf.

67.   In California, for example, the board does not attend the hearings; however,
the board votes on whether to adopt the administrative law judge's decision. Hon.
Susan L. Formaker (general division chief administrative law judge for the Office
of Administrative Hearings for the State of California), in discussion with the author, March 2022. See also Federation of State Medical Boards, *US Medical Regulatory Trends and Actions,* 66.

68.   Tennessee Department of Health v. Collins, No. 18-492-IV, F.O.-6 at * 6 (Tenn.
Ct. App. 2019) ("The Court may not substitute its judgment for that of the agency,
even when the evidence could support a different result.") (citing *Wayne County*

*v. Tennessee Solid Waste Disposal Control Bd.*, 756 S.W. 2d 274, 279 [Tenn. Ct. App. 1988]).

69. Mark T. Law and Zeynep K. Hansen, "Medical Licensing Board Characteristics and Physician Discipline: An Empirical Analysis," *Journal of Health Politics, Policy, and Law* 35, no. 1 (February 2010): 84. Elizabeth Graddy and Michael B. Nichol, "Structural Reforms and Licensing Board Performance," *American Politics Quarterly* 18, no. 3 (July 1990): 395–396.

70. Head of investigations, Tennessee Department of Health, in discussion with the author, May 2019; member, Tennessee Board of Medical Examiners, in discussion with the author, September 2019.

71. Medical consultant, Tennessee Board of Medical Examiners, in discussion with the author, April 2018.

72. Richard L. Abel, *Lawyers in the Dock: Learning from Attorney Discipline* (New York: Oxford University Press, 2008), 502 (noting that only about 10 percent of complaints against lawyers come from other lawyers, including judges).

73. Brendan Martin et al., "Patient Safety Culture and Barriers to Adverse Event Reporting: A National Survey of Nurse Executives," *Journal of Nursing Regulation* 9, no. 2 (2018): 9–17.

74. Melissa McPheeters and Mary K. Bratton, "The Right Hammer for the Right Nail: Public Health Tools in the Struggle between Pain and Addiction," *University of Memphis Law Review* 48, no. 4 (Summer 2018): 1334.

75. Interview not for attribution, in discussion with the author, June 2019.

76. David B. Wilkins, "Who Should Regulate Lawyers?," *Harvard Law Review* 105, no. 4 (February 1992): 824–829.

77. Wilkins, "Regulate Lawyers."

78. "File a Complaint," Board of Professional Responsibility of the Supreme Court of Tennessee, https://www.tbpr.org/for-the-public/file-complaint; "Complaints about Lawyers," Virginia State Bar Association, https://vsb.org/site/forms/intake .aspx.

79. "State Report Card: Wyoming," *Atlanta Journal-Constitution*, accessed July 16, 2022, https://doctors.ajc.com/states/wyoming_sex_abuse/.

80. Emrys Eller, "Did New York Let Doctors Get Away with Sexual Misconduct?," *Type Investigations*, February 21, 2021, https://www.typeinvestigations.org /investigation/2021/02/21/did-new-york-let-doctors-get-away-with-sexual -misconduct/.

81. Interview not for attribution, in discussion with the author, March 2021.

82.  Louisiana Legislative Auditor, *Louisiana Board of Massage Therapy: Regulation of the Massage Therapy Profession* (March 3, 2021), https://app.lla.state.la.us /PublicReports.nsf/0/D1EF459AE075E0058625868D008254D5/$FILE /00022E61A.pdf. According to the massage board, they do not use the sites because "establishments do not have control over what is posted on these websites and there are so many of these websites it would be hard to know which ones to search."

83.  US Attorney's Office for the Eastern District of Kentucky, "Pain Management Physician Resolves False Claims Act Allegations," press release, February 1, 2017, https://www.justice.gov/usao-edky/pr/pain-management-physician-resolves -false-claims-act-allegations.

84.  Darrel Rinehart MD, Docket No. 17.18-146184A (Tennessee Department of Health, November 20, 2018): 1, 12, ¶¶ 13–14, 17, https://apps.health.tn.gov /DisciplinaryExclusion/boardorder/display/1606_15431_112018. *See also* Brett Kelman, "After 5 Deadly Overdoses, Tennessee Doctor Now Practicing in Indiana," *Tennessean,* January 24, 2019, https://www.tennessean.com/story/news/investi gations/2019/01/24/opioid-overdose-deaths-tennessee-doctor-darrel-rinehart -indiana/2452093002/.

85.  November 14, 2018, Tennessee Board of Medical Examiners (contested case of Dr. Darrel Rinehart).

86.  Darrel R. Rinehart, MD, Docket No. 17.18-146184A (Tennessee Department of Health, November 20, 2018), https://apps.health.tn.gov/DisciplinaryExclusion /boardorder/display/1606_15431_112018; Kelman, "After 5 Deadly Overdoses,"; Brett Kelman, "One Doctor, Five Deadly Overdoses: What We Know about the Victims, *Tennessean,* January 24, 2019, https://www.tennessean.com/story/money /2019/01/24/darrel-rinehart-investigation-victims-fatal-opioid-prescription -drug-overdose-what-we-know/2515684002/; August 1, 2018, Tennessee Board of Medical Examiners; September 26, 2018, Tennessee Board of Medical Examiners; November 14, 2018, Tennessee Board of Medical Examiners.

87.  Docket No. 17.18-139095A (Tennessee Department of Health, March 1, 2019), https://apps.health.tn.gov/DisciplinaryExclusion/boardorder/display/1606 _27530_030119.

88.  Stephen Gillers, "Lowering the Bar: How Lawyer Discipline in New York Fails to Protect the Public," *New York University Journal of Legislation & Public Policy* 17, no. 2 (2014): 496.

89.  Steve Miller, "Questionable Doctors Keep Licenses Because of Drawn-Out Investigative Process," *Florida Times-Union,* October 24, 2013, https://www .jacksonville.com/story/news/2013/10/24/questionable-doctors-keep-licenses -because-drawn-out-investigative-process/15811782007/.

90. Schware v. Board of Bar Examiners of New Mexico, 353 U.S. 232, 238–239 (1957); Keney v. Derbyshire, 718 2d. 352, 354 (10th Cir. 1983).

91. Frank E. Cooper, *State Administrative Law* (Indianapolis: Bobbs-Merrill Company, 1965), 1:145.

92. Former member, Tennessee Board of Massage Licensure, in discussion with the author, June 2021.

93. Tennessee Department of Health v. Collins, No. 18-492-IV, F.O.-6, at *6–7 (Tenn. Ct. App. 2019).

94. Samson Orusa, MD, Docket No. 17.60-150338A (Tennessee Department of Health, August 21, 2018) (order no longer available on state website, copy on file with author).

95. Attorney specializing in professional discipline defense, in discussion with the author, March 2018.

96. Michael S. Frisch, "No Stone Left Unturned: The Failure of Attorney Self-Regulation in the District of Columbia," *Georgetown Journal of Legal Ethics* 18, no. 2 (2005): 351–353.

97. For proposals for a more proactive disciplinary system, see Robert C. Fellmeth, "Physician Discipline in California: A Code Blue Emergency," *California Regulatory Law Reporter* 9, no. 2 (April 1989): 28; Lucian L. Leape and John A. Fromson, "Problem Doctors: Is There a System-Level Solution?," *Annals of Internal Medicine* 144, no. 2 (January 2006): 109. A study comparing states with and without proactive enforcement through prescription drug-monitoring databases found that those with a proactive system for identifying overprescribers had slower growth in the availability of prescription pain killers. Prescription Drug Monitoring Program Center for Excellence at Brandeis, *Briefing on PDMP Effectiveness*, last updated September 2014, 6, https://dhhs.ne.gov/DOP%20document%20library/PDMP%20Center%20of%20Excellence%20Briefing.pdf.

98. Stephen Seeling (executive director, South Carolina State Board of Medical Examiners), in discussion with the author, November 2018.

## 7. RECOVER AND REPAIR

1. Brad Schmitt, "Outgoing Tennessee Opioid Czar Calls for Using Controversial 'Harm-Reduction' Drugs," *Tennessean*, February 7, 2018, https://www.tennessean.com/story/news/health/2018/02/07/tennessee-opioid-czar-controversial-drugs-recovery/315463002/.

2.  Dr. Stephen Loyd (member, Tennessee Board of Medical Examiners), in discussion with the author, July 2019.

3.  Dr. Stephen Loyd, in discussion with the author, August 2021.

4.  Courtnee Melton, *The Opioid Epidemic in TN (1 of 3): Key Policy Milestones and Indicators of Progress* (Nashville, TN: Sycamore Institute, August 3, 2017), https://www.sycamoreinstitutetn.org/opioid-epidemic-tn-milestones-progress/.

5.  Melissa McPheeters and Mary K. Bratton, "The Right Hammer for the Right Nail: Public Health Tools in the Struggle between Pain and Addiction," *University of Memphis Law Review* 48, no. 4 (Summer 2018): 1323–1325, 1328.

6.  Tenn. Code Ann. § 53-10-305(a)-(b) (2022); Tenn. Code Ann. § 53-10-304(c) (2022).

7.  Controlled Substances—Prescriptions, Tenn. Pub. Ch. 1039 (2018); Joel Ebert and Anita Wadhwani, "Gov. Bill Haslam Unveils $30 Million Plan to Combat Opioid Crisis in Tennessee," *Tennessean,* January 22, 2018, https://www.tennessean.com/story/news/politics/2018/01/22/gov-bill-haslams-plan-combat-opioid-crisis-include-boosts-prevention-treatment-and-law-enforcement/1054217001/.

8.  Schmitt, "'Harm-Reduction' Drugs."

9.  Tennessee Office of the Governor, "Haslam Signs TN Together Legislation," press release, June 29, 2018, https://www.tn.gov/former-governor-haslam/news/2018/6/29/haslam-signs-tn-together-legislation.html.

10.  US Attorney's Office Eastern District of Tennessee, "Nine Medical Practitioners Indicted in Conspiracy to Distribute Controlled Pain Medicine as Employees of Breakthrough Pain Therapy Center in Maryville," press release, October 16, 2014, https://www.justice.gov/usao-edtn/pr/nine-medical-practitioners-indicted-conspiracy-distribute-controlled-pain-medication.

11.  Barry Meier, *Pain Killer: An Empire of Deceit and the Origin of America's Opioid Epidemic,* 2nd ed. (New York: Random House, 2018).

12.  Complaint, State ex rel. Slatery v. Purdue Pharma LP, Case No. 1-173-18 (Tenn. Cir. Ct. 2018).

13.  Christina K. Collins, APRN, License No. 132524, Docket No. 17.19-138846A (Tennessee Department of Health, March 5, 2018) (order no longer available on state website, copy on file with author).

14.  April 6, 2018, Tennessee Board on Physician Assistants; Walter Blankenship, PA, Case No. 201701728 (Tennessee Department of Health, May 23, 2018), https://apps.health.tn.gov/DisciplinaryExclusion/boardorder/display/3628_1171_051018.

15. Thomas K. Ballard, III, MD, License No. 16530, Docket No. 17.18-150781A (Tennessee Department of Health, November 15, 2018), https://apps.health.tn.gov /DisciplinaryExclusion/boardorder/display/1606_16530_111418; Indictment, United States v. Ballard, Cr. No.: 1:19-cr-10042-STA, at 1, 7 (W.D. Tenn. 2019); US Attorney's Office for the Western District of Tennessee, "US Attorney Dunavant along with Federal, State and Local Partners Continue Efforts to Combat the Opioid Crisis," press release, April 18, 2019, https://www.justice.gov/usao-wdtn/pr /us-attorney-dunavant-along-federal-state-and-local-partners-continue-efforts -combat.

16. *Controlled Substances: Hearing on S. 0777 before the S. Health & Welfare Comm.*, 2018 Leg., 110th Sess. (Tenn. 2018) (statement of Senator Ferrell Haile); Tenn. Code Ann. § 63-1-162(e) (2021).

17. Tenn. Comp. R. & Regs. 0880-02-.25 (2019).

18. Board member, Tennessee Board of Medical Examiners, in discussion with the author, May 2018.

19. Board member, Tennessee Board of Medical Examiners, in discussion with the author, September 2019.

20. Board member, Tennessee Board of Medical Examiners, in discussion with the author, September 2019.

21. May 29, 2019, Tennessee Board of Medical Examiners (contested case of a physician accused of prescribing fentanyl, morphine, and ketamine without preforming exams, taking histories, or keeping documentation in seventy-five patient charts).

22. Ron Ben-Ari, MD, et al., "The Costs of Training Internal Medicine Residents in the United States," *American Journal of Medicine* 127, no. 10 (October 2014): https://www.amjmed.com/article/S0002-9343(14)00596-8/pdf.

23. Board member, Tennessee Board of Medical Examiners, in discussion with the author, September 2019.

24. President, Tennessee Board of Medical Examiners, in discussion with the author, September 2019.

25. Board member, Tennessee Board of Medical Examiners, in discussion with the author, September 2019. In Dr. LaPaglia's case, Dr. Loyd said something similar about Dr. LaPaglia's resume, "[T]hey don't let just anyone into the two programs you trained in." July 31, 2019, Tennessee Board of Medical Examiners.

26. Former member, Tennessee Board of Chiropractic Examiners, in discussion with the author, June 2018. Likewise, a member of the midwifery board told me that her colleague had asked her to stay on top of a dangerous midwife because her malpractice was making midwives look bad. Certified nurse-midwife, member of the Tennessee Council of Certified Professional Midwifery, in discussion with the author, April 23, 2019.

27. March 13, 2018, Tennessee Board of Funeral Directors and Embalmers.

28. Board member, Tennessee Board of Medical Examiners, in discussion with the author, September 2019.

29. Board member, Tennessee Board of Medical Examiners, in discussion with the author, September 2019.

30. Michael S. Frisch, "No Stone Left Unturned: The Failure of Attorney Self-Regulation in the District of Columbia," *Georgetown Journal of Legal Ethics* 18, no. 2 (2005): 331.

31. Oliver Wendell Holmes Jr., "The Path of the Law," *Harvard Law Review* 10, no. 8 (March 1897): 459.

32. Council on Scientific Affairs, "Drug Abuse Related to Prescribing Practices," *Journal of the American Medical Association* 247, no. 6 (February 1982): 864; Donald R. Wesson and David E. Smith, "Prescription Drug Abuse: Patient, Physician, and Cultural Responsibilities," *Western Journal of Medicine* 152, no. 5 (May 1990): 614.

33. Rima Sirota, "Can Continuing Legal Education Pass the Test? Empirical Lessons from the Medical World," *Notre Dame Journal of Law, Ethics, and Public Policy* 36, no. 1 (2022): 4–5.

34. Christina K. Collins, APRN, License No. 132524, Docket No. 17.19-138846A (Tennessee Department of Health, March 5, 2018).

35. Case No: 42345 (Washington Co. Criminal Court, August 23, 2017).

36. Case No: 201602805 (Tennessee Department of Health, September 27, 2017), https://apps.health.tn.gov/DisciplinaryExclusion/boardorder/display/1606_49214_092717.

37. Danny Robbins, "Repeat Offender Still Licensed to Treat Georgia Patients," *Atlanta-Journal Constitution,* https://doctors.ajc.com/georgia_doctor_sex_abuse/?_gl=1*cf9x7l*_ga*MTExMzYxMjAyMS4xNjY1NDQ4NTU4*_ga_6VR7Y4BTY5*MTY2NTQ0ODU1OC4xLjEuMTY2NTQ0ODU4OC4wLjAuMA; "About PBI Education," PBI Education, Professional Boundaries Inc., https://pbieducation.com/about/.

38.  Federation of State Medical Boards, "Report and Recommendations of the FSMB Workgroup on Physician Misconduct," *Journal of Medical Regulation* 106, no. 2 (May 2020); "What It Means to be a Monitor," Physician Health Services, Inc., accessed November 12, 2022, https://www.massmed.org/Physician_Health _Services/Helping_Yourself_and_Others/What_it_means_to_be_a_Monitor/# .X4DNbZNKhsY.

39.  Attorney specializing in professional discipline defense, in discussion with the author, July 2021.

40.  July 30, 2019, Tennessee Board of Medical Examiners.

41.  "The Other Person in the Room," *PBI Education* (blog), archived November 25, 2020, at the Wayback Machine, https://web.archive.org/web/2020112 5161301/https://pbieducation.com/the-other-person-in-the-room/; "The Value of a Well-Trained Medical Chaperone," *PBI Education* (blog), January 2020, https:// pbieducation.com/the-value-of-a-well-trained-medical-chaperone/?highlight =chaperone.

42.  September 2019, Tennessee Board of Medical Examiners.

43.  James M. DuBois et al., "Sexual Violation of Patients by Physicians: A Mixed-Methods, Exploratory Analysis of 101 Cases," *Sexual Assault* 31, no. 5 (August 2017): 518.

44.  People v. Nassar, No. 345699, 2020 WL 7636250, at *1 (Mich. Ct. App. Dec. 22, 2020); Christine Hauser, "At Larry Nassar's Sentencing, Parents Ask: 'How Did I Miss the Red Flags?,'" *New York Times,* January 24, 2018, https://www.nytimes.com /2018/01/24/sports/larry-nassar-parents.html.

45.  Dr. John Hall (former executive director, Mississippi Board of Medicine), in discussion with the author, July 2018.

46.  Ron Paterson, *Independent Review of the Use of Chaperones to Protect Patients in Australia* (Melbourne, Australia: National Health Practitioner Ombudsman, 2017), 7, 10, https://www.nhpo.gov.au/sites/default/files/2020-08/Chaperone -review-report-WEB.pdf.

47.  March 20, 2018, Tennessee Board of Medical Examiners.

48.  License No. 26618, Docket No. 17.18-144262A (Tennessee Department of Health, September 27, 2017), https://apps.health.tn.gov/DisciplinaryExclusion /boardorder/display/1606_26618_092717.

49.  Motion of Government for Revocation of Release, United States v. Young, Cr. No.: 1:19-cr-10040-JDB at 2, 9 (W.D. Tenn. May 2, 2019) (No. 58).

50. Kara Schmitt, *Demystifying Occupational and Professional Regulation* (Orlando: Professional Testing Inc., 2015), 122.

51. Danny Robbins, "Doctor Accused by 17 Females Loses License after Male Patient's Accusation of Sexual Impropriety," *Atlanta Journal-Constitution*, July 13, 2018, https://www.ajc.com/news/public-affairs/limiting-doctor-male-patients -failed-stop-sex-abuse/lu2GbV9GxSNlkujDCI0AAN/.

52. A study of medical board discipline, for example, revealed that more than half of disciplined providers were suspected to have a personality disorder or substance abuse disorder. James M. Dubois et al., "Serious Ethical Violations in Medicine: A Statistical and Ethical Analysis of 280 Cases in the United States from 2008–2016," *American Journal of Bioethics* 19, no. 1 (January 2019): 25.

53. Michael R. Oreskovich et al., "The Prevalence of Substance Abuse Disorders in American Physicians," *American Journal on Addictions* 24, no. 1 (January 2015): 37; Patrick R. Krill, Ryan Johnson, and Linda Albert, "The Prevalence of Substance Use and Other Mental Health Concerns among American Attorneys," *Journal of Addiction Medicine* 10, no. 1 (January / February 2016): 51.

54. Catherine M. Welcher et al., "Programs and Resources to Alleviate Concerns with Mental Health Disclosures on Physician Licensing Applications," *Journal of Medical Regulation* 105, no. 2 (July 2019): 28.

55. March 20, 2018, Tennessee Board of Medical Examiners. I know of two other occasions where a board member expressed the expectation that a troubled doctor would be back before the board. Consumer member, Tennessee Board of Medical Examiners, in discussion with the author, May 2019; March 20, 2019, Tennessee Board of Medical Examiners.

56. Medical director, Tennessee Medical Foundation, in discussion with the author, May 2018; Robert L. DuPont et al., "Setting the Standard for Recovery: Physicians' Health Programs," *Journal of Substance Abuse Treatment* 36, no. 2 (2009): 162. For general information on Lawyer Assistance Programs (the equivalent of a PHP in the legal field), see American Bar Association Commission on Lawyer Assistance Programs, *2014 Comprehensive Survey of Lawyer Assistance Programs* (2015), https://www.americanbar.org/content/dam/aba /administrative/lawyer_assistance/ls_colap_2014_comprehensive_survey_of _laps.pdf.

57. J. Wesley Boyd, "Doctors Pay Up or Else Don't Work," *Psychology Today*, December 1, 2019, https://www.psychologytoday.com/us/blog/almost-addicted /201912/doctors-pay-or-else-dont-work.

58. P. J. Randhawa, "Doctor Left Destitute after Seeking Help from Physician Health Program," KSDK, May 21, 2019, https://www.ksdk.com/article/news /investigations/doctor-left-destitute-after-seeking-help-from-physician-health -program/63-99720f38-5c5c-43c6-9c4c-c0f522ddc8c4?fbclid=IwAR3kRLMkltL 4hjXH0UThrOjlxJiEaPz7Ib39jmoNfBqgFlKHMM8SigbJUkY.

59. Director of Tennessee Professional Assistance Program, in discussion with the author, June 2019.

60. For example, Florida's PHP and medical association use the same mailing address on their tax returns, and the PHP contracts with the association for "accounting services and management of employee benefits." Steve Miller, "Questionable Doctors Keep Licenses Because of Drawn-out Investigative Process," *Florida Times-Union*, October 24, 2013, https://www.jacksonville.com/story/news/2013 /10/24/questionable-doctors-keep-licenses-because-drawn-out-investigative -process/15811782007/.

61. Co-director, Center for Professional Health at Vanderbilt University Medical Center, in discussion with the author, August 12, 2019.

62. Wesley Boyd and John R. Knight, "Ethical and Managerial Considerations regarding State Physician Health Programs," *Journal of Addiction Medicine* 6, no. 4 (December 2012): 245.

63. Attorney specializing in professional discipline defense, in discussion with the author, July 2021.

64. July 31, 2019, Tennessee Board of Medical Examiners.

65. Boyd and Knight, "Ethical and Managerial Considerations"; Robert L. DuPont et al., "How are addicted physicians treated? A national survey of Physician Health Programs," *Journal of Substance Abuse Treatment* 37, no. 1 (July 2009): 1, 3–4.

66. Psychiatrist, in conversation with author, August 2021.

67. Bill Wilkinson, "(MedEd)itorial: The Dark Side of Physician Health Programs," *Blueprint* (blog), January 31, 2017, https://blog.blueprintprep.com/medical /mededitorial-the-dark-side-of-physician-health-programs/.

68. Boyd, "Doctors Pay Up."

69. Dinah Miller, "Physician Health Programs: 'Diagnosing for Dollars'?," *Perspectives* (blog), MDedge Psychiatry, December 5, 2017, https://www.mdedge.com /psychiatry/article/153573/depression/physician-health-programs-diagnosing -dollars.

70. For a public-protection critique of PHPs, see Elizabeth Chiarello, "Barriers to Medical Board Discipline: Cultural and Organizational Constraints," *Saint Louis*

*University Journal of Health Law and Policy* 15, no. 1 (2021): 78 (arguing that PHPs "fail to provide evidence-based care" and, ultimately, "appear to be mechanisms for maintaining the white wall of science more than they look like effective remedies for preventing patient harm").

71. Executive director and founder of the Tennessee Colleague Assistance Foundation, in discussion with the author, July 2019.

72. Samantha Wilson, "The Rise of the Lawyer Counseling Movement; Confidentiality and Other Concerns regarding State Lawyer Assistance Programs," *Georgetown Journal of Legal Ethics* 27, no. 3 (Summer 2014): 951–966.

73. Medical director, Tennessee Medical Foundation, in discussion with the author, June 2019.

74. Consumer member, Tennessee Board of Medical Examiners, in discussion with the author, April 2018.

75. July 31, 2019, Tennessee Board of Medical Examiners.

76. License No. 26618, Docket No. 17.18-144262A (Tennessee Department of Health, September 27, 2017), https://apps.health.tn.gov/DisciplinaryExclusion/boardorder/display/1606_26618_092717.

77. Complaint ¶¶ 474–531, State ex rel. Slatery v. Purdue Pharma LP, Case No. 1-173-18 (Tenn. Cir. Ct. 2018).

78. Anna Lembke, MD, *Drug Dealer, MD: How Doctors Were Duped, Patients Got Hooked, and Why It's so Hard to Stop* (Baltimore: Johns Hopkins University Press, 2016); Barry Meier, *Pain Killer: An Empire of Deceit and the Origin of America's Opioid Epidemic* (New York: Random House, 2018).

79. Thomas Catan and Evan Perez, "A Pain-Drug Champion Has Second Thoughts," *Wall Street Journal*, updated December 17, 2012, https://www.wsj.com/articles/SB10001424127887324478304578173342657044604.

80. Catan and Perez, "A Pain-Drug Champion"; Federation of State Medical Boards, *Model Guidelines for the Use of Controlled Substances for the Treatment of Pain*, 1998 (no longer publicly available; copy of policy on file with the author).

81. Federation of State Medical Boards, *Model Guidelines*.

82. David E. Joranson et al., "Pain Management, Controlled Substances, and State Medical Board Policy: A Decade of Change," *Journal of Pain and Symptom Management* 23, no. 2 (February 2002): 144.

83. Federation of State Medical Boards, *Model Policy for the Use of Controlled Substances for the Treatment of Pain*, May 2004, 1.

84. Jack Richard and Marcus M. Reidenberg, "The Risk of Disciplinary Action by State Medical Boards against Physicians Prescribing Opioids," *Journal of Pain and Symptom Management* 29, no. 2 (February 2005): 206–207.

85. The CDC says that since 1999 more than one million American have died from an overdose, most of which involved opioids. "Drug Overdose Death Rate Remained High in 2021," Center for Disease Control and Prevention, https://www.cdc.gov/nchs/data/databriefs/db457.pdf.

86. Dr. Stephen Loyd (member, Tennessee Board of Medical Examiners), in discussion with the author, September 2019 and August 2021.

87. Booker v. LaPaglia, 617 Fed. Appx. 520, 522 (6th Cir. 2015).

88. Gulley v. LaPaglia, No. 3:12-CV-371, 2013 WL 6713565, at *1 (E.D. Tenn. 2013); Booker v. LaPaglia, 617 Fed. App'x 520 (6th Cir. 2015).

89. States v. Booker, 728 F.3d 535, 540 (6th Cir. 2013).

90. Booker v. LaPaglia, 617 Fed. App'x 520 (6th Cir. 2015); (Gulley v. LaPaglia, No. 3:12-CV-371, 2013 WL 6713565, at *1 (E.D. Tenn. 2013). For further information, see Jamie Satterfield, "Knox Doctor with Penchant for Paralyzing Cavity Searches Admits Selling Prescriptions for Cash," *Knoxville News Sentinel,* November 30, 2018, https://www.knoxnews.com/story/news/crime/2018/11/30/knox-doctor-known-paralyzing-searches-admits-selling-prescriptions-cash/2117791002/.

91. Notice of Charges and Allegations, In re: Michael Anthony LaPaglia, MD (North Carolina Medical Board, February 25, 2002); Notice of Dismissal, In re: Michael Anthony LaPaglia, MD (North Carolina Medical Board, September 21, 2005).

92. Tennessee Board of Medical Examiners, Application of Michael Anthony LaPaglia for Licensure as a Medical Doctor, May 7, 2007, 9–10, 14.

93. Final Order, In the Matter of the Application to Practice Medicine and Surgery of Michael A. LaPaglia, MD, at 4 (Pa. Dep't of State 2008).

94. John Holmes, Affidavit of Complaint at 1, State of Tennessee v. Michael A. LaPaglia, No. 103051 (Knox Co. Cir. 2014).

95. July 30–31, 2019, Tennessee Board of Medical Examiners.

## 8. THE FALLEN PROFESSIONAL

1. July 31, 2019, Tennessee Board of Medical Examiners.

2. "Doctor Being Sued in Fed Court Charged with Weapons, Drug Charges," *OakRidger,* September 6, 2013, https://www.oakridger.com/story/news/courts/2013/09/06/doctor-being-sued-in-fed/44291482007/.

3. Art Van Zee and David A. Fiellin, "Proliferation of Cash-Only Buprenorphine Treatment Clinics: A Threat to the Nation's Response to the Opioid Crisis," *American Journal of Public Health* 109, no. 3 (March 2019): 393 ("Some practices have adopted a model of buprenorphine provision that does not accept any insurance and requires patients to make out-of-pocket (i.e., cash) payments.").

4. Voluntary Petition for Individuals Filing Bankruptcy, Michael Anthony LaPaglia (E.D. Ky. 2016) (No. 3:16-bk-30370-SHB) (listing a mortgage, student loans, and taxes among his debts).

5. US Department of Health and Human Services, Office of the Surgeon General, *Facing Addiction in America: The Surgeon General's Spotlight on Opioids* (Washington, DC: HHS, 2018), https://www.hhs.gov/sites/default/files/OC_Spotlight OnOpioids.pdf.

6. Marisa Crane, "Can Suboxone Get You High?," *American Addiction Centers,* September 15, 2022, https://americanaddictioncenters.org/suboxone/get-high.

7. Jermaine D. Jones, Shanthi Mogali, and Sandra D. Comer, "Polydrug Abuse: A Review of Opioid and Benzodiazepine Combination Use," *Drug and Alcohol Dependence* 125, no. 1–2 (2012): 8, https://www.ncbi.nlm.nih.gov/pmc/articles /PMC3454351/.

8. Indeed, the risk of overdosing on opioids is ten times higher when mixed with benzos. Nabarun Dasgupta et al., "Cohort Study of the Impact of High-Dose Opioid Analgesics," *Pain Medicine* 17 (2016): 85.

9. July 31, 2019, Tennessee Board of Medical Examiners; March 21, 2019, Tennessee Board of Medical Examiners.

10. Michael LaPaglia, MD, Case No. 201802040 (Tennessee Department of Health, January 1, 2019), https://apps.health.tn.gov/DisciplinaryExclusion/board order/display/1606_42617_010219.

11. Dr. Michael LaPaglia (internist facing board discipline), in discussion with the author, July 2019.

12. "License Verification," Tennessee Department of Health, modified October 10, 2022, https://apps.health.tn.gov/Licensure/.

13. "Online Tennessee Attorney Directory," Tennessee Board of Professional Responsibility, accessed October 11, 2022, https://www.tbpr.org/for-the-public /online-attorney-directory. In this way, Tennessee goes further than many states that do not allow clients to search for their lawyer's disciplinary record. For a discussion of the relative lack of transparency of lawyer discipline, see Leslie C. Levin, "The Case for Less Secrecy in Lawyer Discipline," *Georgetown Journal of Legal Ethics* 20, no. 1 (2007). For professions outside of health and law, consumers

must comb through monthly reports with no search function from the Department of Commerce and Insurance, see "Disciplinary Actions," Tennessee Department of Commerce and Insurance, https://www.tn.gov/commerce/dar.html.

14. John Fauber and Matt Wynn, "Doctors Who Surrender a Medical License in One State Can Practice in Another—and You Might Never Know," WYKC Studios, November 30, 2018, https://www.wkyc.com/article/news/nation-world /doctors-who-surrender-medical-license-in-one-state-still-practice-in-others /507-619081091.

15. "About Us," National Practitioner Data Bank, United States Department of Health and Human Services, https://www.npdb.hrsa.gov/topNavigation/aboutUs .jsp.

16. For lawyers, the ABA maintains a national database of board discipline. "National Lawyer Regulatory Data Bank," Center for Professional Responsibility, American Bar Association, https://www.americanbar.org/groups/professional _responsibility/services/databank/. Information in the lawyer data bank is shared with courts and agencies as a matter of course and can be obtained by the general public—for an undisclosed fee—if they submit a written request about a particular lawyer. Unlike on the medical side, the lawyer data bank contains only regulatory actions, not information about malpractice or adverse employment events. Thus, compared with the medical Data Bank, the lawyer version is slightly more accessible to the public but has significantly less useful information.

17. Almost half of American medical boards checked the National Practitioner Data Base fewer than 100 times in 2017; thirteen of those boards didn't check it once. Matt Wynn, "There's a Tool to Help States Find Problem Doctors. Why Do So Few Use It?," *Milwaukee Journal Sentinel,* March 7, 2018, https://www.jsonline .com/story/news/investigations/2018/03/07/theres-tool-help-states-find -problem-doctors-why-do-so-few-use/400723002/; Sidney Wolfe and Robert Oshel, *Ranking of the Rate of State Medical Boards' Serious Disciplinary Actions, 2017–2019* (Washington, DC: Public Citizen Health Research Group, March 31, 2021), https://www.citizen.org/wp-content/uploads/2574.pdf.

18. Empirical researchers, describing their project and paying a fee, can apply for access to anonymized data from the Data Bank, and the Data Bank itself has an in-house research team. Robert Oshel (former associate director for research and disputes, National Practitioner Data Bank), in discussion with the author, December 2021.

19. Alan Judd, "Condemnation without Action," *Atlanta Journal-Constitution,* https://doctors.ajc.com/ama_sex_abuse_doctors/.

20. Adam Smith, *The Theory of Moral Sentiments*, 6th ed. (1790): 165. ("They are led by an invisible hand to make nearly the same distribution of the necessaries of life . . . and thus without intending it, without knowing it, advance the interest of the society, and afford means to the multiplication of the species.")

21. David Hyman, Mohammad Rahmati, and Bernard Black, "Medical Malpractice and Physician Discipline: The Good, the Bad, and the Ugly," *Journal of Empirical Legal Studies* 18, no. 1 (April 5, 2021): 155.

22. David Hyman (professor, Georgetown University Law Center), in discussion with the author, May 2021. Similarly, when I interviewed the former director for research at the National Practitioner Data Bank, he told me: "Some people with really bad records go to rural areas or places where it's hard to recruit physicians," where an employer thinks "it's better to have a physician with a bad record than to have no physician at all." Robert Oshel (former associate director for research and disputes, National Practitioner Data Bank), in discussion with the author, December 2021.

23. Attorney specializing in professional discipline defense, in discussion with the author, July 2021.

24. Attorney specializing in professional discipline defense, in discussion with the author, July 2021.

25. Tenn. Comp. R. & Regs. 0880-06-.02(1) (1987).

26. Attorney specializing in professional discipline defense, in conversation with the author, July 2021.

27. Veterans Affairs self-insures. Donovan Slack, "VA Knowingly Hires Doctors with Past Malpractice Claims, Discipline for Poor Care," *USA Today*, December 3, 2017, https://www.usatoday.com/story/news/politics/2017/12/03/usa-today-investigation-va-knowingly-hires-doctors-past-malpractice-claims-discipline-poor-care/909170001/. The same is true of the Indian Health Service, where the Federal Tort Claims Act puts the federal government on the hook for malpractice payments. 28 U.S.C. §§ 1346(b), 2401(b), 2671–2680.

28. Hyman, Rahmati, and Black, "The Good, the Bad, and the Ugly," 153.

29. Matt Wynn and John Fauber, "More than 200 Doctors Stay on Medicare Rolls Despite Disciplinary Action," *Milwaukee Journal Sentinel*, May 17, 2018, https://www.jsonline.com/story/news/investigations/2018/05/17/doctors-keep-practicing-after-falling-afoul-state-regulators/609534002/; Charles Ornstein, "Medicare Billing Outliers Often Have Disciplinary Problems, Too," ProPublica, June 20, 2014, https://www.propublica.org/article/among-doctors-with-unusual-billing-patterns-disciplinary-actions-common.

30. Slack, "VA."

31. Danny Robbins, "Georgia Hires Prison Doctors with Troubled Pasts," *Atlanta Journal-Constitution,* December 12, 2014, https://www.ajc.com/news/state--re gional-govt--politics/georgia-hires-prison-doctors-with-troubled-pasts/ihz49ty MbWg9dKLu1vt2CI/#:~:text=An%20Atlanta-Journal%20Constitution%20in vestigation,most%20vulnerable%20groups%20of%20people.

32. Christopher Weaver, Dan Frosch, and Lisa Schwartz, "The US Gave Troubled Doctors a Second Chance. Patients Paid the Price," *Wall Street Journal,* November 22, 2019, https://www.wsj.com/articles/the-u-s-gave-troubled-doctors-a -second-chance-patients-paid-the-price-11574439222.

33. Attorney specializing in professional discipline defense, in discussion with the author, July 2021.

34. Gideon v. Wainwright, 372 U.S. 335 (1963).

35. For example, in a county in Michigan, appointed lawyers are paid $56 an hour while their private-practice counterparts make about $285 an hour. Justin A. Hinkley and Matt Mencarini, "Court-Appointed Attorneys Do Little Work, Records Show," *Detroit Free Press,* November 3, 2016, https://www.freep.com/story/news /local/michigan/2016/11/03/court-appointed-attorneys-ingham-michigan /93228990/.

36. Samantha Hogan, "Maine Hires Lawyers with Criminal Records to Defend Its Poorest Residents," ProPublica, October 6, 2020, https://www.propublica.org /article/maine-hires-lawyers-with-criminal-records-to-defend-its-poorest -residents.

37. Hogan, "Maine."

38. Nicole C. Brambila, "Disorder in the Court: Troubled Attorneys Often Take on Capital Cases," *Reading Eagle,* October 25, 2015, https://www.readingeagle.com /2015/10/25/disorder-in-the-court-troubled-attorneys-often-take-on-capital -cases/ ("People are being represented by the absolute dregs in the profession that nobody with money would hire."); Galia Benson-Amram, "Protecting the Integrity of the Court: Trial Court Responsibility for Preventing Ineffective Assistance of Counsel in Criminal Cases," *New York University Review of Law and Social Change* 29, no. 2 (2004): 432, 432n35.

39. Iowa Sup. Ct. Att'y Disciplinary Bd. v. Moothart, 860 N.W.2d 598, 612 (Iowa 2015). The other client was facing charges for prostitution. When she asked Moothart how much he charged for his services, he said "it depends on how much cleavage you show me." Iowa Sup. Ct. Att'y Disciplinary Bd. v. Moothart, 860 N.W.2d 598, 613 (Iowa 2015).

40. Kyle Rozema, "Professional Discipline and the Labor Market: Evidence from Lawyers," *Journal of Law and Economics* (forthcoming) (manuscript at 23).

41. Nicole L. Piquero et al., "Exploring Lawyer Misconduct: An Examination of the Self-Regulation Process," *Deviant Behavior* 37, no. 5 (2016): 3. The same effect is present in medicine, and there is evidence that physicians turn to solo practice *after* discipline. David M. Studdert et al., "Changes in Practice among Physicians with Malpractice Claims," *New England Journal of Medicine* 380, no. 13 (March 2019): 1250.

42. For a discussion of how solo legal practice leads to negligence (and a defense of regulators' disciplinary focus on solo practitioners), see Richard L. Abel, *Lawyers in the Dock* (New York: Oxford University Press, 2010), 506.

43. Board member, Tennessee Board of Medical Examiners, in discussion with the author, September 2019.

44. Anne Lembke, *Drug Dealer, MD: How Doctors Were Duped, Patients Got Hooked, and Why It's So Hard to Stop* (Baltimore: Johns Hopkins University Press, 2016), 120; Christine A. Sinsky and David C. Dugdale, "Medicare Payment for Cognitive vs. Procedural Care: Minding the Gap," *Journal of the American Medical Association, Internal Medicine* 173, no. 18 (October 14, 2013): 1734.

45. Lembke, *Drug Dealer,* 118–123.

46. William J. Stuntz, "The Uneasy Relationship between Criminal Procedure and Criminal Justice," *Yale Law Review* 107, no. 1 (October 1997): 10–11.

47. Stephanos Bibas, "Shrinking *Gideon* and Expanding Alternatives to Lawyers," *Washington and Lee Law Review* 70, no. 2 (2013): 1292.

48. Tenn. Sup. Ct. R. 13 § 2(d)(5)(B).

49. Former member, Tennessee Board of Medical Examiners, in discussion with the author, July 2019.

50. Patient of over-prescribing physician, in discussion with the author, July 2019.

51. Docket No. 17.18-139095A (Tennessee Board of Medical Examiners, July 19, 2017).

52. License No. 27530, Docket No. 17.18-139095A (Tennessee Department of Health, March 1, 2019), https://apps.health.tn.gov/DisciplinaryExclusion/board order/display/1606_27530_030119.

53. March 20, 2018, Tennessee Board of Medical Examiners.

54. John Hall (former executive director, Mississippi State Board of Medical Licensure), in discussion with the author, July 2018.

55. OBGYN facing board discipline, in discussion with the author, March 2018.

56. Sometimes these concerns even make it into the language of board orders, as in the case of an improperly prescribing doctor in Indiana whose license was reinstated because "since [his] suspension, the delivery of medical services in this rural community has been severely compromised." Jing Liu and David A. Hyman, "Physician Licensing and Discipline: Lessons from Indiana," *Journal of Empirical Legal Studies* 18, no. 3 (September 2021): 648.

57. Carrie Teegardin et al., "License to Betray," *Atlanta Journal-Constitution*, https://doctors.ajc.com/doctors_sex_abuse/?ecmp=doctorssexabuse_microsite _nav.

58. July 30, 2019, Tennessee Board of Medical Examiners.

59. May 28, 2019, Tennessee Board of Medical Examiners; September 17, 2019, Tennessee Board of Medical Examiners.

60. Cindy Chang, "Many Doctors Treating State's Prisoners Have Disciplinary Records Themselves," *New Orleans Times-Picayune*, July 29, 2012, https://www .nola.com/news/crime_police/article_98a136d7-c201-5b55-a7f5-5428b4be1439 .html. The Georgia medical board puts an even finer point on it, sometimes re- stricting licenses to "correctional facilities." Robbins, "Prison Doctors with Trou- bled Pasts."

61. Chang, "Disciplinary Records."

62. Chang, "Disciplinary Records."

63. Addy Baird, "Louisiana Bars Problem Doctors from Practicing Medicine in Most Hospitals. So They Treat Incarcerated People Instead," BuzzFeed News, May 10, 2021, https://www.buzzfeednews.com/article/addybaird/louisiana-prison -doctors-licenses-suspended. The prison system has been sued over the matter. See also *Lewis v. Cain*, No. 3:15-CV-318, 2021 WL 1219988 (M.D. La. 2021). Court documents in that case show that the medical director of Angola served thirty months in prison for dealing methamphetamine before taking the helm of med- ical provision at Angola. Complaint at Exhibit C, Lewis v. Cain, No. 3:15-CV-318, 2021 WL 1219988 (M.D. La. 2021) (report on the state of health care at Angola, by experts Madeleine LaMarre MN, FNP-BC, Mike Puisis DO, and Susi Vassallo MD).

64. Deborah Sontag, "Addiction Treatment with a Dark Side," *New York Times*, November 16, 2013, https://www.nytimes.com/2013/11/17/health/in-demand-in -clinics-and-on-the-street-bupe-can-be-savior-or-menace.html.

65. As Dr. Loyd, told me, "You charge someone $125 a week for something you'll get sick if you don't have, you'll get rich quick." Stephen Loyd (member, Tennessee Board of Medical Examiners), in discussion with the author, July 2021.

66. Sontag, "Dark Side."

67. Consider, for example, the neurosurgeon with a history of gruesomely incompetent surgeries who asked the medical board to lift his probation order because it inhibited his employment prospects. When the board refused, he applied for his Suboxone license. May 28, 2019, Tennessee Board of Medical Examiners.

68. Suboxone is also an attractive drug to prescribe for profit because these it can fly under the radar of the licensing boards in a way that traditional pill mills cannot. Federal law provides special privacy protections to patients seeking addiction treatment, making it difficult for Tennessee's Department of Health to obtain their medical charts when investigating unethical prescribing. Without that evidence, the boards say they cannot pursue complaints against doctors running Suboxone pill mills. Medical consultant, Tennessee Board of Medical Examiners, in discussion with the author, August 2019.

69. "Revelstoke Capital Partners Close 50th Transaction in 5 Years," *Revelstoke Capital Partners*, November 20, 2018, https://www.revelstokecapital.com/news /revelstoke-closes-50th-transaction-in-five-years/; Claimants' Motion to Dismiss Complaint for Forfeiture under Supplemental Rules G(8)(b) and G(2)(f), United States v. Knoxville, Knox County, Tennessee et al., Cr. No.: 6:18-cv-00315-REW-HAI at 17 (E.D. Tenn. March 30, 2020) (No. 89).

70. Dawn Deaner (founder and executive director, Choosing Justice Initiative), in discussion with the author, February 2021.

71. Jeffrey L. Kirchmeier, "Drink, Drugs, and Drowsiness: The Constitutional Right to Effective Assistance of Counsel and the Strickland Prejudice Requirement," *Nebraska Law Review* 75, no. 3 (1996): 427.

72. James M. Anderson and Paul Heaton, "How Much Difference Does the Lawyer Make? The Effect of Defense Counsel on Murder Case Outcomes" (working paper WR-870-NIJ, RAND Corporation, Santa Monica, CA, December 2011), 24–25, https://www.rand.org/pubs/working_papers/WR870.html.

## 9. CRIME AND PUNISHMENT

1. United States v. LaPaglia (Amending Pretrial Release), No. 3:18-CR -172-KAC-DCP (E.D. Tenn. 2021); "Elite Healthcare, LLC," National Provider Identifier Database, accessed November 9, 2022, https://npidb.org/organizations /ambulatory_health_care/primary-care_261qp2300x/1023665403.aspx (Michael LaPaglia—Medical Director).

2.	Failure to go along with the program could land them back in jail. For a discussion of the problems with using sober living facilities as a means of addiction treatment and as an alternative to incarceration, see Mara Silvers, "The Unregulated World of Montana's Sober Living Homes," *Montana Free Press,* January 1, 2023, https://montanafreepress.org/2023/01/03/the-unregulated-world-of-montanas -sober-living-recovery-homes/.

3.	United States v. LaPaglia, No. 3:18-CR-172-KAC-DCP (E.D. Tenn. 2021) (Hearing on the Petition for Action on Conditions of Pretrial Release) (Day 1).

4.	United States v. LaPaglia (Amending Pretrial Release), No. 3:18-CR-172-KAC -DCP (E.D. Tenn. 2021).

5.	United States v. LaPaglia, No. 3:18-CR-172-KAC-DCP (E.D. Tenn. 2021) (Hearing on the Petition for Action on Conditions of Pretrial Release) (Day 2).

6.	United States v. LaPaglia, No. 3:18-CR-172-KAC-DCP (E.D. Tenn. 2021) (Hearing on the Petition for Action on Conditions of Pretrial Release) (Day 2).

7.	United States v. LaPaglia (Amending Pretrial Release), No. 3:18-CR-172-KAC -DCP (E.D. Tenn. 2021).

8.	US Department of Justice, "Appalachian Regional Prescription Opioid (ARPO) Strike Force Takedown Results in Charges against 60 Individuals, Including 53 Medical Professionals," press release no. 19–391, April 17, 2019, https://www.justice.gov/opa/pr/appalachian-regional-prescription-opioid-arpo -strike-force-takedown-results-charges-against; "60 arrested in Appalachian opioid operation," WKRC, April 26, 2019, https://youtu.be/QQRf7l1n3_k.

9.	For more information about Nurse Young's case, see Olga Khazan, "The Hard-Partying, Rock-Obsessed Nurse at the Center of a Massive Opioid Bust," *Atlantic,* January 28, 2021, https://www.theatlantic.com/health/archive/2021/01 /rock-doc-opioids/617405/.

10.	United States v. Young, No. 1:19-cr-10040-JDB (W.D. Tenn. 2019) (Government's Motion Pursuant to 18 U.S.C. § 3145(a)(1) for Revocation of Magistrate's Release Order and Request for Evidentiary Hearing).

11.	United States v. Young, No. 1:19-cr-10040-JDB (W.D. Tenn. 2019) (Hearings before J. Daniel Breen).

12.	United States v. Young, No. 1:19-cr-10040-JDB (W.D. Tenn. 2019) (Hearings before J. Daniel Breen on May 13, 2019) (testimony of nursing board investigator, reading from the letter).

13.	United States v. Young, No. 1:19-cr-10040-JDB (W.D. Tenn. 2019) (Hearings before J. Daniel Breen on May 13, 2019) (testimony of nursing board investigator).

14. United States v. Young, No. 1:19-cr-10040-JDB (W.D. Tenn. 2019) (Hearings before J. Daniel Breen on May 13, 2019) (testimony of nursing board investigator).

15. United States v. Young, No. 1:19-cr-10040-JDB (W.D. Tenn. 2019) (Hearings before J. Daniel Breen on May 20, 2019).

16. Jeffrey W. Young, APRN, Docket No. 17.19-151799A (Tennessee Department of Health, November 7, 2018).

17. Member, Tennessee Board of Nursing, in discussion with the author, May 2019.

18. United States v. Young, No. 1:19-cr-10040-JDB (W.D. Tenn. 2020) (Government's Response to Defendant's Objections).

19. United States v. Young, No. 1:19-cr-10040-JDB (W.D. Tenn. 2019) (Hearings before J. Daniel Breen on May 13, 2019); Brett Kelman and Cassandra Stephenson, "The Tennessee Rock Doc: Sex, Drugs, and a 'Costly Mistake,'" *Tennessean,* updated October 22, 2021, https://www.tennessean.com/story/news/health/2019/08/12/nurse-practitioner-rock-doc-jeffrey-young-prescribing-opioids-sexual-assault-preventagenix/1269483001/.

20. United States v. Young, No. 1:19-cr-10040-JDB (W.D. Tenn. 2020) (Detention Hearing, May 20, 2020); United States v. Young, No. 1:19-cr-10040-JDB (W.D. Tenn. 2020) (Order Denying Defendant's Appeal of Magistrate Judge's Order on Release to Home Confinement).

21. Orusa v. Tennessee Board of Medical Examiners, No. 19-391-III (Ch. Ct. for Davidson Cnty., Tenn. 2019) (Petition for Judicial Review of Interlocutory Administrative Order).

22. Corey S. Davis and Derek Carr, "Self-Regulating Profession? Administrative Discipline of 'Pill Mill' Physicians in Florida," *Substance Abuse* 38, no. 3 (April 2017): 265–268.

23. Tenn. Code Ann. § 4-5-320 (2020).

24. Michael LaPaglia, MD, Case No. 201802040 (Tennessee Department of Health, January 2, 2019), https://apps.health.tn.gov/DisciplinaryExclusion/boardorder/display/1606_42617_010219; Charles Brooks, MD, Case No. 201001017 (Tennessee Department of Health, January 2, 2019), https://apps.health.tn.gov/DisciplinaryExclusion/boardorder/display/1606_16587_091012.

25. Member, Tennessee Board of Nursing, in discussion with the author, May 2019.

26. Board member, Tennessee Board of Medical Examiners, in discussion with the author, September 2019.

27. May 28, 2019, Tennessee Board of Medical Examiners.

28. Head of investigations, Tennessee Health Licensing Boards, in conversation with the author, June 9, 2019.

29. Assistant United States attorney, in discussion with the author, April 10, 2019.

30. "60 Arrests Made in Largest Opioid Takedown in History," WDTNTV (April 17, 2019), https://youtu.be/laqokr_W7Eg.

31. For example, see N.J. Stat. Ann. § 45:1–22 (2002) ("In any administrative proceeding commenced on a complaint alleging a violation of an act or regulation administered by a board, such board may issue subpoenas to compel the attendance of witnesses or the production of books, records, or documents at the hearing on the complaint.").

32. Federation of State Medical Boards, *Standard of Proof: Board-by-Board Overview* (January 2023), https://www.fsmb.org/siteassets/advocacy/key-issues /standard-of-proof-by-state.pdf.

33. Head of investigations, Tennessee Health Licensing Boards, in discussion with the author, June 2019.

34. *Dr. Death,* season 1, episode 1: "Three Days in Dallas," at 23:15 (Wondery: September 4, 2018), https://wondery.com/shows/dr-death/season/1/.

35. *Dr. Death,* season 1, episode 2: "Chris and Jerry," at 00:41 (Wondery: September 4, 2018), https://wondery.com/shows/dr-death/season/1/.

36. *Dr. Death,* season 1, episode 1: "Three Days in Dallas," at 26:07 (Wondery: September 4, 2018), https://wondery.com/shows/dr-death/season/1/.

37. Saul Elbein, "Anatomy of a Tragedy," *Texas Observer,* August 28, 2013, https:// www.texasobserver.org/anatomy-tragedy/.

38. Elbein, "Anatomy."

39. *Dr. Death,* season 1, episode 4: "Spineless," at 05:37 (Wondery: September 11, 2018), https://wondery.com/shows/dr-death/season/1/.

40. *Dr. Death,* season 1, episode 4: "Spineless," at 30:41 (Wondery: September 11, 2018), https://wondery.com/shows/dr-death/season/1/ (for dinner details); *Dr. Death,* season 1, episode 5: "Free Fall," at 12:50 (Wondery: September 18, 2018), https://wondery.com/shows/dr-death/season/1/ (Henderson and Kirby call the district attorney).

41. Michelle Shughart (prosecutor of Dr. Duntsch), in discussion with the author, December 2021.

42. *Dr. Death,* season 1, episode 3: "Occam's Razor," at 01:14 (Wondery: September 7, 2018), https://wondery.com/shows/dr-death/season/1/.

43. Michelle Shughart (prosecutor of Dr. Duntsch), in discussion with the author, December 13, 2021.

44. Laura Beil, "A Surgeon So Bad It Was Criminal," ProPublica, October 2, 2018, https://www.propublica.org/article/dr-death-christopher-duntsch-a-surgeon-so-bad-it-was-criminal. According to the Wondery podcast, Dr. Duntsch was first doctor in the nation to receive a life sentence for his practice of medicine.

45. 21 U.S.C. § 841.

46. United States v. Godofsky, 943 F.3d 1011 (6th Cir. 2019).

47. Defense attorney, in discussion with the author, September 2021.

48. Ruan v. United States, 142 S.Ct. 2370 (2022).

49. US Attorney's Office for the Middle District of Tennessee, "Jury Convicts Clarksville Doctor of 36 Counts Related to Pill Mill Operation," press release, September 27, 2021, https://www.justice.gov/usao-mdtn/pr/jury-convicts-clarksville-doctor-36-counts-related-pill-mill-operation; Brett Kelman, "Doctors Rush to use Supreme Court Ruling to Escape Opioid Charges," *CBS News,* September 19, 2022, https://www.cbsnews.com/news/doctors-opioid-charges-supreme-court-ruling-ruan-v-united-states/#:~:text=Martin%20Escobar%20cited%20the%20Ruan,the%20deaths%20of%20two%20patients.

50. United States v. Orusa, No. 3:18-cr-00342 (M.D. Tenn. 2023) (order granting new trial); *Orusa* (order granting government's motion to dismiss remaining counts).

51. US Attorney's Office for the Middle District of Tennessee, "Celina Physician Arrested on Federal Drug Distribution Charges While Preparing to Leave the United States," press release, May 17, 2019, https://www.justice.gov/usao-mdtn/pr/celina-physician-arrested-federal-drug-distribution-charges.

52. United States v. Young, No. 1:19-cr-10040-JDB (W.D. Tenn. 2020) (May 13 Hearing, Page 18, Line 22). Likewise, Dr. LaPaglia's lawyer made a similar argument in his case about the judge imposing restrictions on his practice. United States v. LaPaglia, No. 3:18-cr-172-KAC-DCP (E.D. Tenn. 2021) (Pretrial Release Hearing at 01:12:21) (arguing that "[t]he court is not constituted to make a ruling that's purely a professional . . . matter").

53. Brett Kelman, "This Tennessee Doctor Helped Defraud the Military out of $65M—But He Can Keep His Medical License," *Tennessean*, August 25, 2019, https://www.tennessean.com/story/news/health/2019/08/26/tennessee-doctor-carl-lindblad-defrauded-military-marines-skin-cream/2018882001/.

54. May 28, 2019, Tennessee Board of Medical Examiners.

55. Deborah L. Rhode, *The Trouble with Lawyers* (New York: Oxford University Press, 2015), 111.

56. Rhode, *Trouble,* 114.

57. United States v. LaPaglia, No. 3:18-CR-172 (E.D. Tenn. 2021) (Sentencing Hearing at 15:16).

58. Patient of Dr. Michael LaPaglia, in discussion with the author, June 2021.

59. United States v. LaPaglia, No. 3:18-CR-172 (E.D. Tenn. 2021) (Sentencing Hearing at 01:43:12).

60. Michael LaPaglia, MD, Case No. 17.18–211536A (Tennessee Department of Health, July 21, 2021).

61. July 21, 2021, Tennessee Board of Medical Examiners.

## CONCLUSION

1. US Department of Labor, "US Labor Department Awards $7.5M to Fund Research for Improving Geographic Mobility for Workers in Licensed Occupations," news release no. 17-0049-NAT, January 12, 2017, https://www.dol.gov/newsroom/releases/eta/eta20170112-0; "Occupational Licensure Policy: DOL Consortium," Council of State Governments, accessed October 7, 2022, https://licensing.csg.org/the-consortium/.

2. Advisor, Teaching Compact Technical Assistance Group, at the National Occupational Licensing meeting held by the National Conference of State Legislatures with the author in attendance, June 2022.

3. Ariz. Rev. Stat. Ann. § 32-4302 (2022).

4. Council of State Governments, *Promising Practices on Licensure Mobility* (April 2019), https://issuu.com/csg.publications/docs/promising_practices_licensure_mobil?e=31863820/69362714.

5. National Conference of State Legislatures, "Sunset and Sunrise in Occupational Licensing Policy," April 22, 2022, https://www.ncsl.org/research/labor-and-employment/sunset-and-sunrise-in-occupational-licensing-policy.aspx. Research

shows that sunrise review can help slow the spread of professional licensing to professions where it is not necessary. Kathy Sanchez, Elyse Smith Pohl, and Lisa Knepper, *Too Many Licenses? Government "Sunrise" Reviews Cast Doubt on Barriers to Work* (Arlington, VA: Institute for Justice, February 2022), 6, 47–50, https://ij.org/wp-content/uploads/2022/02/Too-Many-Licenses_-Sunrise-Reviews-Cast-Doubt-on-Barriers-to-Work.pdf.

6. "Sunrise, Sunset, and State Agency Audits," Council on Licensure, Enforcement and Regulation, accessed October 30, 2022, https://www.clearhq.org/RAG #Sunrise-Sunset-Agency-Audits; Robert J. Thornton and Edward J. Timmons, "The De-Licensing of Occupations in the United States," *Monthly Labor Review* 138, no. 5 (May 2015): 2, 12.

7. 2018 Tenn. Pub. Acts Ch. 834; 2021 Pub. Acts Ch. 527.

8. Sanchez, Pohl, and Knepper, *Too Many Licenses?*; Dick M. Carpenter II, Lisa Knepper, Kyle Sweetland, and Jennifer McDonald, *License to Work: A National Study of Burdens from Occupational Licensing,* 2d ed. (Arlington, VA: Institute for Justice, November 2017), 38–39, https://ij.org/wp-content/uploads/2022/11/License_to_Work_2nd_Edition.pdf.

9. National Conference of State Legislatures, *Occupational Licensing: Assessing State Policies and Practices Final Report* (December 2020), 10, https://documents.ncsl.org/wwwncsl/Labor/NCSL_DOL_Report_05_web_REVISED.pdf. Likewise, the number of bills increasing licensing requirements or fees within a profession (218) exceeded bills rolling back requirements or fees (166).

10. National Center for Interstate Compacts, *Fact Sheet: Interstate Licensure Compacts and Universal Licensure Recognition Laws, National Center for Interstate Compacts* (May 2022), https://otcompact.org/wp-content/uploads/2022/06/Compacts-and-Universal-Licensure-Laws-June-2022.pdf.

11. Mike Bell (Tennessee state senator, chair of the Government Operations Committee), in discussion with the author, June 2018.

12. Tennessee Senate Government Operations Committee, March 14, 2018.

13. Ariz. Rev. Stat. Ann. § 32-4301(E), (F) (2020).

14. June 21, 2022, National Conference of State Legislatures, "The National Occupational Licensing Meeting," Las Vegas, NV.

15. North Carolina Board of Dental Examiners v. Federal Trade Commission, 574 U.S. 494 (2015).

16. State v. Berry, 2020 WL 260426 (Ariz. Ct. App. 2020); Colorado Real Estate Commission v. Vizzi, 488 P.3d 470 (Colo. App. 2019).

17. Teladoc, Inc. v. Texas Medical Board, 2015 WL 8773509 (W.D. Tex. 2015); SmileDirectClub, LLC v. Battle, 969 F.3d 1134 (11th Cir. 2020).

18. Federation of Associations of Regulatory Boards Forum, September 2018, Portland, OR. The case was the subject of a presentation to the veterinary board (April 11, 2018, Tennessee Board of Veterinary Medical Examiners). In another meeting the lawyer for the board warned them of an "FTC situation" as they were deciding which providers to approve for continuing education courses (June 1, 2018, Tennessee Board for Licensed Professional Counselors, Licensed Marital and Family Therapists and Licensed Clinical Pastoral Therapists).

19. Tenn. Code Ann. § 71-3-501; Tenn. Comp. R. & Regs. 1240-04-01.

20. I interviewed an ALJ who told me about a trial over a bad haircut, the only case he could recall before the cosmetology board about service quality. Tom Stovall (Administrative Law Judge), in discussion with the author, November 2021.

21. Institute for Justice, *License to Work* (November 2017), https://ij.org/report /license-to-work-2/ltw-occupation-profiles/ltw2-auctioneer/; "States with No Auction Law," National Auctioneer License Law Officials Association, https://nalloa .org/state-with-no-auction-law/.

22. Tenn. Code Ann. § 62-5-201 (statute establishing the funeral board and determining its composition—seven members total, four required to be funeral directors, two either a funeral director or embalmer, and one layperson).

23. "Funeral Directors, Embalmers, & Burial Services," Tennessee Department of Commerce and Insurance, https://www.tn.gov/commerce/regboards/funeral. html (describing the composition of the Burial Services Section of TDCI); Tenn. Comp. R. & Regs. 0780-05-09 (the general rules and regulations for cemeteries— describing the role of the "commissioner," or more likely the commissioner's designee, in the regulation of cemeteries).

24. Tenn. Code Ann. § 62-5-401; Tenn. Code Ann. § 62-5-305.

25. "Regulatory Board Disciplinary Actions, 2019," Tennessee Department of Commerce and Insurance, https://www.tn.gov/commerce/dar/rb.html (containing disciplinary data for the Board of Funeral Directors—In 2019, of the twelve filed complaints regarding unlicensed activity, eleven received a penalty. In comparison, of the thirty-nine filed complaints regarding safety, fourteen received a penalty).

26. Tenn. Code Ann. § 46-1-214 (financial reporting requirements for trusts operated by cemetery owners); Tenn. Code Ann. § 46-1-215 (financial reporting requirements for cemetery owners); "Regulatory Board Disciplinary Actions, 2019,"

Tennessee Department of Commerce and Insurance, https://www.tn.gov/commerce/dar/rb.html (containing disciplinary data for burial services. In 2019, of the thirty-seven total disciplinary actions, nineteen were due to failure to properly maintain a statutory required trust fund or financial report. The remaining were either failure to maintain cemetery grounds or violation of a pre-need sale regulation).

27.   Several advocates call for a more "fine-grained" kind of periodic review that does more than threaten to abolish a board. Corey Everett (director, Colorado State, Latino Coalition for Community Leadership), in discussion with the author, October 2018; Alex Adams (executive director, Idaho Board of Pharmacy), in discussion with the author, October 2018.

28.   One sign that a profession probably does not need to be licensed to protect the public is that it is licensed in some but not all states, like auctioneers, court reporters, and florists.

29.   For example, the University of California system has recently paid close to $700 million to settle lawsuits "brought by hundreds of alleged victims of a former UCLA gynecologist." Richard Winton, "UC Pays Record $700 Million to Women Who Accused UCLA Gynecologist of Sexual Assault," *Los Angeles Times,* May 24, 2022, https://www.latimes.com/california/story/2022-05-24/heaps-settlement-312-patients-takes-cost-of-his-abuse-to-700-million.

30.   "Opioids," Tennessee Hospital Association, https://tha.com/quality/opioids/; Holly Fletcher, "Drug, Alcohol Abuse Saps $2 Billion from Tennessee Annually—an Under-the-Radar Impact of Opioid Epidemic," *Tennessean,* updated December 4, 2017, https://www.tennessean.com/story/money/industries/health-care/2017/12/04/drug-alcohol-abuse-saps-2-billion-tennessee-annually-under-the-radar-impact-opioid-epidemic/909253001/.

31.   Tenn. Code Ann. § 68-201-104 (2022).

32.   Monti Herring (Narcan trainer for Prevention Partnership), in discussion with the author, October 2019.

33.   Some states, if not enough, already do this; more should follow suit. See, for example, "Filing a Grievance—Other FAQs," North Carolina State Bar, https://www.ncbar.gov/for-the-public/i-am-having-a-dispute-with-a-lawyer/filing-a-grievance/ ("Individuals who file grievances in good faith against a North Carolina lawyer are protected by statute from retaliation.").

34.   Federation of State Medical Boards, *US Medical Regulatory Trends and Actions* (2018), 67 https://www.fsmb.org/SysSiteAssets/advocacy/publications/us-medical-regulatory-trends-actions.pdf.

35.  "About DORA," Colorado Department of Agencies, accessed November 12, 2022, https://dora.colorado.gov/about-dora. *See also* Morris M. Kleiner, *Reforming Occupational Licensing Policies* (Washington, DC: Brookings Institution, January 2015), 17, https://www.brookings.edu/wp-content/uploads/2016/07/reform _occupational_licensing_policies_kleiner_v4.pdf.

36.  For example, for "Sexual Impropriety Involving Current Patients," the guidelines provide a minimum of a $1,000 fine, a course on boundaries, and a maximum of suspension of practice authority. 24 Del. Admin. Code § 1700-17.7.6 (2013).

37.  For a detailed description of the British medical regulatory system and how it compares to an American state, see Rebecca Haw Allensworth and Cathal T. Gallagher, "Doctors Playing Lawyers: Lessons for Professional Regulation in Crisis," *American Journal of Legal Medicine* (forthcoming, manuscript on file with the author).

38.  UK General Medical Council, *Our Annual Report 2019* (August 2020), https://www.gmc-uk.org/-/media/gmc-site/about/how-we-work/annual-report -2019/documents/annual-report-2019.pdf.

39.  Medical Practitioners Tribunal Service (UK), *Criteria for the Appointment of Tribunal Members,* accessed November 12, 2022, https://www.mpts-uk.org/- /media/mpts-documents/dc8375---criteria-for-the-appointment-of-tribunal -members_pdf-64048192.pdf.

40.  "Medical Practitioners Tribunals—How They Work," Medical Practitioners Tribunal Service (UK), accessed November 12, 2022, https://www.mpts-uk.org /hearings-and-decisions/hearing-types-and-how-they-work/medical-practi tioners-tribunals.

41.  "Who Makes the Decisions," Medical Practitioners Tribunal Service (UK), accessed November 12, 2022, https://www.mpts-uk.org/hearings-and-decisions /who-makes-the-decisions.

42.  Medical Act, 1983, c.54, § 40 (UK).

43.  Allensworth and Gallagher, "Doctors Playing Lawyers."

44.  Paul Bennett Marrow, "New York's Unified System for Professional Misconduct and Discipline," Westchester Bar Journal, vol. 29 (Spring 2002).

45.  Marrow, *Unified System.*

46.  A legal challenge to a hypothetical federal professional licensing law would probably argue that it violates the Tenth Amendment, which reserves to the states any powers not enumerated by the Constitution as belonging to the federal gov-

ernment. US Const. amend. X. Such an argument is unlikely to succeed, however. While the Court has shown an unwillingness to allow the federal government to intrude on areas of regulation traditionally left to the states (which would include professional licensing), their cases usually find no federal authority because the regulated activity does not affect interstate commerce, an argument that would be hard to make about licensing laws. Only very rarely has the court invalidated legislation otherwise authorized by the commerce clause because it violates the Tenth Amendment, and almost all of these cases are "anticommandeering" cases in which the federal government has improperly demanded that state government regulate according to federal policy (which would not describe a federal professional license). The only case I was able to find in which the Court invalidated a statute, valid under the commerce clause, that did not allege commandeering, was *Bond v. United States*, 572 U.S. 844, 845 (2014), which overturned a woman's federal criminal conviction for using "chemical weapons" to poison her husband's mistress on the grounds that assault by poisoning is the kind of crime traditionally handled by state, not federal, law.

47.   Tennessee Elevator and Amusement Device Safety Board, June 5, 2018, https://www.tn.gov/content/dam/tn/workforce/documents/Contact/MinutesEle vator&AmusementDeviceSafetyBoard060518copy_cond_N_ex2.pdf ("this group right here is in charge of everything that goes up and down and round and round.").

48.   Tenn. Code Ann. § 68-121-102 (2022).

49.   Vt. Stat. Ann. tit. 26 §§ 1733, 1351(e) (2020).

50.   Brett Kelman, "COVID-19: Medical Board Deletes Anti-Misinformation Policy Amid GOP Pressure," *Tennessean,* updated December 10, 2021, https://www .tennessean.com/story/news/health/2021/12/07/medical-board-deletes-anti -misinformation-policy-amid-gop-pressure/6416959001/.

# Acknowledgments

I owe the biggest debt of gratitude to the hundreds of people who agreed to talk to me about our broken professional licensing system. There are too many to list here, from licensing board members and staff to professionals locked out of their livelihood or facing discipline. Without their candor, the research for this book would not have been possible. I would like to extend a special thanks to those people who opened up to me about abuse at the hands of professionals, and to the professionals who were willing to talk to me about their struggles with substance use and mental health. I owe an especially big thanks to Dr. Stephen Loyd, whose generous and open spirit I cannot hope to capture on the page.

Thank you to the friends and colleagues who read drafts, shared their research with me, or provided me with encouragement when I needed it. These contributors include Annie Berry, Ed Cheng, Joe Fishman, Chad Hindman, Morris Kleiner, Terry Maroney, Sara Mayeux, Will McLemore, Kate Nicholson, Dan Sharfstein, Lauren Sharp, and Adam Tillinghast. Thank you to the Informed Patient Institute and the law faculties at UCLA, Northwestern, and Vanderbilt for helping me workshop chapters, and to my dean, Chris Guthrie, for generous research funds and teaching leave in support of this project. And thanks to those who helped me get my proposal into the right hands, most especially Michael Kaler at Basic Books and my colleague Ganesh Sitaraman.

For invaluable research assistance, thanks to Meredith Barrow, Elise Blegen, Margherita Capolino, Elodie Currier, Harrison Elbert, Izzy Fishbach, Ari Goldfine, Tyler Greek, Sean Horan, Peter Lee, Seamus McDonough, Mark Mehochko, Andrew Merritt, Jackson Miner, Amber Otto, Madison Perry, Chase Pritchett, Michael Regard, Sara Smith, Sarah

Staples, Nic Vandeventer, Joey Vettiankal, Becky Villanueva, Jae Yoon, and Hannah Zhuang. Thanks to the research librarians at Vanderbilt Law School who provided incredible support for this work: Mariah Ford and Katie Hanschke.

Thank you to Audra Wolfe, of the Outside Reader, and Meribah Knight, who both provided editing services and much-needed cheer-leading. Thanks to my editors at Harvard University Press, Sharmila Sen and Sam Stark, and to my agent, Jill Marsal, who believed in this book.

Thank you, Dad, for always saying the perfect thing when I was losing hope. And thanks to my children, Ronan and Ingrid, for taking this ride with me. This book is yours, too.

And finally, thank you to my husband, Will Allensworth. You are my favorite.

# Index

Abbott, Timothy, 181–182

access-to-care: post-discipline employment and, 17, 151, 153–154, 161–164; quality of service and, 67, 151, 163; in rural and inner-city communities (*see* inner-city communities; rural communities); scarcity effects on, 63–64, 71–72, 78, 161–163 (*see also* scarcity of professional services)

access-to-justice: post-discipline employment and, 17, 153, 154–155, 166–167; scarcity of professional services and, 64

accountants, 15, 31, 86, 150

acupuncturists, 49, 221n24

addiction and recovery. *See* substance use disorders

administrative law judges, 118, 201, 202, 246n67

advanced practice registered nurses. *See* nurse practitioners

advisory licensing boards, 30, 205–206

African Americans: discrimination and, 85, 87, 90–92; hair braiders, hair professionals, and, 23, 95–99 (*see also* hair braiders); prestige from licenses among, 42–43, 96–99

agreed disciplinary orders, 118, 122–123, 186, 200

Akerlof, George, 60

Alabama, 231n48

alarm systems contractors, 26, 45, 46, 47, 53–54, 222n4

Alaska, 229n33

alcohol and drug abuse counselors, 25, 27, 40–41

Almon, William, 135

American Bar Association (ABA), 114, 141, 259n16

American Indians, professional services for, 154

American Medical Association (AMA), 72, 75, 134, 142, 146, 151

antitrust liability, 192

Appalachian Region Prescription Opioids (ARPO) Strike Force, 170, 176, 181

appointment process for licensing boards, 9, 31, 211n21, 215n34

architects, 28, 47, 188

Arizona, 189, 191, 231n48

art therapists, 27, 30

Asian Americans, 93, 235n9

associations, professional: about, 28; board deference and delegation to, 31–39, 134, 138; board member participation in, 9, 15, 31–34, 211n21; lobbying by, 29–32, 79; medical, 44,

Data Bank: National Lawyer Regulatory, 259n16; National Practitioner, 150–152, 179–180, 198, 201, 259nn17–18

Deaner, Dawn, 166–167

Delaware, 202

delays in discipline, 12, 106, 112, 121–122, 124, 173–176, 179–180

dental assistants, 92

dental hygienists, 25, 28, 220n22

dentists, 33, 49, 64, 111, 192, 220n22

*Dent v. West Virginia* (1889), 211n12

Department of Regulatory Agencies (DORA), 201–202

dietitians, 37

Diouf, Fatou: effects of discipline on, 22, 23–24, 56–57, 84–85, 96; licensing as obstacle for, 16, 21–24, 26; licensing reform advocacy by, 22–24, 39, 84–85, 95–97, 100

disciplinary procedure: board lack of expertise in, 125–126, 133–134, 140, 142–143, 146, 201; details of, 117–123; reform of, 200–203

discrimination, 85, 89–94. *See also* inequality; racial effects of licensing

District of Columbia, 138, 229n33

Dr. Death. *See* Duntsch, Christopher

doctors / physicians: associations for, 44, 75–79, 82, 232n63; bargaining power of, 94; as board members, 11–13, 33, 203; competition among, 26–27; continuing education for, 35, 128, 135; criminal charges against, 105, 108–110, 114–117, 121, 135, 146, 168–171, 176–186; foreign-trained, 72, 93; licensing barriers for, 37, 44, 72; licensing reform for, 190, 201–203, 206; medical residency of, 25, 72, 145; post-discipline employment of, 17,

148–154, 156–157, 160–166, 168–169, 260n22, 262n41, 263n56, 264nn67–68; prescribing by (*see* prescribing); primary care, 229n38; professional discipline against, 12–13, 17, 105–110, 113–117, 119–154, 158–160, 174–176, 179, 186, 198, 201–203, 206, 240n7, 241n12, 241nn14–15, 245–246n60, 254n52, 254n54, 273n36; professional health programs for, 139–142, 144, 145, 146, 169, 186, 255n60; reapplication after license revocation by, 12–13, 109; scarcity of, 16, 59, 63–64, 67, 69–79, 93, 161–163, 225n7, 260n22, 263n56; scope of practice of, 48–49, 72–74, 219n13, 221n23; supervision of other professionals by, 73–79, 81–82, 152, 228–229n33, 231n48; telemedicine by, 26–27, 75, 213n15

drugs: abuse of (*see* substance use disorders); counselors for (*see* alcohol and drug abuse counselors); opioid (*see* opioid crisis); prescribing of (*see* prescribing)

due process, 119, 122, 174, 201

Duntsch, Christopher, 178–181, 268n44

economies of scale in regulation, 29, 38, 143, 203–204

education, professional: continuing (*see* continuing education); cosmetology, 39, 89, 97, 193, 235n5; as disciplinary sanction (*see under* continuing education); foreign, 38, 72; hairbraiding, 23, 25, 42, 100; as licensing barrier, 23–25, 35, 37–41, 72, 86–89, 94, 97, 100–101, 188, 193; licensing requiring, 3, 196; medical, 35, 44, 72, 128, 135 (*see also* medical residency); schools, 39, 50, 71; scope of practice effects of,

50; student debt for, 71, 72, 86, 89, 149; unions providing, 94; verification of, 37–38

electricians, 25

emergency (summary) suspension, 149, 174

engineers, 47, 51–52, 61, 188

entrepreneurship, 4, 24, 49, 52–53, 98

ethics rules: competition and, 26; discipline for breach of, 107–108, 111, 119, 167, 170; good moral character requirements as, 66, 87; as licensing barriers, 34–35; licensing requirements as, 57; politicization of, 206; prestige and, 27; professional judgment and, 196

evidentiary burdens, 177–178, 200

examinations: associations administering, 37; for hairbraiding, 23, 42; as licensing barriers, 1–2, 37, 72, 86–87, 93; licensing requiring, 1, 196

expertise, board members: in discipline, 125–126, 133–134, 140, 142–143, 146, 201; in professional practice, 11, 43, 48, 183–184, 205; as regulators, 10, 37, 142–143, 146, 201, 205

externalities, as reason for licensure, 60–62, 193

federal licensing. *See* national licensing

Federal Trade Commission (FTC), 98, 192

Federation of Associations of Regulatory Boards (FARB), 14, 38, 58, 192

Federation of State Medical Boards (FSMB), 38, 75, 143

federations, 14, 38–39, 58, 75, 143, 192

fees: boards funded by, 8, 34; board surplus of, 34, 216n50; examination, 37, 87; legislation about, 270n9; lobbyists

paid via, 32; professional health program, 139, 141

felony records. *See* criminal records

fences: history of professions and, 43–44; scope of practice determining, 45, 48–55; unlicensed practitioners outside, 44–47, 49. *See also* barriers to entry

fines: as disciplinary sanction, 111; for unlicensed practitioners, 45, 47, 52, 57, 84, 88, 96

First Amendment, 224n24

Florida, 93, 122, 140, 255n60

4D model of professional discipline, 134–138. *See also* American Medical Association (AMA)

fraud: consumer protection laws about, 64; criminal charges for, 172, 178, 182; healthcare, 106, 108–110, 115, 119, 121, 123, 172, 178, 182, 203; licensing alternatives to address, 194; professional discipline for, 46, 106, 108–110, 115, 119, 121, 123, 203

free riding, regulatory, 175–176, 184

free speech. *See* First Amendment

funeral directors: as board members, 31, 271n22; disciplinary procedures for, 111, 132, 150, 271n25; licensing alternatives for, 194–195; scope of practice of, 54–55

Georgia, 113, 135, 154, 162, 263n60

*Gideon v. Wainwright* (1963), 154, 166

Gluzman, Maximiliano, 38

Go Build Tennessee, 34, 216n50

good moral character requirements, 66, 87

grandfathering, 29

guilds, 43–44

judgment, professional, 195–196
judicial review of disciplinary decisions, 9, 112, 118, 122, 201

Kansas, 231n48
Kentucky, 113, 182
Kleiner, Morris, 4–5, 94
Koch Brothers, 4

L&B Healthcare, 106–107, 127, 146, 149, 186
language, as licensing barrier, 1–2, 11, 93
LaPaglia, Michael: criminal charges against, 105, 145–146, 168–169, 185–186; discipline against, 105–107, 125–126, 127, 141, 144–147, 148, 174, 186, 251n25; post-discipline employment of, 148–150, 165, 168–169; professional health program for, 141, 145, 169; reinstatement of license of, 107, 146–147; repeat offenses of, 105–106, 109, 186
lawfare, 84–85, 100, 187–188
lawyers: access to, lack of, 64, 88 (*see also* access-to-justice); bargaining power of, 94; as board members, 7, 11, 31, 201, 203; competition among, 26; court-appointed, 111, 112–113, 154–155, 156, 158, 166–167, 261n35; criminal charges against, 113–114, 178, 184–185; discipline against, 17, 107, 111–114, 119–122, 132–133, 139, 141, 150, 154–155, 167, 184–185, 240n7, 243n32, 243n35, 247n72, 259n16; disciplinary hearing representation by, 122–123, 152; ethical issues for, 26, 206; licensing barriers for, 38, 193; post-discipline employment of, 17, 153, 154–156, 166–167,

258n13, 259n16; professional health programs for, 139, 141
legislation: effecting licensing reform, 67, 188–191, 270n9; about hair-braiding, 66, 84–85, 95–97, 99, 100; lawfare to induce, 84–85, 100, 187–188; licensing barriers and, 25, 57; licensing board influence on, 31–34; licensing board interpretive authority over, 34–39; lobbying for, 28–32, 188–190; on opioid crisis, 126–127, 129; political economy of, 29–30, 34, 99–100, 190, 214n28; practice acts, 7, 29; product liability, 59, 61; about professional discipline, 126–127, 129, 190; about scope of practice, 50–52, 219n13; about supervision, 78
Lembke, Anna, 157
lemons problem, 60, 62
libertarianism, 4–6, 11, 13, 15–16, 66, 84, 188, 191
lobbying, 28–32, 49, 79, 188–190
locksmiths, 189
Louisiana, 66, 120, 163–164, 225n7, 231n48, 248n82, 263n63
Louisiana Board of Massage Therapy, 120
Loyd, Stephen, 125–127, 139, 141, 144–147, 149, 202, 251n25

Maine, 155, 231n48
malpractice: discipline for, 12, 114, 116, 120, 132, 201, 252n26; insurance for, 63, 153; transparency of records on, 151, 201, 259n16
manicurists, 93, 223n12
market failures, as reasons for licensure, 60–62, 193
Maryland, 44, 221n24
Massachusetts, 64, 231n48

professional associations. *See* associations, professional

professional health programs (PHPs): criminal charges and, 169; professional discipline and, 139–142, 144, 145, 146, 186, 255n60, 255–256n70

psychologists, 30, 138, 141, 191, 206

public board members, 130, 141, 161, 199, 202–203

public defenders, 154–155, 166–167

Purdue Pharmaceuticals, 127–128, 142–144

quality and safety effects of licensure: access-to-care and, 67, 151, 163; constitutional law and, 65–67; continuing education and, 35; difficulty of measuring, 62–63; empirical evidence of, 62–63; for externalities, 60–62, 193; unlicensed practice and, 46–47, 57, 96

racial effects of licensing, 16, 87, 89–99. *See also specific minorities*

rational basis review, 65–67, 100, 224n24. *See also* constitutional law

real estate agents, 25, 34, 35, 45, 150

recidivism after professional discipline. *See* repeat offenses, discipline for

reciprocity, 2, 82, 189, 191. *See also* portability, licensure

record keeping, falsified or poor, 108, 172, 178, 182

records, criminal. *See* criminal records

Redbird, Beth, 238n36

red tape, 4–6, 11, 16

reforms: of licensing system generally, 5, 17–18, 67, 187–207; to licensure burdens, 39–41, 57–59, 65–67, 187–197; to professional discipline, 123–124, 198, 200–201

reinstatement after license revocation or suspension, 12–13, 107–108, 110, 126, 128, 138, 141, 146–147, 161–163

repeat offenses, discipline for, 105–113, 138, 145–146, 186, 241nn14–15. *See also* reinstatement after license revocation or suspension

resources, board: lack of, 7–8, 17, 36, 47, 108, 118–119, 133–134, 142–143; reform requiring adequate, 123–124, 197–198, 201–202

respiratory therapists, 25

revocation of license, as disciplinary sanction, 12, 78, 105, 109, 112–113, 121, 123–124, 130–131, 153–154, 160, 170, 184, 186, 203

Rhode, Deborah, 184–185

Rhode Island, 231n48

Rinehart, Darrel, 121, 171, 181

Rock Doc, The. *See* Young, Jeff

*Ruan v. United States* (2022), 182

rules of practice: as alternative to licensure, 194–195, 197, 205, 273n36; board interpretation of, 34–39, 198, 201, 202–203; competition and, 26; innovation hampered by, 32; scope of practice and, 49. *See also* ethics rules

rural communities: post-discipline employment in, 148, 154, 156, 162–163, 260n22, 263n56; scarcity of professional services in, 64, 71–72, 74, 78, 160, 162–163, 263n56

safety. *See* quality and safety effects of licensure

Salcedo, Jose, 91

Sarver, Jason Allen, 113

scarcity of professional services: as a consideration in discipline, 78, 131, 160, 161–163, 260n22, 263n56; dis-